What is Web design?

Design depends largely on constraints
Charles Eames

A RotoVision Book

Published and distributed by RotoVision SA

Route Suisse 9, CH-1295 Mies, Switzerland

RotoVision SA, Sales, Editorial & Production Office,

Sheridan House, 112/116A Western Road, Hove,

East Sussex BN3 1DD, UK

Tel: +44 (0)1273 727268

Fax: +44 (0)1273 727269

Email: sales@rotovision.com

www.rotovision.com

10 9 8 7 6 5 4 3 2 1

ISBN 2-88046-686-5

Production and separations
by ProVision Pte. Ltd. in Singapore

Tel: +65 6334 7720

Fax: +65 6334 7721

Opposite:
A visualisation of the National
Science Foundation-funded
element of the Internet,
undertaken by Donna Cox
and Robert Patterson of the
University of Illinois National
Center for Supercomputing
Applications (NCSA) in 1992.
Images from this series were
used in the publicity of the
American Center for Design's
ground-breaking 1995 'Design
for the Internet' conference.

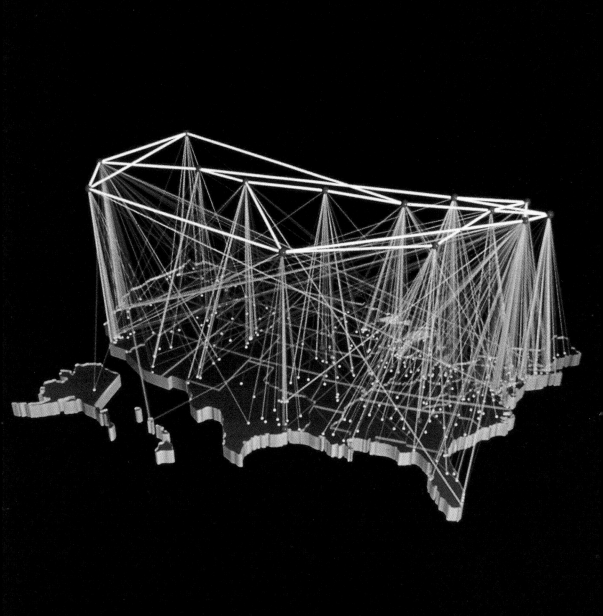

Issues

Anatomy

Practice

Etcetera

What is Web design?

Design for the Web is the most significant new area of design practice of the last 20 years. Learning to work in a new medium is both exciting and challenging, and forces us to restate what design is. The fluidity this new area of activity presents may allow design to assume a more prominent role in business and society.

It is easy to be daunted by the challenge of this new medium. In fact, design for the Web shares with other disciplines a view of design as a way of thinking, a service provided to a client for the benefit of others, an understanding of constraints, a series of problem-solving methods and processes, and an activity whose success is, to some degree, measurable.

It also draws on skills from many of these other design disciplines, and some beyond it, building on a rich tradition of design of graphical user interfaces and interaction design. More than other designers, Web designers also need to collaborate with people who have these skills.

What is different about Web design?

While Web design has much in common with the approach to other areas of design there are also some important differences. Many of the challenges of Web design are about creating an effective interface between people and technology. At present this is focused on giving people access to tasks and presenting them with information that will allow them to achieve goals that are meaningful to them, and which have value to clients.

A Web site is not a fixed entity and changes according to the device by which it is accessed. It may also change as a result of user interaction, and with the passing of time. It has dimensions not found in other areas of design, making it more difficult to envision and describe. While Web design is often considered to be aesthetically unpleasing, the 'beauty' of the Web is in its dynamism and interaction, both of which contribute to the users' quality of experience.

Web designers also need to go beyond the implementation of their design solutions to explain and document them in a way they can be built on. The solution is secondary to this.

Clients

In the early days of Web design clients understandably knew little about design in the medium and good designers were in demand. This is no longer the case and the relationship of designer and client is tending towards that found in other areas of design. Web designers now need to be savvier and more knowledgeable.

To be able to work effectively with clients they need a good understanding of business models and processes, and to be clear for each project they engage in what their client will consider to be a success and how this might be measured.

And being a good designer is not enough. Designers need to be able to manage the design process and deal with the political aspects of projects. They need to have a good idea who has an interest in a project beyond their immediate client contact and who really makes the decisions. They need insights on the working of the client organisation so they can ensure that their design solutions can be sold and adopted effectively. And they need to be vigilant to ensure projects are fulfilling their objectives and that the products will be sustainable.

Real people

At the other pole of effective working are the people who will use the final product, which includes people in the client organisation who maintain it as well as those for whom it is formally intended. The intended users are often the best foil for deciding what really works, as their satisfaction stands above the particular interests of the groups involved in creating the product.

Engineering

While design and engineering are distinct activities, with the Web they are closer than in other areas of design. Although early Web designers created Web sites by learning to code and adapting other people's sites, today it is not necessary to be an engineer to design for the Web. However, more than almost any area of design, it is critical to have a good understanding of the medium and the available tools.

Design in the business process

Good design ideas without a good process for implementation are almost useless. A good process is particularly important with Web design as Web products tend to involve more people in an organisation than other kinds of design projects, and their commitment to the solution will determine whether it lives or dies.

It is valuable to involve clients closely in a design project, so they are clear the brief has been understood and how solutions were reached. Presenting the design process as a mysterious 'black box' from which solutions magically appear limits a client's ability to learn about design and advocate for its value.

The other key elements of any Web design project are effective collaboration, communication and information sharing between the designer, the client, the engineering team and others who have a stake in the project.

Reflection is also crucial. Throughout a project the success of the design process should be reviewed, and the design solution should be assessed against the project goals and users' needs. After the launch these can be considered more broadly and should lay the basis for continued collaboration with the client, improvement of the product and future projects.

Towards the future

The forces that have shaped Web design are moving the discipline on and we need to look at these trends so that designers can be effective in the future. As more people have access to the Web and it becomes part of everyday life there will be new audiences with more varied needs and greater variations of skill and experience to design for. Designers should also be aware that the current state of technology is not permanent and that the best solution today may not be the most appropriate tomorrow.

Designers need to think about design for the *Internet* rather than the Web, for connected interactive devices rather than just computer-based Web browsers, many of which will allow new uses and contexts of use, and new technological constraints and possibilities.

The approach of *What is Web Design?*

This book begins from the assumption that the reader needs to understand design for the Web. Although most design challenges require solutions in more than one medium it would not be practical to extend beyond the Web, though we do digress where appropriate.

See *What is Graphic Design?* for a more specific discussion of graphic design.

Web design has much in common with other areas of design and this book begins by establishing general design principles and applying them to the Web. These principles will be equally applicable to the technologies and platforms that support online interaction in future, and to an extent to other areas of design. This book doesn't advocate absolute rules, as rules are specific to particular scenarios. Likewise it advocates a general model for the design process rather than an absolute approach. It doesn't address technical issues such as coding and programming, as these change from month to month and can be better learned online. Nor does it address how to be

creative, improve your aesthetic skills or master time-based media. These things cannot be learned from a book. It does provide pointers for those who have specific interests or concerns.

The nine case studies are based on interviews with people involved in commissioning, designing and engineering. They were selected on the basis that the projects showcase good design thinking and intelligent practice, and are intended to be informative rather than critical, showing in practice many ideas we discuss.

Technical notes

Smaller, indented text indicates additional information or related examples. Further information on each chapter in the book can be found in Further reading (page 244), while technical terms are explained in the Glossary (page 249). Screen grabs are taken with the URL field visible, so you can easily visit the site yourself. Sites will look different on different browsers and platforms – that is the nature of the Web. All are likely to have changed to some extent by the time you visit them (and some may even not exist). URLs referenced in this book are also available via the accompanying Web site.

Questions about, and comments and constructive criticism of this book are welcome. Please post them at www.whatiswebdesign.com or email Nico Macdonald at nico@spy.co.uk

John Maeda:
Created for the Japanese beauty and fashion company Shiseido and based on the game of strategy and vertigo. "When a path travelled through interactive space is not in a planned horizontal or vertical motion, there can be a sense of thrill similar to riding a rollercoaster," writes Maeda.

A short history of the Internet and digital computing

The development of digital computing and of the Internet represent two of mankind's greatest technological achievements and, though they are thoroughly modern, their development can be traced back over decades and even centuries. And while many inspired individuals are associated with them, they are also the work of a collective and worldwide imagination. This imagination is still hard at work and if its current and future ideas meet the right economic forces and are combined with innovative and creative thinking about how we might live and work, we shall continue to be involved in wonderful developments.

Computing captured the public imagination in the late 1950s and early 1960s with the image of the mainframe computer attended by white-coated technicians pointing the way to a future of corporate and social efficiency focused around 'Organisation Man'. This positive, if rather technocratic, view of computing acquired a dystopic aspect as, later in the 1960s, computers became associated with militarism, and particularly the Vietnam War.

In the United States, computers were also associated with a faceless, grey corporatism that constricted the human spirit and robotic production lines that did workers out of jobs. By the mid-1970s, however, the younger siblings of the anti-War protesters were using their wits to master information technology and subvert 'the system'. Engineering genius Steve Wozniak, who went on to co-found Apple Computer, cut his teeth in the world of 'phone phreaks', people using electronics to fool AT&T's US telephone network into placing free long-distance calls, not for want of free phone time but rather to prove they could do it, and put one in the eye of corporate America.

As the rebellions of the 1960s lost their idealistic edge, computers came to be seen as alternative tools for human advancement. Steve Jobs, with whom Wozniak teamed up to found Apple, summed up this change when he noted that "I'm one of those people who think that Thomas Edison and the light bulb changed the world a lot more than Karl Marx ever did". And thus, many of the best and the brightest of Jobs' generation built new computers based on technology from corporate and government-sponsored research and development, aided by high-quality modern manufacturing techniques. This took place in the context of a modern West coast economy primed by military spending (both Wozniak's and Jobs' fathers worked in the defence industries), and delivered them to the de-industrialising, paper-driven companies of Reaganite America.

Over a century before computers came to the attention of the public, Charles Babbage devised a mechanical computer, or more precisely a calculator, known as The Difference Engine. There is no continuous line of development to the next major breakthrough in computing which took place during the Second World War, at places such as Bletchley Park in the UK. These developments were driven by very different needs from Babbage's: the decrypting of enemy communications.

A Bletchley luminary, Alan Turing, proposed one of the earliest philosophical theories of computing, known as the Turing Test.

These machines were entirely mechanical as were their IBM equivalents, used on the Pacific front by the US military, which used a punch card, a Babbage-era technology originally developed to 'program' Jacquard looms. The first electronic computers included ENIAC (Electronic Numerical Integrator Analyzer and

Computer), completed in 1945 at the University of Pennsylvania's Moore School of Electrical Engineering, and 'Baby', developed at Manchester University in 1946. With the pump primed and the Cold War under way, computer-related technologies developed rapidly. These included the development of the transistor by John Bardeen, William Shockley and Walter Brattain at AT&T's Bell Labs in New Jersey; the launch in 1953 of the IBM 650, the first mass-produced computer; and in 1959 the simultaneous announcement by Fairchild Semiconductor and Texas Instruments of the development of integrated circuits. In 1967, Texas Instruments produced the first hand-held calculator, the same year that Douglas Engelbart, working at the Stanford Research Institute in California, presented a computer-based word processor, an early hypertext system and a collaborative application.

As far back as 1950, it had occurred to Engelbart that computers might have a graphical interface (rather than displaying results by punching cards or printing on paper). He had been a radar technician during the Second World War and reasoned that if radar could drive an oscilloscope, a computer "could draw things on the screen". Engelbart also developed the mouse, another concept fundamental to the development of modern computing and to the use of the Web.

The dynamic in computing moved from mainframe computers and 'batch processing', to mini-computers, which allowed large numbers of people to use a single computer via remote terminals. Commercial mini-computing was pioneered by Digital Equipment Corporation (DEC), founded by two Massachusetts Institute of Technology (MIT) researchers. Meanwhile, in the early 1970s, two Bell Labs researchers began working on Unix, the operating system that more than any other has shaped the development of the Internet.

The next breakthrough was personal computing. Many, including Bill Gates, envisioned "a computer on every desk and in every home" and were inspired by the Altair 8800, built on the 8080 from Intel, founded by veterans of the Fairchild Semiconductor. Jobs' and Wozniak's Apple II, running new VisiCalc spreadsheet software, was the success story of the early years of personal computing, while IBM weighed in in 1981 with its PC running Bill Gates' and Paul Allen's PC DOS. ➔

1940s
Foundations of computing:
Alan Turing, British mathematician, cryptographer and computing pioneer. ENIAC, one of the first electronic computers, completed at the University of Pennsylvania in 1945.

Human-size computing:
The first transistor, invented by John Bardeen, William Shockley and Walter Brattain at AT&T Bell Labs in 1947. The transistor facilitated the miniaturisation of computers, leading to the creation of the first integrated circuit just over a decade later.

 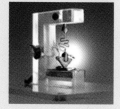

1950s
Commercialisation:
The UNIVAC (Universal Automatic Computer), launched in 1951, the first mass-produced electronic computer. It used punch cards, originally developed to 'program' looms in the early 19th century.

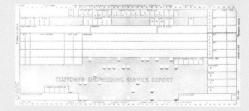

1960s
The computer industry:
Thomas Watson Jr led IBM from the early 1950s, taking it from the age of mechanical tabulators and typewriters into the computer era. The IBM 360, introduced in 1964, became the industry standard mainframe computer.

Mini-computing:
The Digital Equipment Corporation, founded by MIT alumni Ken Olsen and Larry Clark, developed the PDP series of mini-computers that enabled simultaneous use by multiple operators. A PDP-1 was purchased by BBN, who developed the first router.

Human factors:
Working at the Stanford Research Institute in California, Douglas Engelbart pioneered many developments that made computers more usable. Human factors in software became established in the 1980s as human-computer interaction.

1960s

New digital generation:
In the 1960s, many people saw liberating potential in computing and telecommunications. Some computing pioneers, including Steve Wozniak, cut their teeth 'phone phreaking', using devices such as the 'blue box'.

1970s

Affordable computing:
The Altair 8800, introduced in 1975, was an affordable computer for these pioneers, including Microsoft founders Bill Gates and Paul Allen, many of whom were involved in the Homebrew Computer Club.

Killer applications and PCs:
With his friend Steve Jobs, Steve Wozniak founded Apple Computer and in 1977 launched the Apple II, the first computer to feature colour graphics. The VisiCalc Apple II spreadsheet software convinced many people they needed a personal computer.

Pioneering user interfaces:
The Palo Alto Research Center (PARC), founded by Xerox with Bob Taylor as its first director, pioneered many developments in computing including the graphical user interface, Ethernet and laser-printing.

1980s

PC gets corporate:
IBM addressed the personal computing market with the 1981 PC Jr, which ran the Disk Operating System (DOS) from Gates' Microsoft. The IBM PC used an Intel chip and created a standard platform for personal computing.

Operating systems for all:
Steve Jobs, inspired by the work at PARC, led the development of the Apple Macintosh, launched in 1984. Susan Kare designed elements of the user interface including screen graphics and fonts. Steve Wozniak provided the engineering genius.

Up to this point there had been little focus on ease of use in computing. The Xerox Star, launched the same year, changed this emphasis. Developed at Xerox's Palo Alto Research Center (PARC) in California the Star built on concepts for an 'office' computer – using icons, graphics and a mouse – initiated by Alan Kay (often referred to as the 'father of the PC') while working at PARC. Among other PARC breakthroughs were Ethernet networking, laser-printing and the PostScript page description, all of which have been fundamental to the development of the Internet, office working, and design and publishing.

Xerox was a major investor in Apple Computer and, in 1979, invited Steve Jobs and a group of his employees to see the Star, which inspired the development of the graphical user interface (GUI) for Apple's Macintosh computer, launched in 1984. Despite its enormous head start over the IBM-type PCs and its great early success, MacOS was eclipsed in the early 1990s by PCs running Microsoft's Windows. This pattern could be seen when Microsoft overtook IBM in dominance of computer operating systems, and Compaq (now HP) overtook IBM in PC hardware manufacturing, closing the loop on the previous generation of computing in 1988 by acquiring Digital (as DEC became known). With the development of networking, and particularly the Internet, the mini-computer model of client-server reasserted itself, albeit this time the clients were powerful personal computers rather than 'dumb' terminals.

The development of the Internet goes back further than many would expect, partly because the Web (which was developed more recently and works over the Internet) is often confused with the Internet. It can be argued that, in compressing space and time, the telegraph, pioneered by Samuel Morse and others in the mid-19th century, is the true progenitor of the Internet, and Tom Standage refers to it as "the mother of all networks" in his book *The Victorian Internet*.

Concepts of networked information didn't develop much until well after the Second World War. However, in 1945, Vannevar Bush, Director of the US Government's Office of Scientific Research and Development, published a seminar article, 'As We May Think', in *The Atlantic Monthly*, that proposed a device, which he called the Memex. The Memex would store information on a kind of microfilm, which would be interlinked to make it 'browsable' (in the current parlance). Bush had half anticipated the computer and half anticipated a Web site, albeit one that could only be used by one person at a time. The term 'hypertext' was first coined in 1965 by Ted Nelson, referring to "text that diverges and allows choice to the reader, that's best read at an interactive screen" and Nelson developed the Xanadu project to promote his hypertext model. ➔

Hypertext can also be thought of as a network of information elements, all of which can link to one another to enable the information to be read in many ways, with easy access to references.

Launch of the Macintosh: Ridley Scott directed the advert, which was broadcast only once, during the US football 'Super Bowl'. It played up the liberating aspects of the Macintosh in contrast to the Orwellian and corporate world of IBM.

The concept of hypertext took hold in academia and research circles and even saw the commercial light in products such as Apple's HyperCard information organising software, developed by Bill Atkinson in the mid-1980s. However, the factors that would help hypertext come of age, most notably a universal network, weren't yet in place.

Although the need for new forms of global communication were becoming apparent soon after the Second World War, the initiatives that led to the establishment of the precursor to the Internet didn't begin until the late 1950s. In 1957 President Eisenhower proposed the Advance Projects Research Agency (ARPA) to advance high-tech research, ostensibly in response to the USSR's lead in the space race emphasised by the successful launch of Sputnik that year.

In 1962, MIT Professor and computer-science pioneer JCR Licklider published his 'Galactic Network' memos, which are the first recorded vision of a global computer network accessible from virtually any computer. That year, Licklider became head of computer research at ARPA and moved its emphasis to advanced research in computer science in the newly formed Information Processing Techniques Office (IPTO). Much of IPTO's work involved funding computer-based research in universities throughout the US. IPTO's third director, Bob Taylor (who went on to be the first director of Xerox PARC), became interested in why, with so many computers at his disposal in the organisation's IPTO, they were unable to communicate with each other. While inter-computer networking was being demonstrated, Taylor decided to devote $1 million to funding the development of an integrated messaging

processor (IMP), essentially a router, to facilitate the interconnection of these computers. The contract was won by Cambridge, Massachusetts-based Bolt Beranek & Newman (now part of Genuity), and the first network connection was made between BBN and UCLA in December 1969, against the background of Neil Armstrong's moon landing, enormous civil unrest in the US and a flourishing counter-culture. The ARPANET, as it became known, soon connected the University of California Santa Barbara, the Stanford Research Institute and the University of Utah. ➜

Inventing the Internet:
(left to right) In 1945 US Government adviser Vannevar Bush proposed the Memex – half-computer, half-Web site. Post-War President Eisenhower (not shown) established a high-tech research agency, and early head JCR Licklider moved its focus to information processing; here, Bob Taylor commissioned the ARPA network. In the mid-1960s Ted Nelson developed the concept of hypertext.

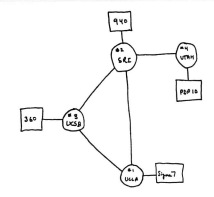

A nascent network:
By December 1969 the ARPANET had four nodes (above). It also embraced other institutions conducting ARPA research (left). By 1973 it connected to sites in the UK and Norway (below).

Soviet first:
Celebrating the launch of the Sputnik satellite (top).

The first router:
The room-height Interface Message Processor (IMP) engineered by BBN and used to connect the early ARPANET (above).

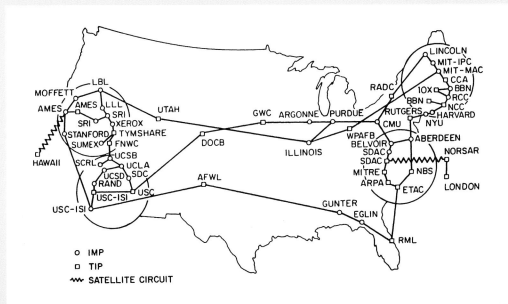

By the mid-1970s, Vinton Cerf and Bob Kahn had created a set of protocols (TCP/IP) that managed the structuring and movement of data between computers, and as early as 1982 the newly formed Sun Microsystems, whose catchphrase was "The network is the computer", was building TCP/IP into its Unix-based workstations. In 1972, Ray Tomlinson, working at BBN, created an email application, which went on to become the 'killer application' of the Internet (as ARPANET came to be known), and the following year a connection was made to University College London, and the network continued to spread via cable and satellite.

For many years the Internet was all but unknown beyond universities and other research-related institutions. However, by the late-1980s, the ground had been laid for the commercial use of the Internet, and services such as MCI Mai, Prodigy, Compuserve and AOL were offering access to email and online information, albeit using their own proprietary protocols and networks. In the mid-1990s the US Government funding for the Internet ceased.

The concept of hypertext hadn't gone away, and in 1990 an Oxford physics graduate, Tim Berners-Lee, working at the European Nuclear Research Organisation, CERN, in Geneva, invented the World Wide Web (with considerable support from his colleague Robert Cailliau). The first Web browser was created on a NeXT, the computer Steve Jobs created when he was forced out of Apple (and to which he subsequently returned when Apple acquired NeXT), and it was able to both view and edit Web pages. With a wide installed base of Internet-connected computers and a demand for up-to-date information in the worlds of science and engineering, the Web acquired a critical mass. The code for creating Web pages, Hypertext Markup Language (HTML), was easy to author, and a Web site could be created by anyone who had access to the right software.

The first Web browsers were 'text-only', not unlike early personal computers, prompting students at the University of Illinois' Center for Supercomputing Application (NCSA), led by Marc Andreesen, to create a graphical browser known as Mosaic. Although the research work was part-funded by Apple, it passed up the opportunity to commercialise Mosaic, which was instead taken up by ex-Stanford Professor and Silicon Graphics co-founder Jim Clark who, with Andreesen and some of his colleagues, founded Netscape Communications Corporation in Silicon Valley. The ability to download its Navigator browser led to its rapid establishment as the browser of choice for Internet users, and in 1995 the company launched what was to be the highest profile initial public offering since Apple Computer. The Web, as we know it, had been born.

From Internet to Web:
(left to right) Vinton Cerf and
Bob Kahn co-created TCP/IP,
the core Internet protocols.
Tim Berners-Lee proposed the
World Wide Web and created
the first Web browser (right)
and server. Marc Andreesen
pioneered the Mosaic
graphical browser (below).

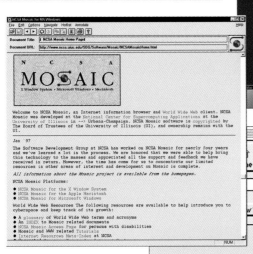

From textual to graphical:
Andreesen co-founded
Netscape, while Microsoft
tried to compete with AOL
and others, launching its
proprietary online service in
1995. The Web became the
dominant online platform,
epitomised by services such
as Amazon.com, and AOL
and Microsoft embraced it
to varying degrees.

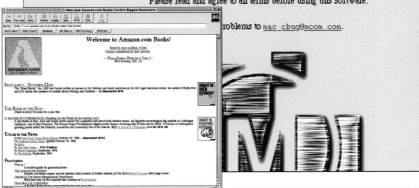

Background of Web design

While design for the Web is a new area of practice, it can draw from many other areas of design, and we should not treat it as if we are starting from scratch. The most fundamental aspect of design – communication-based problem solving for a client – exists logically prior to the choice of media in which the problem might be solved. And while the Internet and the Web are innovative, they and their associated design practices draw heavily on existing knowledge. The domains and skills from which Web design draws are extensive.

The design of graphical user interfaces for software, which encompasses screen-based tools with which users interact, is a close precursor to Web design. Anyone who has used a computer for some time will be familiar, perhaps unconsciously, with the conventions in this kind of design. The other similarity with software is that Web sites generally require the assistance of software engineers to be able to move from design solution to implementation. However, software is very task oriented and tends to focus on a document work area at which tools appear (a 'bring me' model). The Web, by contrast, is broader in its applications, and these are often more content-led and less task-centric (think of an online newspaper) and its client-server model mandates a 'go to', rather than the 'bring me', model in which users have to move to a new page with every action. Library science and information design are closer precursors here.

Product design also has a lot in common with Web design. Like software, products tend to be task-oriented, though they interface with the user in more dimensions to communicate what they can do and how they can be used. Like the Web, product design and development is more likely to be a core business activity than print design and thus requires more extensive negotiation – with, among others, engineering, sales and marketing, customer support and many other parts of the organisation.

Both product and software design (and thus Web design) draw on knowledge of the human's physical and psychological abilities and limitations. Physical aspects are addressed by ergonomics and the psychological by human cognition and, in the case of computing, by human-computer interaction (HCI). The design of the mouse or of a keyboard is the ergonomist's focus, while the human cognition expert would have a view on how many items in a menu someone could take in, or the time it would take for a user to lose focus or to begin feeling frustrated waiting for a Web page to load.

Architecture extensively informs Web design (note the adoption of the term 'information architecture') particularly in its approach flagging the function of a building, the layout of and relationships between the elements that make up three-dimensional spaces, orientation, direction-finding and navigation, interaction with physical objects and the creation of workable environments. As with product design, architecture requires a knowledge of materials and of the complex processes used to move a design solution from idea to reality.

From the real to the imaginary, the design of games has many lessons for design on the Web. In games the quality and shape of the interaction with the user is critical, and the structure of the interaction between people rather than the graphics is key. Tools have to be easy to learn and actions intuitive to control; environments have to be convincing and the narrative compelling. Games also deal with non-linear narrative where users can freely navigate through the game 'content', and even manipulate or change it.

In another imagination-driven area of our culture, film and other time-based media bring to Web design an understanding of narrative and story-telling, scene-setting and -changing, pace and drama. (Ted Nelson argued that "interaction design is a subset of film-making".) These characteristics will be more important for Web design as the Internet becomes useful beyond its initial commercial applications.

Back in the world of commercial design, the mastery of visual communication and typography inform design for the Web, particularly at the level of the text- and image-driven page. The particular skills associated with information design are also invaluable for creating intelligible and usable products given the information-intense nature of the Web. Appropriately learning from other skills and disciplines can be useful in developing an understanding of Web design, and will be useful in developing the discipline. Web development is a complex business requiring multi-disciplinary input and, along with their particular solutions, we can learn about the processes these other disciplines have developed, and the ways they collaborate with other parties, to turn their creativity into reality. However, design for the Web is not simply the sum of a number of skills that preceded it. The significance of the the Internet and digital computing are so great that in the long term we shall have to go far beyond what we can learn from other disciplines to be able to realise the possible benefits, and these developments are already underway.

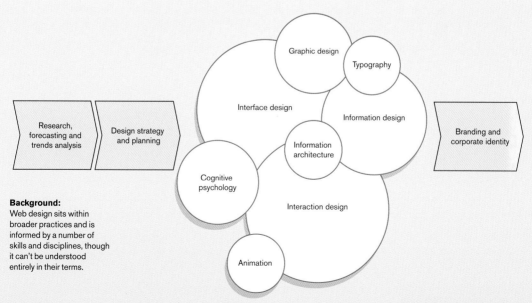

Background:
Web design sits within broader practices and is informed by a number of skills and disciplines, though it can't be understood entirely in their terms.

Research, forecasting and trends analysis

Design strategy and planning

Graphic design

Typography

Interface design

Information design

Information architecture

Branding and corporate identity

Cognitive psychology

Interaction design

Animation

Product design:

As with Web design, product design requires an understanding of people, engineering and business models. It is more complex in some ways, also requiring a knowledge of materials, manufacturing and distribution, as well as health and safety, and regulatory issues. Sony's Airboard email and Web device (top right), which also communicates with a TV, needs to fit the situation of someone relaxing in their living room. The personal and portable nature of the Palm V (top far right) has to support intense and frequent use in many contexts.

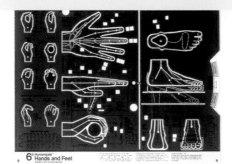

Physical ergonomics:

A clear understanding of the nature of the subject for which a product is being created is vital. Ergonomics looks at the 'measure of man' to understand the best fit for products we will use. For a project to develop a syringe for diabetics IDEO London considered that the best design would be held in the fist and squeezed. At the point they need to inject insulin diabetics are often feeling weak and can put more force into contracting a fist than pushing a traditional 'plunger' syringe. As injections are often in the arm, a fist-held device is also easier to hold in position.

Architecture:

Foster and Partners' Hong Kong International Airport pays close attention to navigation, important in a location with which most visitors will be unfamiliar and many will be feeling under pressure. The space is uncluttered and visitors are able to see and orientate themselves to the land and water. Good signage is also vital in these spaces.

Games design:
In Capcom's Street Fighter II, as with all good video games, the connection between the player's action and response on screen is one key to the creation of compelling experiences (even for non-players). The maturation of the video games industry, which has a greater turnover than Hollywood, provides many lessons for the Web design industry.

Information design:
A very broad field, information design covers the presentation of tabular data, information diagrams, product specifications and signage. The work of designers Jock Kinneir and Margaret Calvert on the UK highway signage, from 1964, is a wonderful example of an information and navigation system that is clear, readable, elegant and extensible.

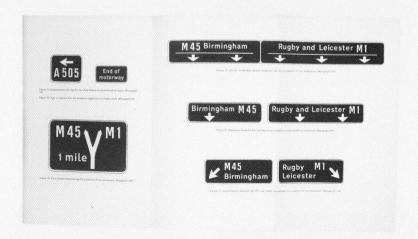

Technical platforms

Just as it is important for designers working in print to understand what is possible with page makeup tools and offset litho presses, so it is important for designers working with the Internet to understand the technologies and processes for prototyping and implementation that underpin it. Although there are characteristics of the Web which will be familiar to software interface designers and to designers who have worked with TV graphics and with interactive CD-ROMs and kiosks, many of its characteristics have no precedent.

Firstly it is important to understand the relationship between the network, the Internet and the Web. A network is a medium over which data can move, and includes cables, telephone lines, and wireless or satellite connections.

Here, a comparison with human verbal communication may be appropriate. The primary medium over which verbal communication takes place is the air, though it can be transmitted through solid materials. Sound is created by vibrating the larynx, thereby creating sound waves. These are modulated by the mouth, tongue and lips to create speech. Speech takes the form of languages. Within each language there are particular vocabularies that may be

professional, regional or cultural, while conversation follows protocols such as question and answer.

The Web is just one of many services that can run over the Internet, and for designers it is currently the most important, but this may not always be the case. There are important design considerations for email, another service that runs over the Internet, and for Wireless Application Protocol and its associated Wireless Markup Language which enable interaction via a mobile phone.

The Linotype:
The need to understand technology is not new to design, though the more established a technology becomes the more this understanding becomes second nature.

How the Internet works:
These media are 'enabled' to physically transmit data using standards such as Ethernet, Point-to-Point Protocol (PPP), and Digital Subscriber Line (DSL).

Data is transmitted according to protocols that are often specific to the device or type of device being connected, which for data transmission over the Internet is TCP/IP (Transmission Control Protocol/Internet Protocol). The Transmission Control Protocol element manages the disassembly and reassembly of data sent from one machine to another, while the Internet Protocol element is responsible for routing those packets to their destination as quickly as possible. This will typically involve packets of data taking different routes over the Internet, a technique known as 'packet switching'. Many other protocols exist including

Apple's AppleTalk and those used by Novell's Netware, but increasingly TCP/IP is being used for all computer networking.

On top of these many layers are the protocols that control the services we are familiar with on the Internet – for instance, sending emails or accessing Web pages. The protocol for the latter is Hypertext Transfer Protocols, abbreviated to the 'http' that prefixes Web addresses in a browser.

Finally, each of these services has its own data structure. For email this structure includes the sender and recipient email addresses, subject line, message body and much else. For the Web it includes the page title, the hierarchy of information on the page, links, images, forms and so on, and is referred to as Hypertext Markup Language (HTML).

How the Internet works:
The Internet is not just about desktop PC browsers connected via modems to the Internet. Almost any kind of data can be routed over the Internet 'cloud', made up of interconnected networks, routers and servers.

	A Web page being browsed on a personal computer attached to a fixed office network	Email being sent and received from a typical ISP on a personal computer from home	Email being sent and received from a typical ISP on a mobile phone in the street
Data element	HTML	Email	Email
Protocol element	HTTP	POP/SMTP	POP/SMTP
Data transmission element	TCP/IP	TCP/IP	TCP/IP
Transport element	Ethernet	PPP (Point-to-Point Protocol)	GPRS
Physical element	Category 5 cable	Copper telephone line	Wireless connection

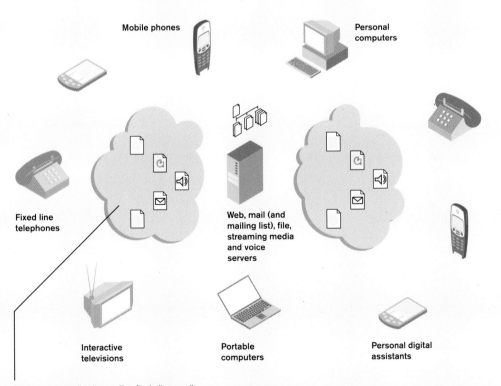

Mobile phones

Personal computers

Fixed line telephones

Web, mail (and mailing list), file, streaming media and voice servers

Interactive televisions

Portable computers

Personal digital assistants

Web pages, emails, diverse files (including email attachments), audio and video files and streamed media

Computers and operating systems

Just as the Internet has many layers of abstraction, so do computers. In the current model of computing there is a hardware layer based around a micro-processor, which could be designed by Intel, Motorola and many others. In a personal computer the hardware includes the micro-processor, storage (usually a hard disk), input devices (keyboard, mouse, a microphone), output devices (the screen, a speaker), a network connection and connection for peripherals (printers, digital cameras, PDAs). The operation and coordination of these hardware elements is done by the operating system, the most widely used of which are Windows, MacOS and various versions of Unix (which includes Linux). The operating system creates an environment in which software applications – which might be a word-processor, a browser or a Web page editor – can perform, with the operating system managing file storing and naming, input from the operator, access to fonts, screen display, and connections to networks and to peripheral devices. The computer and operating system have a significant impact on the experience of using a Web site (see illustration opposite).

Programming and coding

These terms are often conflated or interchanged and it is important to understand the conceptual differences. Programming produces code that can act on an input to create an output. Programming has languages, such as C and Java, which are used to create operating systems and software. Coding produces a set of instructions that structure and manipulate data, and control its display. The display of Web pages is controlled by HTML, and Flash is also coded. XML is used to structure data, and is manipulated by XSLT. Some types of coding, known as 'scripts', are also able to perform complex operations. Examples include Javascript (no relation to Java), which is embedded in Web pages, and PHP, used on Web servers.

Client-server architecture

The core of the Internet is based around a client-server system where information is stored, and heavy processing executed, on a 'server' and the results delivered to the 'client', which is traditionally a personal computer but could be anything from a mobile phone or PDA to a public display. This is the model for email and for the Web, though there are also 'peer-to-peer' systems in which the 'client' computers interact directly. The file-sharing service Napster partly used this model, while the workgroup system Groove is entirely peer-to-peer based.

How a Web page builds:
The Web is a 'deliver and print' medium and many factors determine the speed at which a page reaches the user and renders on their screen, its size and colour reproduction, typography and page layout, and its functionality. Designers can't assume that their audiences will see what they see.

Server
Its speed, the complexity of pages and services it delivers, and the demands of others' tasks partly determine delivery speed

Client computer
Processor speed partly affects speed of page rendering

Speed of server's and client's network connections determine page delivery speed

Fonts
Browsers look for fonts specified in a Web page on the client computer, substituting others if they are not available

Operating system
Partly determines browser functionality (Java, ActiveX) and page and rendering speed. Determines aspects of the colour gamut and physical size of type. Partly determines which plug-ins can be used

Web browser
Partly determines page rendering speed. Determines whether and how the page renders (HTML and CSS version and compatibility). Determines whether and how well scripts work (Javascript). Partly determines which plug-ins can be used

Plug-ins and helper applications
Determine whether some content types (Flash, RealAudio, QuickTime) can be accessed

Graphics card
Partly determines colour depth, resolution and speed of screen drawing

Display
Size and resolution determine how much of page is visible and scale of elements. Type (LCD, CRT) determines visibility, and partly determines image quality and colour depth

'Classic' computing:
Conceived by Presper Eckert and John Mauchly, Univac pre-dated the client-server separation pioneered by mini-computers such DEC's PDP series (overleaf).

Technical platforms 27

Browsers and plug-ins

A Web browser is a piece of software created to run on a particular operating system. The basic job of a browser is pretty simple: to talk to a Web server and request specific Web pages, to display in an appropriate way the page and the associated elements that are delivered, and when a link is selected or a form submitted, to go back and talk to the server (which may not be the same as the previous one) and display the next page. This is essentially what the NCSA Mosaic browser did, but there is much more to browsers today. They can display varied content, including time-based media and interactive formats such as Flash (typically by way of a 'plug-in'), they can process scripts such as Javascript, and they can interpret code that makes pages dynamic. They can also have more complex 'conversations' with Web servers and make those conversations secure. They can 'auto-fill' forms and auto-complete URLs. And of course they can download files. Browsers display a variety of bitmap images (stored pixel by pixel), most commonly GIF and JPEG, and are beginning to support geometrically stored (vector) images. In the 'browser wars' Microsoft's Internet Explorer won over Netscape's Navigator, but both are still important, as are the light-weight Opera from Norway and AOL's quirky browser.

Web servers and caching

In essence, a Web server is a relatively simple product. Its primary role is to serve up requested Web pages (including graphics) and process submitted forms, but as with the modern Web browser, in reality its role is more complex. It can recognise the type and platform of the browser requesting a page and adapt what is delivered.

It serves other content types that browsers can display and download, makes secure connections and manages restricted site areas, integrates with databases and other systems, generates Web pages on the fly and enables searching. Web servers also have to perform, delivering hundreds or thousands of pages an hour to a multitude of users. One way they achieve this is by 'caching' frequently requested or complex pages in memory so they can be delivered more quickly at the next request. This activity is also carried out network-wide by Internet service providers and Web publishers, using 'proxy' servers. To improve loading speed, browsers also cache page elements, to avoid downloading them again if they are used elsewhere. Whole pages are cached as well, to speed loading if a user returns to that page.

Content publishing systems

In the early days of the Web, a site rarely consisted of more than a handful of pages. Such sites performed a simple role and were typically managed by one person. (The browser Tim Berners-Lee first created was also a Web page editor.) As the Web addressed more ambitious challenges, sites became larger and more complex, and as they played a more important role in organisations their management moved to teams of people, often in different locations. New solutions for the organisation, management and publishing of content were needed, which were addressed by products from Mediasurface to Vignette's StoryServer, and later by 'blogging' tools such as Radio Userland. At their core these content publishing systems' role is to allow individual elements of Web content to be created, edited and approved by the appropriate people (often referred to as 'workflow') and delivered in the appropriate parts of the Web site. Content publishing systems may also bring in content from other sources, interface with tools that can customise content based on the interests of particular users, act as a conduit for advertising or integrate with e-commerce systems.

Template-driven systems

Across a Web site there are many standard elements which appear on many pages, from site navigation to logos and boilerplate legal disclaimers, and pages themselves are typically standard elements. Updating each instance of such elements when they change proved to be very laborious, and Web editing systems were developed based on 'libraries' of elements and 'template' pages. These elements can quickly be applied and, if modified, updated throughout the site. This approach is taken by simpler site editing tools such as Adobe GoLive and Macromedia Dreamweaver, and by the many content publishing systems. These template and library elements are either saved in the Web page, or added to the page as 'includes' when it is requested from the Web server.

Database-driven systems

Databases are not new in the world of computing but it became clear early on in the development of the Web that many of the tasks it would support would involve manipulation of large information sets, a job typically done by a database. They have since been integrated into the 'back-end' of Web sites for functions including retailing, travel and financial services. Both database-driven and content publishing systems separate content from presentation, and often the latter is built upon the former.

Screen displays

This is the primary medium through which we receive 'output' from a computer – for instance, a Web page is a screen – though computers also have an aural channel, and non-computer devices such as games often use physical channels (typically force feedback through a joystick). Screens have varied characteristics which influence the display of these outputs, primarily their colour 'depth' (from black and white to full colour), their size, their resolution and their display technology (typically cathode-ray tube or LCD in the case of flat screens).

Domain and host names

Every device connected to the Internet (and this doesn't just mean computers) has an Internet Protocol (IP) address that takes the form of a 'dotted quad' such as 18.29.1.35. These addresses tell routers where packets of data need to get to. However, like phone numbers, these addresses are hard for people to remember and to differentiate. The Domain Name System was devised to allow names to be used instead of numbers, for instance www.w3.org. A domain name is a name (such as 'w3') with one or two suffixes, indicating either type of organisation or country location or both. For instance, the World Wide Web Consortium has the domain name w3.org as it is an organisation, the Nobel e-Museum has the domain nobel.se as Sweden doesn't use organisation suffixes, and Barclays Bank has the domain barclays.co.uk as it is a company operating in the UK. Servers on the Internet are identified by a host name that is prefixed to the domain name and which maps to an IP address. Thus www is the host name for the w3.org Web server, and www.w3.org is its address.

Conclusion

The key technical concepts behind the Internet and the Web are not complex, but it is important for designers to grasp them if they are to create successful and satisfying products, and see them effectively and efficiently implemented. These concepts affect the design process at a number of levels and determine the nature of the product that will be delivered.

The client-server architecture of the Web and the characteristics of Web servers affect the experience of using a product from speed of page loading to the effect of page refreshes on a user's focus. The 'distribute and print' model combined with the variation in hardware and software environments on which Web sites (and communications such as emails) are viewed will change what users can see and the ways in which they may interact with it. Systems that integrate with Web servers will affect the way in which interactions can be designed and the ways in which information can be presented. And browser characteristics and functionality have a significant impact on scenarios of use.

Many of the concepts that underlie these technologies have a fundamental beauty and can be appreciated for themselves as well as for their impact on design. Understanding the designerly aspects of engineering can only help collaboration between designer and engineer.

How the Web works:

The Web is more complex than just static Web pages. The conversation between a Web browser and a Web server begins with a negotiation and a request (including information on the browser version and platform, and the last page accessed), follows with delivery of the requested data and ends with acknowledgement of successful delivery. This conversation, framed by the 'hypertext transfer protocol' (http), takes place for every element of a Web page and is recorded as a 'hit' on the Web server. However, the conversations are finite and when the page and all its elements have been delivered communication ends. If the page, or an element of it, changes on the server, this won't be reflected by the browser, and every user interaction with the page will require the server to respond and send a new page. For this reason http is referred to as a stateless protocol, though it is possible to code pages to request periodic updates from the server.

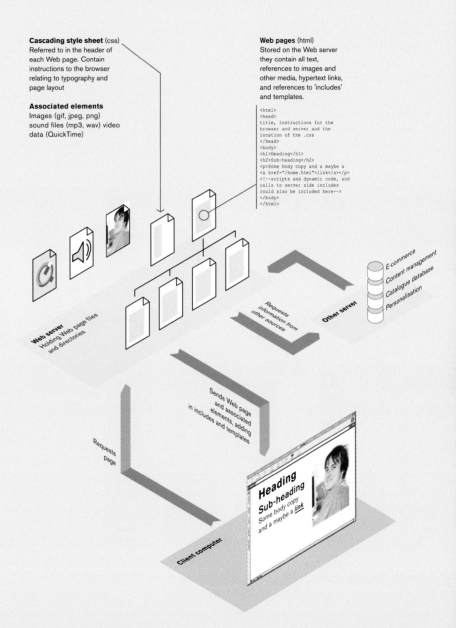

Cascading style sheet (css)
Referred to in the header of each Web page. Contain instructions to the browser relating to typography and page layout

Associated elements
Images (gif, jpeg, png) sound files (mp3, wav) video data (QuickTime)

Web pages (html)
Stored on the Web server they contain all text, references to images and other media, hypertext links, and references to 'includes' and templates.

```
<html>
<head>
title, instructions for the
browser and server and the
location of the .css
</head>
<body>
<h1>Heading</h1>
<h2>Sub-heading</h2>
<p>Some body copy and a maybe a
<a href="/home.html">link</a></p>
<!--scripts and dynamic code, and
calls to server side includes
could also be included here-->
</body>
</html>
```

E-commerce
Content management
Catalogue database
Personalisation

Other server

Requests information from other sources

Web server
Holding Web page files and directories

Sends Web page and associated elements, adding in includes and templates

Requests page

Client computer

Heading
Sub-heading
Some body copy
and a maybe a *link*

Principles of design

The word 'design' is usually associated with a particular domain – graphic design, product design, Web design – but it is important to appreciate that design is bigger than any individual domain in which it is applied. Design is a way of thinking. It is a way of situating and exploring an objective problem. It encapsulates approaches to creating possible solutions to that problem, and processes for evaluating the success of those solutions. And it has methods and processes for communicating solutions and turning them into reality.

Although design processes and methods tend to be specific to one domain, many are, or could be, applied in another, while some have value beyond the domain of design. Here we shall discuss principles applicable across design.

What is design?

The role of design is to help a client achieve a particular goal by addressing communication with, and creating products for, its audiences. A client could be a third-party organisation or a business department employing a designer; it could be an individual or the designer himself. The concept of the goal-oriented client is core to the design process, and is what differentiates design from art. The goal design engages with gives it its objective character, with the client representing the external rein on the design process. By contrast even if art has a client they have no objective goal. As film-maker Orson Welles once remarked, "a major limit of art is having no restrictions", and much of the joy of design is in solving the client's problem within the project's boundaries.

Definitions

It might appear that the people who will use the products of the design process have been left out of this equation. Often it can seem that, as their needs are so concrete, these people *are* the real client of the designer. In fact the immediate client's goals will, of necessity, translate into communicating certain messages to certain groups of people, or enabling them to do certain things, which may be of value to them. As the instigator of the process those things will ultimately be defined by the client and not the users, though in most cases their interests will coincide, and within this framework the designer should act as the user's advocate in the design process.

Successful and satisfying experiences

With respect to users, the goal of design should be to create "successful and satisfying experiences", a formulation proposed by designer Lauralee Alben: successful in that the user can complete his task efficiently; satisfying in that this experience is pleasurable, not merely functional, where pleasure may have aesthetic, poetic and fun elements.

Understanding organisations

For designers to be able most effectively to support a client's goals, they need to be, or to become, familiar with the area in which their client operates, particularly those related to the design project. This might include knowing about the origins and dynamics of the markets or sectors in which they operate; *their* clients, partners and suppliers; the typical operational and manufacturing processes in their industry; existing and possible future competitors; global or economic changes or social trends which affect or might affect their business; and the regulatory environment in which they operate. The designer doesn't need to be an expert on his client's sector but he will be more effective the better informed he is.

Redefining the problem

While the client is the ultimate authority on a design project, and has ultimate responsibility for its outcome, a well-informed designer may be in a position to question some of his client's assumptions, and their strategies based on those assumptions. They may even conclude that there isn't a major *design* problem and that the client's strategic focus should be elsewhere.

Research

Beyond understanding the general context in which the client operates, the designer needs to understand the specifics of a project. This begins with establishing what will constitute success and how this might be measured, finding out who has a stake in the project, who is driving it, who makes the final decisions, and the relationship of these stakeholders. They also need to ascertain how the objectives on which the project is founded are currently addressed, look at the history of the project and review how similar projects fared in the past. And they need to be aware of the constraints on the project, including budgets, availability of client staff and other client initiatives that may impinge on it. There are many ways in which this research might be conducted, from reviewing project documentation to interviewing staff and the company's existing clients, running a competitor analysis to organising a workshop, observing people in action and analysing their task flow to asking them to present their view of their work.

Many of these techniques are 'borrowed' from other fields, such as anthropology, which more acutely understand the power of observation and researching with an open mind.

Users and stakeholders

Some of the people the designer engages with will be involved on a regular basis with the *product* of the design process (supporting or maintaining it), while others will have an interest in its outcome because they are involved in or responsible for its creation. A third group will have an indirect interest in its success (perhaps because they are shareholders in the client company). The interests of all these groups need to be considered, and to varying degrees they need to be convinced of the value of the design solution that is finally proposed.

Context of use

The other key group that needs to be addressed is the users. The designer needs to understand the way these people currently satisfy the need the product addresses, and the context in which they do this. Context is critical. If a product is formally useful to someone but takes no account of where they use it, the constraints on their time and attention, their level of technical ability, or the related tasks they need to perform, then it is unlikely to be used at all.

Analysis

Along with being able to better situate the problem, and understand those who might use the product, design needs to be able to analyse this information to learn from it, using techniques, many of which may be visual, to gain further insights. It also needs to find ways to put itself in the position of the various user groups.

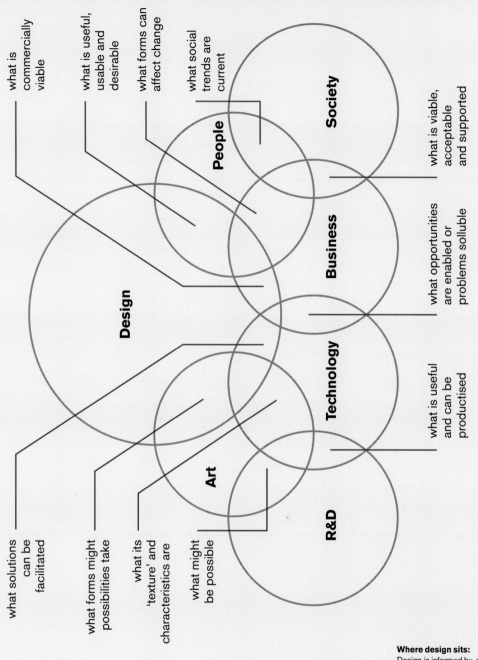

what is
commercially
viable

what is useful,
usable and
desirable

what forms can
affect change

what social
trends are
current

People

Society

what is viable,
acceptable
and supported

Design

Business

what opportunities
are enabled or
problems solluble

Technology

what is useful
and can be
productised

Art

R&D

what solutions
can be
facilitated

what forms might
possibilities take

what its
'texture' and
characteristics are

what might
be possible

Where design sits:
Design is informed by, and
mediates between, many
social activities. While it is
distinct from art the two
interact closely.

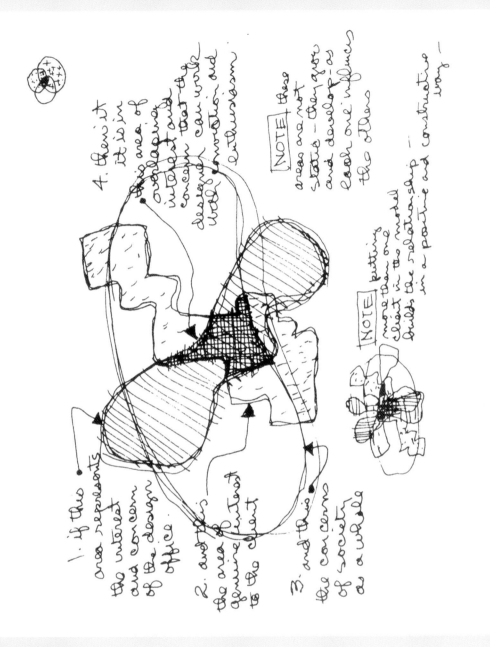

'The area of appropriate practice' for design: Polymath US designers Charles and Ray Eames' sketch of the area in which "the designer can work with conviction and enthusiasm".

Cultural issues and social trends

As well as understanding the specifics of the situation, design also needs to have a broader understanding of the context in which the project exists. It needs to have a knowledge of current and predicted social trends, a familiarity with the culture of the organisation and, where appropriate, of national and global culture.

Human behaviour

Beyond the needs of specific users there are also general human characteristics that need to be considered when designing a product. These include the need for reliability, valuing trust, the desire to connect with other people, and to be engaged by good use of language and strong opinion. Needs at this level are above and beyond the specifics of the project brief and should inform any design solution.

Understanding technology

To proceed, design also needs to have a firm grasp on technology, and also on the ways it is developing. An intimate understanding of technology gives designers more possible avenues for solving a problem. Technology is also one of the constraints on the design solution and this understanding will facilitate a more creative and effective implementation of the solution. Designers who succeed in this regard are often those who have extensively experimented with a technology, or are able to perceive its core dynamics.

Design as synthesiser and driver

While design needs to understand technology it shouldn't be driven by it, either to use it for its own sake, or submit unnecessarily to limitations it might impose. The design process is one of synthesising business goals, audience needs and requirements, and overall constraints to create an appropriate solution within them. This solution necessarily has technical elements, and it is logical and appropriate that the design process and solution should shape and drive the development of those aspects of a project – though this doesn't mean designers telling technical people what to do.

Brainstorming and lateral thinking

When the extent of the problem and the constraints in which it exists have been mapped, knowledge of the audience established, and the client's brief and the ways in which the success of the project will be evaluated agreed, design can move to investigating solutions. Many techniques are used to facilitate this, from sketching to story-telling, and brainstorming to role playing, with a view to seeing the problem in its full context, making lateral connections, coming up with creative and innovative solutions, and recording ideas in a way that they can be built on. Ideas developed in this way need to be evaluated and tested and there are some basic principles they need to follow.

Designing forward

The design solution that may be appropriate for today might not be appropriate for tomorrow. This may be because technologies might be viable tomorrow that will support a better product, because a new way of working or a new business model comes to the fore or because the client may be able to commit more resources to the project further on which would support a more ambitious solution. Some of these variables may be reflected in the client brief, some may be understood by design and others may need to be teased out from the other project participants. Design needs to consider these future developments and create solutions that can, in due course, take advantage of them.

Simplicity and clarity

Two important principles are simplicity and clarity. A design solution should start from the bare bones and add elements as necessary to ensure that the design (as opposed to the product) is only as complex as it needs to be. However, it is possible to over-simplify, and complexity may be successful if combined with clarity, giving the user a 'way in' to the product. While simplicity is desirable we should not ignore the fact that people are smart and will deal with complexity when they need to. As Albert Einstein posed it: "Things should be made as simple as possible – but no simpler."

Design 'with the grain'

Solutions to the individual elements of a problem should not be considered in isolation. Where possible, if there is a task or an action a person might need to do that can be accomplished simply as the result of his completing another task or action, this will lead to a better overall solution.

Inclusivity and flexibility

Just as the best design solutions start from simplicity so they should also start by imposing as few restrictions on the use of the product as possible. While the design process is effective at identifying people's current, latent and future needs, there will always be unexpected needs or uses for a product that won't have been picked up, and the more restricted a product's uses the less likely it is to be able to support

Culture and context of use: The success of NTT DoCoMo's i-mode phones in Japan (below) is partly a result of the social unacceptability of talking on the phone on public transport. i-mode supports non-verbal communication modes, allowing people to 'talk' while they commute to and from work. Products such as mobile phones provide a challenging context of use (on the move and often outdoors) and a very constrained display (low resolution and usually black and white). However, mobile phones are personal items with 'known' users, and good design can take advantage of this.

"I'd like to build the world a Web site": Just as with advertising and marketing, different design solutions are appropriate to different cultures. Coca-Cola's US Web site has a 'lifestyle' focus, while the Japanese site is more functional and informational (overleaf).

OUR COMPANY   FEATURES   COOL LINKS   SHOP   COUNTRY SITES   CONTACT US   SITEMAP

Coca-Cola Game

Youth Partnership

Vanilla Coke

Cool Coca-Cola Summer Music Promotions.   Click Here!

Privacy Policy | © 2002 The Coca-Cola Company | Terms of Use

these needs. While there are some products which, for reasons of efficiency or safety, need to be very constrained in the ways they can be used, in general the best design approach is to restrict the use of a product only where there is a clear reason for doing so. Of course, unexpected needs can't be anticipated, but by making a product as flexible as it can be – without obscuring its intended use – they might be supported as they arise. While the client's objective will be to support certain explicit tasks if there is no cost to making the product more inclusive and flexible, they can hardly object. And they may find their audience discovers entirely new uses for their product in the future, delivering a lucrative bonus to the client.

Most people's use of spreadsheets doesn't involve any calculation, but the tabular structure they offer is useful for many other purposes, and have established spreadsheets as office tools way beyond the back-room bean counters.

Design patterns

While there may be many formal design solutions to a problem, there may sometimes be approaches that have been used repeatedly to support the same objectives. These approaches are often referred to as 'design patterns', a concept proposed by architect Christopher Alexander who sought to develop a model for creating successful places that blended the application of logic with collective experience. Patterns can be observed in all areas of design and an awareness of their use may lead to the creation of better design solutions.

Designing forward:
Contempt's Web site for eDesign magazine (top right) was designed to be extensible such that it could in future work with a more complex database-backed system.

The complete customer experience:
One of the more successful online, it is clear from using Amazon (below right) that its service has been thoughtfully designed behind the screen as well. A client needs to be able to support its online offer with appropriate fulfilment, logistics, customer service and communication. Designers are likely to be aware of the off-screen implications of what they design on screen and may also have a unique view across their client's organisation.

e design

THE MAGAZINE OF INTERACTIVE DESIGN AND COMMERCE   No.1   Oct 15, 2001

- > NEWS
- > eFEATURES
- > COMMUNITY
- > MAGAZINE
- > SHOP
- > SUBSCRIBE

THIS MONTH IN eDESIGN:

e design
HERE TO STAY!

- + ebay under construction
- + The Urban Market: Creating Community Identity
- + e-Business Innovation: IBM Does Design
- + Tuned in to Antenna Design
- + The Urge to Converge: All-in-One Gadgets

FEATURES

Flash Sites

Lorem ipsum dolor sit amet, consectetuer adipiscing elit, sed diam nonummy nibh euismod tincidunt ut laoreet dolore magna aliquam erat volutpat. /more

Antenna Design

Whether pushing pixels or inventing vending machines, Antenna Design is tuned into users' needs.

Diam nonummy nibh euismod tincidunt ut laoreet dolore magna aliquam erat volutpat. /more

SPOTLIGHTS

 Advice
- + Search for Advice
- + View Issues

 Careers
- + Search for Jobs
- + View a Job Profile

NEWS HEADLINES
- + Lorem ipsum dolor sit amet
- + Adipiscing elit diam
- + Euismod tincidunt
- + Ut laoreet dolore
- + Magna aliquam erat

ADVICE BOARDS
- + Lorem ipsum dolor sit amet
- + Adipiscing elit diam
- + Euismod tincidunt
- + Ut laoreet dolore
- + Magna aliquam erat

REVIEWS
- + Lorem ipsum dolor sit amet
- + Adipiscing elit diam
- + Euismod tincidunt
- + Ut laoreet dolore
- + Magna aliquam erat

EVENTS
- + Lorem ipsum dolor sit amet
- + Adipiscing elit diam
- + Euismod tincidunt
- + Ut laoreet dolore
- + Magna aliquam erat

---

amazon.co.uk

| WELCOME | ☒ | | BOOKS | ELECTRONICS | MUSIC | DVD | VIDEO | SOFTWARE | PC & VIDEO GAMES | TOYS & KIDS! |

| YOUR FAVOURITE STORES | YOUR RECOMMENDATIONS | THE PAGE YOU MADE | N |

Hello **Nico Macdonald**, we have recommendations for you (if you're not Nico Macdo Discover what's New for You

RECOMMENDATIONS

All Products

All Used

Books

Music

DVD

Video

Electronics

Software

PC & Video Games

More to Explore
New for You
New Releases for You

welcome to amazon.co.uk
YOUR RECOMMENDATIONS

Hello, Nico Macdonald. Explore today's featured recommendations. (If you're no Macdonald, click here.)

Music Recommendations
Melody A.M.

Amazon.co.uk Review
Melody AM, the debut from Norwegian outfit Royksopp, is widely being tou "classic" status. Far from "just another chill-out" album, this is a richly texture warm, late-night food for the soul. The songs seem to reflect the extremes of the environs were produced in--the... Read more

▸ See more in Music Bargains for £7.99 & Under, Pop, and other Music Recomme

Books Recommendations
Experiential Marketing

Amazon.co.uk Review
Experiential marketing, a decidedly turn-of-the- millennium form of corporate

Innovation

Design patterns may present appropriate solutions, but the best solutions sometimes require innovation that won't necessarily follow an established pattern. While radical innovation isn't always appropriate, without it there will be no real progress in the development of products, and designers will end up constantly refining the previous generation of innovations.

The whole user experience

The design solutions that most satisfy people are those that address their whole experience of using the product and are not narrowly focused on the explicit tasks it is intended to support. Designers need to ensure they don't get tunnel vision when considering the audience's use of the product. Considering and playing out whole scenarios of use can be very valuable in identifying apparently peripheral experiences that will have a significant impact on people's overall experience of using a product.

Effective process and communication

A number of ideas we have discussed are elements of a design process. The value of process in design is hard to underestimate, particularly where a complex product is being developed, a large number of people are involved in developing the product or a project has many stakeholders. A good process represents a collective subconscious that can ensure that collaboration is effective and the design approach isn't compromised.

An explicit process can also help clients and those who work with design to understand better what it is, and support it more effectively. This understanding is critical to securing client support for a design solution and preparing to work with the people who can ensure its effective implementation.

Effective process sits alongside and is supported by effective communication, which is built on a clear understanding of the design process, of the roles of the people who are also involved in the product development and of the interests of the stakeholders in the process. For communication to be effective it needs to avoid jargon and obfuscation, and present ideas and suggestions in a logical and, where appropriate, objectively supportable manner.

Iterative design and testing

One key aspect of a good design process is regular evaluation. Evaluation techniques are varied but their overall characteristic is to place the product in a real scenario of use and see how it performs. This exercise may be conducted by someone with design expertise, or knowledge of the domain in which the product will be used, who can give an objective assessment of the success of the solution judged against the brief and the other criteria we have outlined. It may also be conducted by members of the design team acting out the use of the design solution while objectively assessing it. Or it can be carried out by asking typical audience members to use it to attempt certain intended tasks. The learning from these exercises becomes part of the next phase, or iteration, of the design process.

Evaluation and reflection

Along with iterative evaluation, designers (and clients and other stakeholders) will benefit from reflecting on and evaluating a project, and the success of the product, when it is formally complete. Were the client's goals met by the product? What worked well and what didn't? Were there incorrect or unrealistic assumptions, or were the conclusions based on them inappropriate? How would such a project be approached if it were started over? This isn't a process of recrimination but one in which designers and others involved in the project actively learn how to work better and create improved products.

Professionalism vs ethicism

Design works within the dynamics created by the client, the audience and what is possible. Design's ultimate role is as an intermediary between the client and the audience. There are a number of tendencies in design that pull against this. These include the desire for self-expression, for originality for its own sake and for solutions that primarily please the designer. This approach betrays the people who will use the product, and ultimately the client. The other tendency is for the designer to know better than the client, or to disapprove of and subvert the client's approach – a tendency expressed in the concept of the ethical designer. This approach betrays the client and can only promote distrust. It also betrays and insults the audience by assuming they are choosing to use ill-conceived products or are dupes of some unethical activity by the client. Ultimately, by conflating the design process with ethics and politics, all three are demeaned, and depth, subtlety and complexity are substituted for bland observations and dictats.

Designing the organisation

The design process is a wonderful thing and has the potential to be applied more widely than it is today. Historically the term 'design' was much broader in its application – consider William Blake's discussion of God's *design* for people's lives – and there may be value in applying it more widely. As economic activity becomes more service-oriented, businesses are taking on some of the characteristics of products in relation to their audiences. Their interactions with them are becoming more subtle and complex, needing greater attention from design. In this situation design processes could be valuable tools for planning businesses and organisations more broadly, and become more important on their own terms.

Elements

Design for the Web draws on many different sources, inspirations, disciplines and skills and it is important to learn about and understand them and take from them what is appropriate. In this chapter we outline these themes, moving from the general to the specific, and broadly follow the order they might be addressed during a project. We refer back to this chapter from the Anatomy section (pages 114–162).

Digital, interactive and network art

As with any new technology, the Internet and the Web have been investigated as media by artists, and some very interesting art has resulted. Art explorations in these media are very important for design, but they are not the same as design.

The role of art is to explore ideas and to stimulate our thinking about our relationships to one another, to society and to the natural world. It is initiated by a thought, not a problem. In the context of the Internet and the Web, art can help us understand their 'texture' and dynamics and think about new ways in which they might create experiences. It can also investigate what constitutes pleasure and delight in our engagement with them.

These kinds of artistic investigations are *of* as opposed to simply being *in* the medium. Just as an Impressionist-style image created in Adobe Photoshop could not be considered to be digital art, so art forms conceived in and shaped by other media but displayed on the Web are not art *of* that medium.

The digital (that is *computing*) is integral to the Internet and the Web, the latter presenting views on to the former and, by extension, digital art can also give us important insights into design on the Web. MIT-based professor John Maeda's investigations into the relationship between computing, programming and graphics have created new aesthetic languages that are integral to the medium, while his playful piece 'The Reactive Square' suggests new ways in which we might interact with digital environments. Tony Dunne and Fiona Raby's FLIRT projects played with location-specific information and mobile networks, emphasising that mobility isn't just about pervasive access to data but can also relate to geography, a person's activity and his associates. It also shows that these interactions can have a poetic quality. Designers should also be alive to developments in art (and not just art that investigates new technologies) as a reminder of the broad context in which they work and the character of the society for which they design.

The network meets the city: Fifty people in Helsinki took part in the FLIRT project 'The Lost Cat'. They received an SMS two days before the event to say the cat had gone missing, and one day before to say where it might be. Depending on their location in the city the cat would appear on people's phones and they could call it up to show it to a friend. "It is not a Tamagotchi," says Raby. "The key is that it has chosen you and you are special."

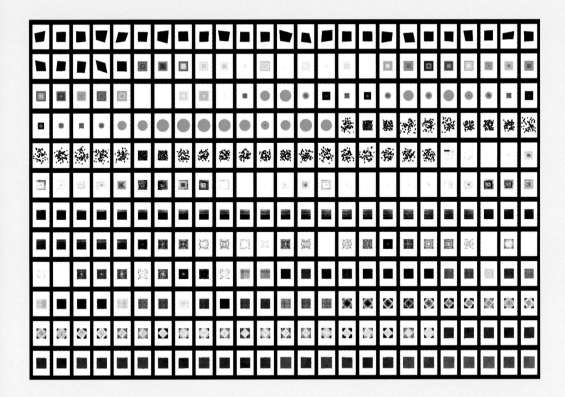

**John Maeda's
'The Reactive Square':**
Maeda's Reactive Books
series began as an experiment
to reconcile print with digital
media. The four squares,
inspired by the simplicity
of Malevich's work, react
to sound. This set Maeda's
children's expectations for
interactivity and they would
yell at computer stores as
they passed.

Forecasting and design trends

Designers need to be aware of the objective and more subjective changes taking place in society. Design is addressed to the goals of business and its audiences, but those audiences represent people whose situation, concerns and self-identity are constantly changing, and a design solution which doesn't take into account these dynamics is likely to fail, if not immediately, then in the short term.

The objective changes people experience can be seen in the world of work where there are developments such as changing levels of self-employment, women making up a larger proportion of the workforce, longer working hours and more working on the move and at home, and a manifold increase in sources of business information. In the home, working parents have less time, managing the home is more complex, and kids have more autonomy. While in the world of leisure, people have more money to spend, and cheaper transportation allows them to go further, or travel more often.

The more subjective changes, often referred to as trends, are the direct or indirect result of these objective changes. Examples in the world of work include greater employer scrutiny of inter-personal relationships, and less decisive and more risk-conscious management. In society, more broadly, subjective changes include a disengagement from politics in favour of more 'tribal' identities, alongside stronger identification with brands, a greater concern about the ethics of business and government, and less trust and greater suspicion of individuals coupled with a reluctance to make inter-personal and long-term commitments.

While these phenomena may be peripheral to many Web design projects today, they fundamentally shape what products people choose to use, and how they use them, and it will be more and more important for designers to understand them and take them into account.

Technology trends

In order for designers to be able to create products that have value for their clients and their clients' audiences, in the longer term they need to be familiar with developments on the technology horizon. These developments might be very practical in their consequences; for instance, improved or faster networking protocols, faster and smaller micro-processors, higher resolution, more flexible display technologies or better and cheaper printers. They may be more fundamental developments around wireless networking, cheap, single-function micro-chips, or electronic paper. In programming and software, they could be breakthroughs related to artificial intelligence, improved voice recognition algorithms, a new scripting or programming language or graphics format, or a proposed standard for storing and interchanging data.

Parallel to technology trends are developments in manufacturing processes and techniques which can make once unaffordable technologies available to larger audiences. The personal computer industry was able to build on manufacturing expertise in industrial electronic tools, while PDAs and mobile phones built on the high standards achieved in the construction of personal electronics.

Alan Kay, one of the most insightful innovators in the world of computing and the Internet, is well known for his observation that "the best way to predict the future is to invent it". However, technology trends cannot simply be

ter was reading, but it had no pictu
the use of a book,' thought Alice
considering in her own mind (
feel very sleepy and stupid
chain would be worth the trouble
, when suddenly a White wi
was nothing so very remar in t
uch out of the way to hear abt
shall be late!' (when she thought it

Playing in the kitchen:
Philips 'Billy' electric wand (left) reflects a preference for more organic forms among some European consumers as well as a trend towards irony. The move away from utility in kitchen products indicates that cooking has become more of a lifestyle and leisure activity. The popularity of Dualit's commercial kitchen products reflects a desire for authenticity over utility.

Phones as jewellery:
Mobile phones are now so small and of such good quality that people purchase them as much for style as for features. This trend towards more individual forms of identity is epitomised by Nokia's snap-on covers (below) and people's willingness to pay for bespoke ring tones.

Writing is on the wall for paper:
Paper that can be updated electronically is a technology trend that has long been anticipated (above). The paper 'metaphor' is well understood and electronic paper could provide a less painful bridge between the worlds of analogue paper and digital displays. Cheap electronic paper could provide an alternative to the limited size of displays and the lack of portability of computers, or a means for displaying time-sensitive or user-specific information in public spaces.

extrapolated from the point of creation of a new technology. The success of one technology is always dependent on the success of others. These successes are also intimately linked to the developments in business (including new business models and practices), to social trends and, often, to global developments and major events.

Designing processes not things

The ability of computing to manipulate information and of networks to connect people and organisations leads to these technologies being applied to the creation of products which are dynamic, rather than self-contained, and which facilitate interaction and transactions that may be commercial but are likely to be much broader.

The experience someone has using the Web is shaped more by interactions with a service, or, more broadly, with an organisation, rather than an interaction with a physical thing. As a result, the areas which designers need to consider are less clearly defined, extend further into the client organisation, and are more concerned with process than artifacts.

With Web design projects it is often the case that clients focus more on the 'site' than on the organisational changes that will be needed to ensure that the offer the site makes to its user can be supported and fulfilled. In these situations it is important that designers play a role in identifying what resources and processes need to be put in place. Design tools that help analyse and represent abstract things can be very valuable in this scenario.

Mapping organisations:
The interaction map for Studio Archetype's Mayo Clinic Pharmacist CD-ROM (designed in the early 1990s) shows how many touchpoints interfaces have with organisational processes. If these aren't supported the design will be undermined.

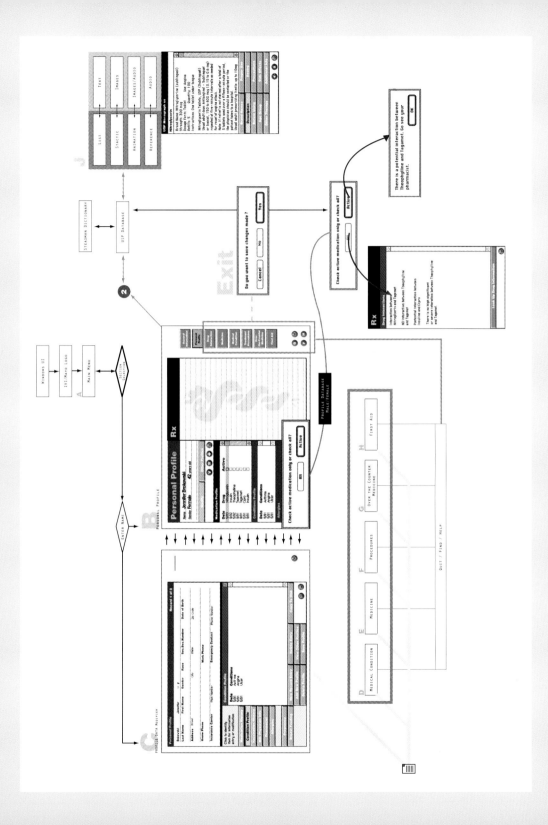

People

Design sits at the centre of the triangle of what is commercially viable and rewarding for business, what solutions can be facilitated technologically, and what is useful, usable and desirable for people. These are the independent variables from which design begins and they are not up for question. As Colin Burns of the user-centred design company IDEO has noted on the latter factor "there are no stupid folks out there, just stupid designers".

We should note that the term 'user' is often used generically to describe people who use interactive products. In reality, users are people (or 'folks') who may be engaged in activities – including reading, learning, transacting, and collaborating – who span the gamut of human life. They may be employees, customers, learners, clients, partners or collaborators. For a particular project we should avoid this de-personalising term but when we are talking about Web interaction in general the term is almost unavoidable, as it best captures the interactive nature of engagement with the medium.

When thinking about users we should also be aware that the user of a product is not always the person who decides to purchase it. The requirements of a corporate IT manager specifying systems for thousands of employees and a parent buying for their teenager will be very different but all need to be addressed.

Human cognition

There is nothing 'natural' about using software or Web sites. All tools, from a Stone Age axe to a 20th-century motor car, provide an interface and a fit between the properties of the natural world and a human's perceptual, physical and cognitive abilities. For both ancient and modern tools this interface communicates both the tool's capabilities and how it is intended to be manipulated. As mass production took over from craft manufacture, tools were no longer made for a specific user, and understanding general human physiology became more important in creating tools that could be widely used.

This 'fit to the body' became formalised as ergonomics (also known as human factors) around the time of the Second World War, driven by the challenges presented by one of the most complex, pressured and dangerous situations in which we interface with a machine: flying a fighter aircraft.

As electronics took over from physical mechanisms in products, it became less easy to perceive their function and how they were intended to be used. Human interaction with products became more an issue of 'fit to the mind' and was investigated through *cognitive* ergonomics. With the development of the micro-processor and the advent of computing, this link became even more tenuous, and electronic devices became 'black boxes' that could take any form. Not only can a computer take any form, it is really a kind of universal tool that can perform myriad functions. ➜

Man-machine interface:
An aircraft cockpit presents a very complex interface that needs to fit the human body, and consider size, reach and movement, as well as issues such as peripheral vision.

Whereas the form of an electronic device might be designed to indicate its function, the physical form of a computer gives away nothing about any specific function and the locus of the interface moves to the screen (and to a lesser extent aural and other channels). To address these challenges, the disciplines of human-computer interaction and interaction design were developed, the former rooted in psychology and computer science and the latter in design.

To understand what is possible and what is happening when they use a computer program or a Web site, people tend to create a mental, or conceptual, model to help them understand and predict how the system will behave. Car drivers also have mental models that help them understand the way their vehicles work but they have the advantage that, unlike computer systems, the internal combustion engine, transmission and steering column have a physical form. Additionally, people will use a number of such systems – from Hotmail to Google – and retain a mental model for each.

There are many other aspects to our understanding of interfaces that need to be considered. There are limits to the amount of information that we can take in at once; for example our ability to differentiate lists, such as menus, starts to diminish if they have over seven entries.

This is reflected in the structuring of telephone numbers into a sequence of three then four, established in the US by research at Bell Labs when it was part of AT&T.

On the other hand we are very good at recognising similarities and patterns, in everything from colour and tone, typeface and type size to spacing, shape and texture.

Human vision also has distinct characteristics. While we tend to focus on a small area, we can see objects in a wide periphery and we are particularly aware of movement in this area. We can survey a screen very quickly and decide what to home in on, moving swiftly from one type of item to the next (on the Web often the hyperlinks) while remaining oblivious to objects that are immediately adjacent (often the adverts).

This behaviour is typically studied using eye tracking tools that enable researchers to correlate eye movements and mouse clicks with screen display. Such tools are also used to study how people read printed publications.

Human vision has a given resolution and a set colour depth that it can perceive. The brain processes what it 'sees' in distinct ways, which can be exploited to enhance our perception.

From their experience with the natural world humans are also familiar with a certain pace of interaction and this translates into expectations of digital systems. It has become axiomatic in HCI that if a software user doesn't get a response to an action in under a second, they are likely to develop a feeling of frustration. It has similarly been argued that Web page download times are an important factor in determining people's experience of the Web.

Identity and preferences

Much human interaction with software and Web sites is focused on executing tasks and if these processes are not well supported people get frustrated or simply fail to achieve their goal. We need to know what the steps are in a process, what is needed to affect each one, how long the process might take and where we are within it. We need to know when we haven't provided enough information, or that the information isn't in a format the system can use. We need to know if and how we can retrace our steps to correct something or reverse a choice we made, or simply how we can back out of an operation.

Web sites which pop up new windows during processes – for instance, to connect to a payment clearing system – may limit a user's ability to retrace their steps. Information on how to leave a mailing list is as important as joining information.

If a serious error does occur we need to be able to recover from it quickly and painlessly. We also need to know when we have completed one task so we can move on to the next.

If a system doesn't make it clear that a user has succeeded, he may waste additional time or have to find some other way of ascertaining what has happened. If a system indicates that a user has completed his task when he hasn't, his expectation – for instance, that something he has ordered will be shipped – will be incorrect.

User dos and don'ts

In general people want to increase certainty and decrease unnecessary repetition of work. People also expect consistency in the way systems operate, and may expect them to follow the pattern of equivalent real-world systems.

Many Web sites undervalue users' input by making them enter information that the system could have inputted for them based on data already obtained. While this can be a result of limited programming and design resources, it sometimes represents a disregard for users' input. The worst examples of this are systems which delete data the user has entered, often in the process of a user trying to correct an error, or as a result of poor system performance.

Cultural issues

Human cognition is not a fixed thing. While much of it is physiologically determined it can also be socially shaped, and we need to be careful not to automatically project conventions we consider to be given on to other cultures. We can't assume, for instance, that red means 'stop' or 'danger' in all cultures, or that a tick means 'correct'.

Multiple users

While the differences in cognition *between* cultures may be the most significant, people within the same culture will also show great variance and design needs to take this into account where appropriate. Even individuals' cognitive abilities and skills change as they become expert at using a software tool and this move from novice to expert is an important dynamic in shaping tools to users' needs.

Reassertion of physical ergonomics

While the 'fit' of software and Web sites mainly focuses on cognitive ergonomics, fit to the physical world isn't entirely absent. Hand-to-eye coordination is needed to operate a mouse or other pointing device and this has a bearing on the ease with which small-screen objects can be selected or clicked. The screen is also semi-physical in the sense that it has limits beyond which a pointer can't be moved.

One consequence of this is that the part of the screen that is quickest to reach is a corner, the next quickest being a location on an edge. This observation is derived from Fitts' Law.

As the Internet becomes more pervasive and connects products beyond personal computers, physical ergonomics will again become an important issue for Web designers. This is already happening with data-enabled mobile phones, portable Web devices such as Pogo and electrical appliances such as Electrolux's Screenfridge.

The need to understand the way a product 'fits' the intended audiences and how 'comfortable' it is to use is critical, and often underestimated, but comes second to designing products that those audiences need or want and which make sense to them overall. Neither should we be too prescriptive, as people often use products in unanticipated ways, or adapt them to their specific needs.

People may use a shopping basket on an e-commerce site to facilitate comparison rather than purchase of similar products, or adapt email to serve as a task list and document repository.

Humans are not simply cognitive machines seeking efficiency. Our behaviour is mediated by subtle social factors and trends which may be elusive but shouldn't be underestimated.

From novice to expert:
The technologies Web sites currently use don't easily support adaptation to users with different levels of skill. However, software and operating systems have been addressing this challenge for some time. On the software side, Microsoft Word is an interesting example of a complex application that tries to support novice users. On installation its menus are relatively short, but if a user holds the menu open other options appear, and if one of these is used it is prioritised in the menu. On the operating systems side, Apple at one time produced an interface for novice users called At Ease, which was intended to replace the Finder for beginners.

Electrolux Screenfridge:
Addressing the best location for access to Internet-based services in the kitchen, Electrolux observed that the fridge was often a focal point, not least for leaving messages. The nature of interactions with such devices is very different from those with a personal computer, not least because of competition for use.

Pogo:
A lightweight, hand-held device combining Web access and email with a phone and an MP3 player. Users of such devices are likely to be standing or outdoors and may only have one hand free, and the interface design needs to address these constraints.

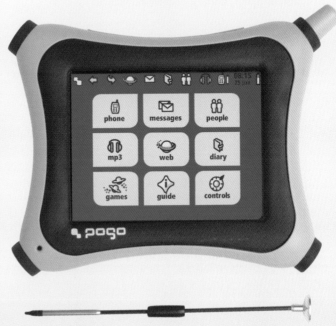

Scenarios and personas

While design mediates between business goals, technology and user needs, in the process of creating interactive products it is very easy for designers to lose their focus on these project determinants as they home in on the detail of specifying the product and related processes.

The use of 'scenarios' is one technique that brings user needs and context of use to the fore. Jack Carroll, director of Virginia Tech's Center for Human-Computer Interaction, has written extensively about scenarios, characterising them as "stories about people and their activities". Scenarios have a setting, they have agents or actors who have goals or objectives, they tell a story which involves actions applied to objects and the events that result, and they have an outcome.

Scenarios that tell stories about the ways a client's intended users might use a product can help evaluate the viability of particular design solutions. They can help people think about the details of a design, where dependencies in the process exist, where there are technical requirements or temporal changes that may affect use of the system, and where and when unexpected or undesired outcomes might be produced. Scenarios may even generate solutions to design problems.

Scenarios allow designers to ensure that all the project requirements ("what the software or Web site enables for whom") have been addressed, and to think about the ways the various aspects of the system will come together and interact. However, they do need to be assigned some priority to facilitate scaling back a project if this becomes necessary. The concept of 'personas' is closely related to scenarios. They focus on describing users and identifying their goals. Personas are portraits of and stories about idealised users, developed around characteristics including a name, picture, job description, age, computer skills, means of accessing the product, goals – and perhaps a 'quote' from the persona.

These personas are developed to the point where they have a presence in the process, and aspects of a product can be discussed in terms of the way a specific persona would use and react to it. Personas force designer and programmers to go beyond subjectivity when thinking about the consequences of their decisions. Personas are also an effective way of connecting with clients, and with their employees who will use the system, as they are likely to be able to identify with well researched personas. They may even adopt them for their own purposes such as staff training and sales.

Scenarios and personas both incorporate aspects of story-telling, one of our most established ways of imagining situations and outlining challenges.

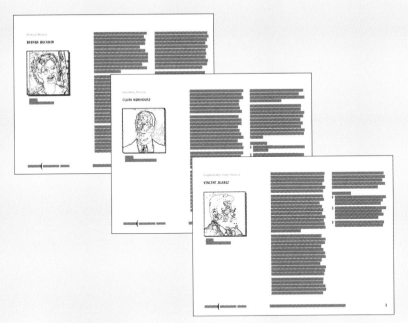

Pervasive personas:
Cooper's personas tell stories
about people's lives, describe
their goals, note their expertise
and form of Web access.

Persona creation
© 2002 Cooper

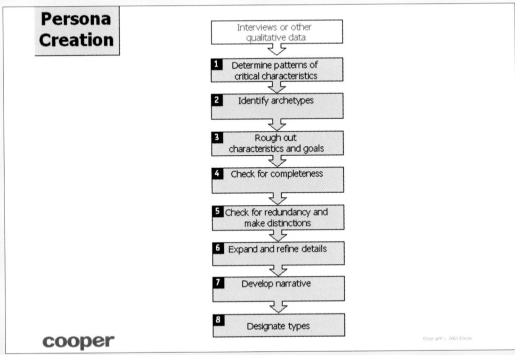

Persona Creation

Interviews or other
qualitative data

1 Determine patterns of
critical characteristics

2 Identify archetypes

3 Rough out
characteristics and goals

4 Check for completeness

5 Check for redundancy and
make distinctions

6 Expand and refine details

7 Develop narrative

8 Designate types

cooper

Copyright 2002 Cooper

User research

Research focused on the people who will use a product is important both for getting to grips with what they would really value and for understanding the context in which they might use it, helping to ensure that the final product can fit appropriately into their lives. It can also lead to inspiration about the forms the product might take.

In order to understand your audience you can learn from what they say, what they do, and from what they make. You also need to understand who they are.

What people *say* can be investigated from questionnaires, one-on-one interviews, focus groups, and other email and Web-based surveys. While these techniques are valuable, they have a number of limitations. People may not be truthful in their answers – they may be led by the question or, in the case of focus groups, by others in the group; often they have difficulty seeing themselves in particular scenarios.

Techniques for understanding what people *do* include ethnography and usability-based research. Ethnography involves observing in context the way that people engage in the activities related to those the product is intended to address. It can be conducted by a researcher directly, or indirectly by asking people to record their activities. Ethnography relies on getting the broadest context in which activities take place, to facilitate the best understanding of people's needs and the factors that any solution will need to take into account. Ethnography can involve asking questions but most insightful answers will be given to 'who, where, why, when and how' rather than 'would you' and 'will you' questions. Usability-related research looks more

specifically at how people use products that address the same need as the product in development. Again it uses open-ended questions and helps to create an understanding of where the product does and doesn't succeed for the user.

What people *make* when presented with the challenge of solving a problem also reveals a lot about their needs and the context into which such a product would have to fit, and may also reveal more than 'do' techniques about their underlying motivations or emotions. Such techniques can be used with quite simple materials, particularly for screen-based solutions, though for physical products the materials needed are more involved.

Understanding who people *are* is the province of quantitative research. For physical products such research might need to be exhaustive, but for a Web-based product there are fewer dimensions of the audiences that are appropriate measures. These dimensions might include age, sex and profession, degree, type and quality of access to the Web (including shared access) and level of skills with the Web and with computers in general.

Innovation beyond research:

The Sony Walkman is an example of a product for which there was no apparent need, but which became one of the most successful electronic products in history. The Short Messaging Service (SMS) element of mobile phones was devised as a channel for network engineers to use and, had they been asked, most mobile phone users would have expressed little need for it. Yet today, SMS generates a significant proportion of mobile phone companies' revenues.

Users as designers:

The first generation Iomega Zip drive was designed by Fitch employing research techniques in which users would make their own solution to the product brief. This led the Fitch designers to include a window in the drive, having appreciated that users wanted to see which disk was inside.

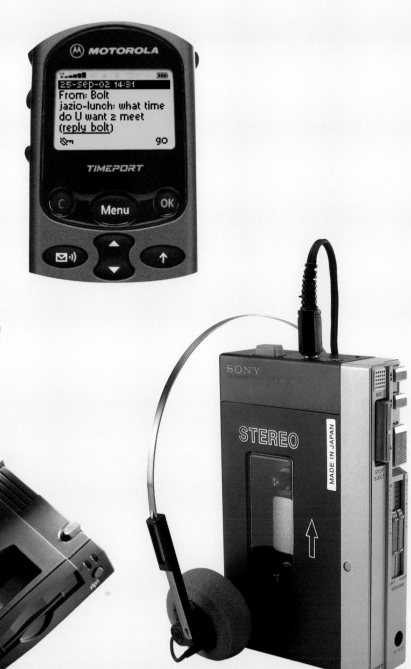

Corporate identity and branding

With any design development, the client's existing corporate identity and branding (if there is one) will be one of the constraints, and starting points, of the design solution. Corporate identity has long been important for businesses wanting to communicate a message to clients and customers, investors and shareholders, and to their own staff, about the company's activities and the way it conducts them. Branding has evolved as an extension of these communications, focused around the products and services a company delivers, but has gone beyond this to address customers' aspirations and the creation of lifestyles.

While branding has become a significant area of design, brands cannot just be created at will. As design critic Stephen Bayley has argued "strong brands are built on the reputation of great products". Effective on- and offline brands grow out of the successful application of design and communication principles and methods. Challis Hodge, a Chicago-based user-experience consultant, notes that "brand equals the sum of the perceptions that result from every point of contact people have with a company, its products and services over time".

The rise of branding has also tended to be in inverse proportion to real innovation in product development. However, the Web is one of the remaining areas in which innovation is still considered to be a more important driver of customer adoption than brand and marketing, and branding should not lead product development. Rather, it should be a part of users' quality of experience of the product.

One area where branding does need to be explicitly addressed is the creation of trust, a critical issue for a number of applications of the Web including e-commerce. If other aspects of the design or performance of the site are poor the brand will be also undermined.

The development of corporate identity for application to the Web needs to be sensitive to the medium, as it would in development for application in print, on clothing, in retail environments or on vehicles. The Web is a malleable medium with multiple dimensions such as time. User interaction is fundamental to it, and users' experience of it extends from an email they receive to a document they may download or Web page they may print. Maintenance of a corporate identity is more in the hands of the company employee who supports the online activity, and in many cases in the hands of third parties who (legitimately or not) integrate a client's brand into their online activities.

Brand extension:
Communications company Orange (top) has a strong brand but may have extended it to the Web too literally, drawing on the image style it uses in print over the functionality and performance of its phone service, or the strong information design of its bills.

Trust and money:
Trust is a key asset of financial institutions. The American Express Web site (above) uses the filigree pattern familiar from cheques, bank notes and its own cards to connect to real-world associations of sound finances.

MSN or iPaq:
Digital products and services are easier to combine to create hybrid products than real-world products and services, making it more difficult to control the 'brand experience'. Who do you praise or blame when this product performs or fails: Compaq or Microsoft? (right)

Elements 63

Metaphors

One way in which designers have addressed the challenge of creating cognitive models of digital systems is through metaphors. As in real life, a metaphor uses one concept to explain another to which it is not literally applicable. They are one example of the mental models we develop to help understand abstract systems.

Examples of metaphors used in computing are 'the desktop', and 'buttons' which use three-dimensional effects (and often sound) to mimic the 'feel' of their mechanical equivalents. On the Web the most pervasive metaphor, dictated by most Web browsers, is 'the page'. As an organising principle for a design solution, metaphors are very appealing, as they appear to provide an understandable and ready-made interface. They are certainly useful for Web design, but they should be used sparingly and we should note some caveats.

One problem with using a metaphor is that some users may not connect with it. Another problem is that if the product being designed really had the behaviour and functionality of its metaphorical counterpart it probably wouldn't be effectively using the technology.

New digital products almost always relate to some existing activity and that activity often suggests the metaphor that might be adopted. However, as soon as that activity moves on to a digital platform new possibilities and forms become apparent and as these couldn't be accomplished with the non-digital tools the metaphor must inevitably break down. Also, while aspects of the original tool can be mimicked in the digital medium, they will often constrain the use of the product, and won't be supported as well as they are in the original tool.

There is a fundamental problem with the basic metaphor used on the Web: the page. The Web fulfils many functions related to printed material, and has adopted many of its characteristics as metaphors. However, it brings new possibilities and forms, including searching and hyperlinking. Here, the page and book metaphors break down immediately, and some of their strongest facets are not well supported. Inserting a bookmark in a page and highlighting text have no direct equivalents, and although we use Web 'browsers', books are much easier to browse than page metaphor-based Web sites.

One vocal commentator on metaphors is Donald Norman. In his book, *The Invisible Computer,* he notes that "use of a metaphor is appropriate in the initial stages of learning. But while those first stages are only there temporarily, the metaphor is with us forever." His advice is to "forget the term metaphor. Go right to the heart of the problem. Make a clean, clear, understandable conceptual model. Make sure the user can learn and understand it. Make all the actions consistent with that conceptual model, the better to reinforce it."

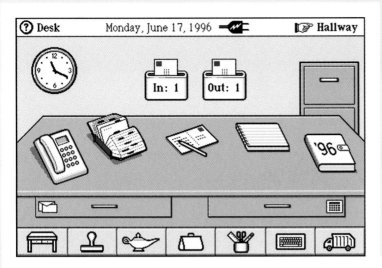

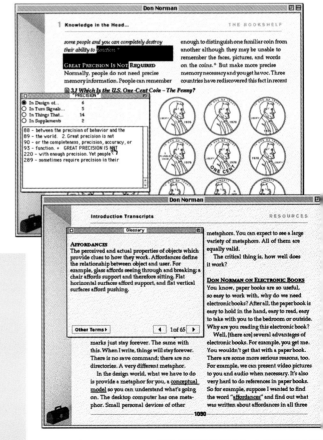

The literal desktop metaphor:
General Magic's MagicCap interface was developed in the mid-1990s by Bill Atkinson and other Apple veterans for portable connected devices (left).

Metaphorical books:
In the early 1990s celebrated CD-ROM publisher Voyager developed the Expanded Book based on Apple's HyperCard hypertext tool. Book metaphors have resurfaced on Apple's Newton PDA, the single-purpose SoftBook, and in Adobe's PC-based eBook format (below).

The home as interface:
Rightly noting that the desktop metaphor is best suited to office workers, Microsoft developed the 'Bob' interface for home users, though it was soon abandoned (above).

Real things:
For its RealThings project, IBM's Ease of Use team adopted a design approach using counterparts that resemble familiar, real-world artifacts. Interfaces were developed for a phone, a CD player and a book (left).

Information architecture

One of the genuinely new skills that has been defined in the area of design for the Web is that of information architecture. This is largely because the Web effectively supports interaction with content, itself a new area, and in this respect it is closely related to navigation (see page 70). Of course, there is an overlap with skills that exist in software development – though software is not usually content-driven – and an overlap with editorial and information design in print – though print is not interactive or as malleable as content on the Web.

Information architecture investigates and scopes the organisation of a Web site, playing a synthesising role between the needs of the project stakeholders and participants (engineering, copywriting, marketing), and the needs of the intended audience, to create detailed plans for the product.

Practised information architects Lillian Svec and Raoul Rickenberg note that they "create plans that describe the underlying organisational structure and navigation for a system of content and interactions" and Jesse James Garrett adds that "our concern is always with creating structures to facilitate effective communication".

In their book *Information Architecture for the World Wide Web* Louis Rosenfeld and Peter Morville discuss the broader roles of information architecture as a process that "clarifies the mission and vision for the site, balancing the needs of its sponsoring organisation and the needs of its audiences. [It] determines what content and functionality the site will contain. [It] specifies how users will find information in the site by defining its organisation, navigation, labelling, and searching systems. And [it] maps out how the site will accommodate change and growth over time."

A major area addressed by information architecture is search. While search may not be appropriate on every Web site, where it is it considers: how data is structured and tagged; the search algorithms that should be used, how search results should be displayed (including their context and prioritisation) and how results may be refined by the searcher.

The activities in which information architecture engages and the tools it uses include taxonomy development and thesaurus design, card sorting and matrix analysis, mapping and flowcharting, storyboarding and navigational planning, organisation modelling and personalisation strategy. The results of these may be presented as schematics, wireframes, prototypes, functional specifications, style guides and site maps.

Information architecture is also focusing on business context, overseeing its practice across an organisation, and is increasingly concerned with content management strategy.

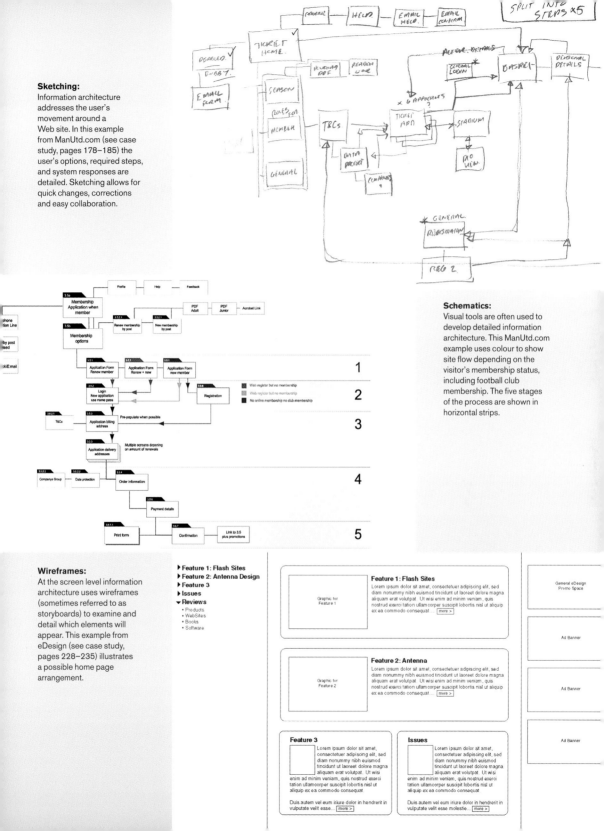

Sketching:

Information architecture addresses the user's movement around a Web site. In this example from ManUtd.com (see case study, pages 178–185) the user's options, required steps, and system responses are detailed. Sketching allows for quick changes, corrections and easy collaboration.

Schematics:

Visual tools are often used to develop detailed information architecture. This ManUtd.com example uses colour to show site flow depending on the visitor's membership status, including football club membership. The five stages of the process are shown in horizontal strips.

Wireframes:

At the screen level information architecture uses wireframes (sometimes referred to as storyboards) to examine and detail which elements will appear. This example from eDesign (see case study, pages 228–235) illustrates a possible home page arrangement.

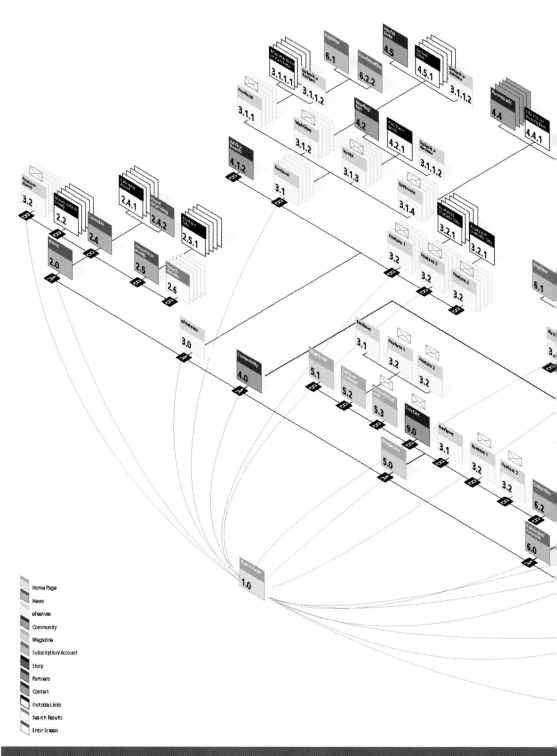

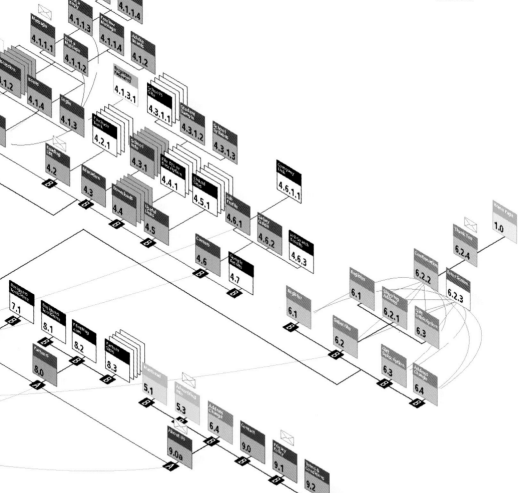

Site maps:
One of the more familiar information architecture artifacts, site maps are sometimes developed as navigational tools for users. This site map from eDesign (inspired by the work of Dynamic Diagrams) uses colour to indicate site sections as well as subscriber-only screens, external links, search results and error screens, with icons indicating email links. The numbering system allows for unambiguous identification of screens.

CONTEMPT.
www.contempt.net

Navigation

Navigation design is intimately linked with and typically flows from information architecture. It also builds on an understanding of user needs and technical possibilities, and flows into interface, interaction and graphic design, but it merits individual attention.

As Web sites tend to be content-led, enabling users to orient themselves and find information is a typical design challenge, and the need for effective navigation is often the first thing that strikes people (and particularly clients) who are new to the Web.

There are a number of major challenges in navigation design, which need to balance client objectives and user needs appropriately. Firstly, the navigation should be clear, and the way it supports activation needs to be appropriate and learnable. It needs to give users a sense of what information or features the site contains and their scope and relevance. It needs to give feedback when it has been activated, and when the user arrives at his destination it should also indicate the nature of the content he has arrived at and reflect its location in the site.

Hierarchical structures are a typical way of organising information on the Web, and the flatness of depth of the hierarchy in a site will affect users' chances of success in finding what they are looking for. Often people will arrive at a page within this hierarchy, rather than at the home page, having followed a link from a search result, a publication such as an email newsletter, an advertisement or a recommendation. Here it is important that the navigation shows the context of the information they have found, which will help them evaluate its relevance.

This is typically achieved with a breadcrumb trail (a navigational device popularised by Yahoo!).

Navigation may also be able to reflect location.

It is generally desirable to allow users to re-orient themselves, if the navigation *has* failed them. A typical solution is to make the organisation's logo a link to the home page. This is an example of a navigation design pattern.

A well-established design pattern is to repeat image-based navigation with a text-based version at the bottom of each page. This may have continuing value for accessibility and for people accessing a site via a device with a restricted display. However, a user may be confused to find the navigation repeated.

The key to navigation design is to understand how much information a user needs at any given point, and it may not be appropriate to give users all possible options at all times. It is important to understand why a user might have accessed a particular page and where he might want to go from there. Scenarios and personas can be useful here (see page 58).

The 30-Year Path of E-Mail

Technology
The New York Times

OPEN SMALL BUSINESS NETWORK™
CLICK TO OPEN

Decoding URLs:

Although intended for machine reading, people using the Internet regularly encounter URLs. Savvy users look at them to understand site structure, and may 'cut back' a URL to get to another site section. They may also move their pointer over a link to see its URL and get an idea where it will take them. (This kind of information forms part of the 'rhetoric of departure'.) On the *New York Times* Web site URLs clearly indicate the article date, section and subsection, and hint at its theme. Page titles are often overlooked in Web site development but are valuable for users who have bookmarked a page, are typing a URL in a browser or are reviewing their browsing history. The *Times'* pages are clearly titled but don't include the publication name, which would provide valuable context in a bookmark list.

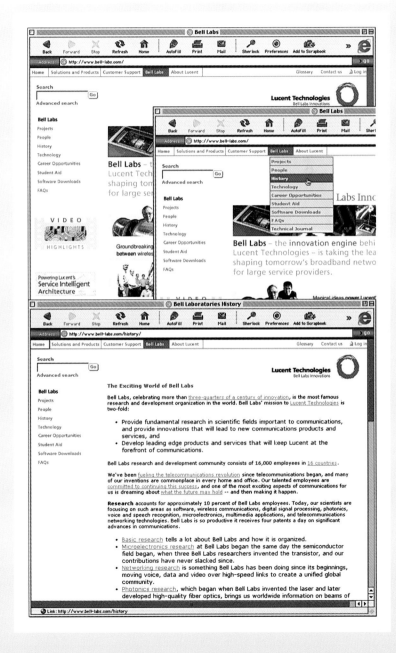

Aping GUIs:

Graphical user interfaces developed drop-down menus to allow screen space to be used economically. As dynamic Web technologies have developed these techniques have been taken up for Web navigation, though it cannot be assumed that they will work as well for this task as they do for software menus.

Breadcrumb trails:
Often people will arrive at a page within a site, rather than at the home page. In these scenarios it is important that the navigation shows them the context of the information they have found, which will help them evaluate its relevance. (This kind of information forms part of the 'rhetoric of arrival'.) This is typically achieved with a breadcrumb trail (a navigational device popularised by Yahoo!).

A breadcrumb trail may very directly reflect the directory structure of the Web site, a connection made clear on the Xplane Web site.

However, well considered navigation may also be able to reflect location. The *Washington Post* navigation uses colour (and reverse colour), indentation and bullets to flag up hierarchical location.

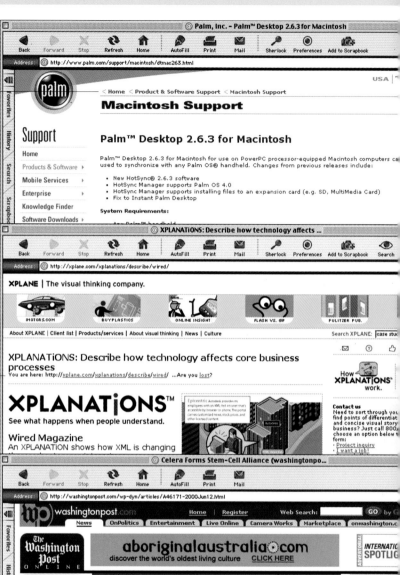

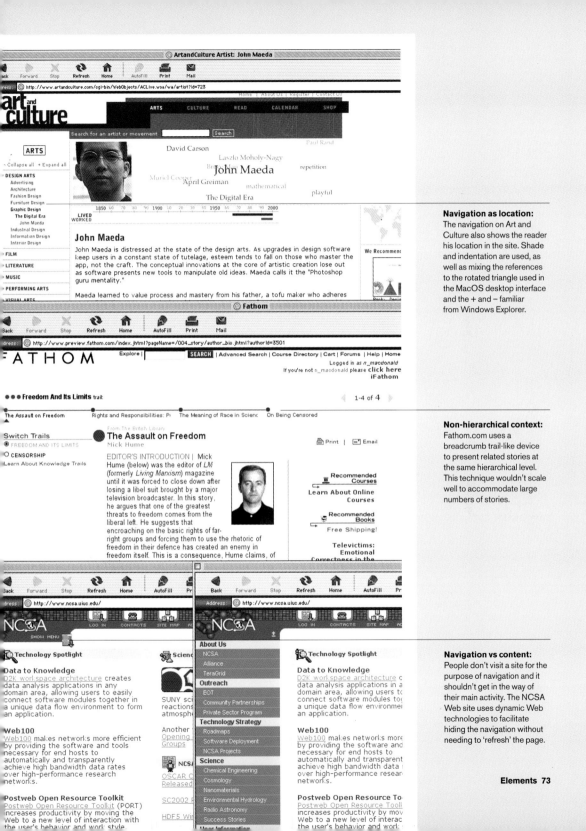

Navigation as location:
The navigation on Art and Culture also shows the reader his location in the site. Shade and indentation are used, as well as mixing the references to the rotated triangle used in the MacOS desktop interface and the + and – familiar from Windows Explorer.

Non-hierarchical context:
Fathom.com uses a breadcrumb trail-like device to present related stories at the same hierarchical level. This technique wouldn't scale well to accommodate large numbers of stories.

Navigation vs content:
People don't visit a site for the purpose of navigation and it shouldn't get in the way of their main activity. The NCSA Web site uses dynamic Web technologies to facilitate hiding the navigation without needing to 'refresh' the page.

Information design and visualisation

Organising information clearly and effectively is just as important on the Web as it is in print and, considering that two of the strengths of the Web are information processing and interfacing with information sources, it is particularly important. Information design is a well-established and mature area of print design and many of its approaches are appropriate for the Web, though some solutions are not appropriate as the medium is malleable, and screen sizes and resolutions are limited.

Information design on the Web draws on information architecture, graphic design and typography. However, it is often undervalued in business or just forgotten. This may be because simply getting information to users is considered sufficient, and also because any kind of structured information is likely to have been produced automatically, for which the output may be more difficult to control.

Good information design allows users to effectively and quickly understand information with which they are presented. This understanding might be about its parameters, the order in which it is displayed or the meaning of each graphical or textual element. Good information design should also facilitate appropriate comparison of information.

While information design is important in presenting information to users, it is also a key skill in information architecture, and facilitating effective communication, particularly with clients and with engineers.

Information design extends into information visualisation, which begins with the graphs and charts with which we are familiar in print, and extends to dynamic and user-manipulable presentations. Ironically, although the Web took

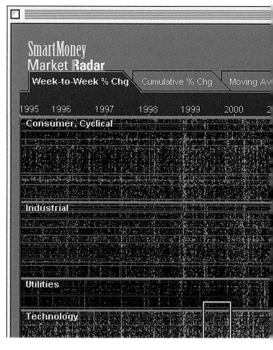

Getting the basics right: British Airways' Web site uses simple information design techniques such as a scale to to present mileage points and status, and colour to indicate variations in ticket price. Overall, its typography and information design is clear and elegant.

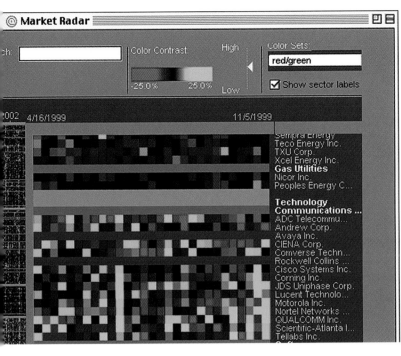

Taking stock of the market: *Smartmoney* magazine's Java-based Market Radar presents an overview of changes in prices for the stock market. The reader can focus in on one industry to see the performance of an individual company in the context of its peers. The macro view makes clear the overall trends in each sector, with the speculation in Internet-related technologies clearly visible. Its approach reflects Ben Shneiderman's mantra "overview, zoom-in, details on demand".

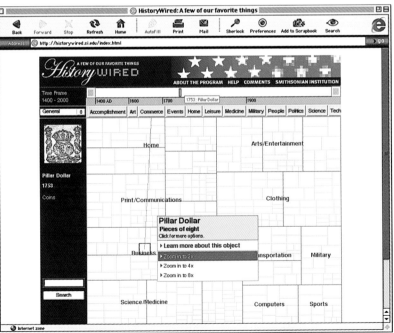

Efficient display: The Smithsonian Institution HistoryWired site adopts an iteration of Shneiderman's 'treemaps' concept to display areas of historical research, and supports drilling-down into material. Treemaps allow information sets to be displayed efficiently while supporting scale comparisons. HistoryWired also uses a timeline to illustrate one dimension of the information.

off with the development of the 'graphical' Mosaic browser, most information on the Web is textual. Even with major bandwidth increases information presentation rarely surpasses print-type graphics to exploit the kinds of information visualisations that are now possible.

The value of information visualisation lies in our visual nature. Our brains are good at processing images, identifying patterns, and distinguishing and grouping by size, colour, shapes and spatial relationships. We are adept in the visual space, but this skill is under-exploited. As Ben Shneiderman, founding director of the University of Maryland's HCI Lab, points out: "Visual bandwidth is enormous and human perceptual skills are remarkable, while human image storage is fast and vast."

Search engines are almost entirely text-driven and are prime candidates for the use of information visualisation techniques, but they are also applicable in many other areas. Visual presentation has an important role to play in the future of online information.

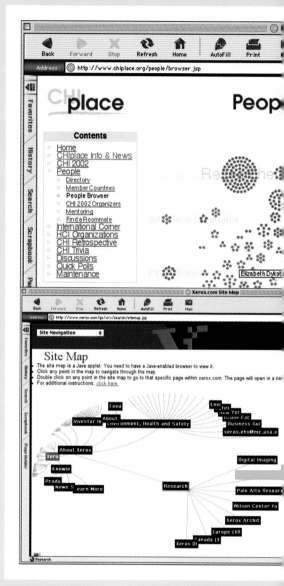

Navigation in context:
Inxight's tool (above), originally developed at Xerox PARC, presents a fish-eye view on a Web site structure, an approach referred to by creator Ramana Rao as a "focus plus context driven".

Direct manipulation:
A researcher at the University of Maryland HCI Lab created an interface for finding films (right). Film Finder presents a range slider that allows filtering by film length (a technique known as 'direct manipulation') and year. Buttons allow for selection by ratings and awards. Query results are immediately displayed as a 'starfield'.

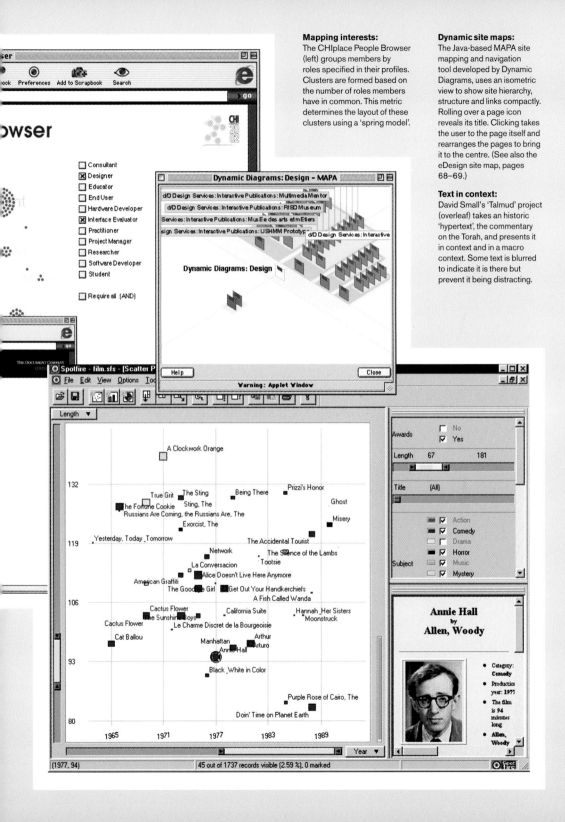

Mapping interests:
The CHIplace People Browser (left) groups members by roles specified in their profiles. Clusters are formed based on the number of roles members have in common. This metric determines the layout of these clusters using a 'spring model'.

Dynamic site maps:
The Java-based MAPA site mapping and navigation tool developed by Dynamic Diagrams, uses an isometric view to show site hierarchy, structure and links compactly. Rolling over a page icon reveals its title. Clicking takes the user to the page itself and rearranges the pages to bring it to the centre. (See also the eDesign site map, pages 68–69.)

Text in context:
David Small's 'Talmud' project (overleaf) takes an historic 'hypertext', the commentary on the Torah, and presents it in context and in a macro context. Some text is blurred to indicate it is there but prevent it being distracting.

CITIES OF REFUGE

(Extract from the Tractate Makkoth 10a...)

These cities (of refuge) are to be made neither into small nor into large walled cities, but medium-sized boroughs; they are to be established only in the vicinity of a water supply, and where there is no water at hand it is to be brought thither; they are to be established only in marketing districts, they are to be established only in populous districts, and if the population has fallen off, more cities are to be brought into the neighbourhood, and if the residents (of any such place) have fallen off, others are brought thither; priests [cohanim,] Levites and Israelites. There should be traffic neither in arms nor in trap-gear there: these are the words of R. Nehemiah but the Sages permit it. They, however, agree that no traps may be set there, nor any ropes left dangling about in the place so that the blood avenger has no occasion to come visiting there.

R. Isaac asked: What is the Scriptural authority [for it — provisions]? - The verse [and] that fleeing unto one of these cities might live (Deuteronomy 4 : 42) which means: provide him with whatever he needs so that he may [truly] live.

A Tanna taught [a baraitha]: A disciple who goes into banishment is joined in exile by his master, in accordance with the text [and] fleeing — he might live... which means: provide him with what he needs to [truly] live. R. Zeira says: a teacher that thou livest a disciple... "Let no one teach" ... Mishnah [the teacher] to a disciple goes into

Whither are they banished? To the three citi[es]
on the yonder side of the Jordan and three c[ities]
in the land of Canaan, as ordained, ye shall g[ive]
cities beyond the Jordan and three cities in th[e]
Canaan; They shall be cities of refuge. Not u[ntil]
cities were selected in the land of Israel did th[e]
three cities beyond the Jordan receive fugitive[s]
ordained. [and of these cities which ye shall g[ive]
cities for refuge shall they be unto you which
that [they did] not [function] until all six cou[ld]
simultaneously afford asylum.
And direct roads were made leading from on[e]
other, as ordained, thou shalt prepare thee a
divide the borders of thy land into three part[s]
[ordained] scholar-disciples were delegated t[o]
manslayer in case anyone attempted to slay h[im]
way, and that they might speak to him.
R. Meir says: he may [even] plead h[is]
is ordained and this is h[...]
Judah says: to h[...]

Interaction design

Interaction design is the aspect of Web design that has least precedent in any existing area of design. The challenges of interaction design are a product of the development of digital computers, and the concept was only formalised in the early 1980s at the time that personal computers were taking off. Bill Verplank, a human factors engineer at IDEO working in this area, notes that: "As soon as there are mapping and modes, built-in behaviour, programmability, that's when really interesting things start to happen. How you manage the complex interactions is interaction design." It is clear that interaction design is important with the Web.

Interaction design draws on other disciplines such as ergonomics, cognitive psychology, human factors and the study of language. One of its most significant theorists, Donald Norman, has a background in cognitive psychology.

While interaction design is new it does build on our understanding of interacting with machines. In *The Design of Everyday Things* Norman outlines four principles that make for a good interaction with a tool's interface: it should be visible (the user should be able to see its current state); it should be easy for the user to form a conceptual model of the tool; there should be a good mapping between the interface and its functions, and there should be feedback to the user on the result of his actions. These principles also apply to design for the Web and provide a good model for thinking about and evaluating design solutions.

Norman has also championed the concept of 'affordances', a term first coined by perceptual psychologist JJ Gibson to describe the actions that a user perceives as being possible with an interface (such as a button which 'affords' pushing.) As screen-based interfaces are not physical, the concept of affordances has limited application and can lead to over-literal design.

While it is important to build on the learning from other disciplines, and from the design of software interfaces, there are some areas with interaction design on the Web that are not well charted. Many applications of the Web allow access to large amounts of information.

The challenges here are addressed by information visualisation, which focuses on visual ways to represent information and support its manipulation. While we address information visualisation elsewhere (see page 74), solutions for the manipulation of large datasets, such as search results, are in the realm of interaction design.

One solution is direct manipulation, a term associated with Ben Shneiderman. This refers to 'live' manipulation of a dataset through direct control of the variables which define it, showing the user the relationship between them.

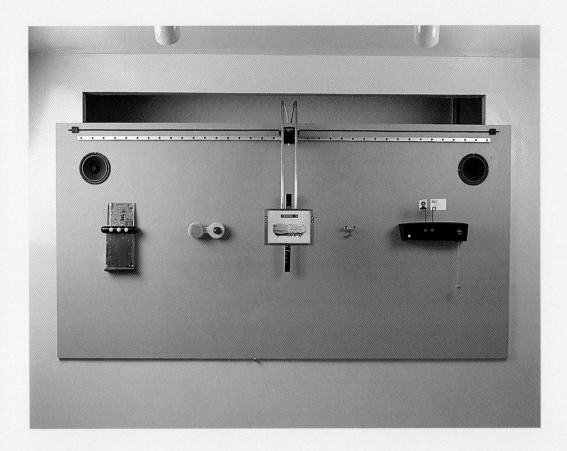

Enhancing the physical with the digital:

While interaction design for the Web is focused on the screen it is not appropriate for all products and services to be entirely screen-based. Durrell Bishop's networked products project for the centenary show of London's Royal College of Art investigates the appropriate relationship between 'soft' and 'hard' interfaces. The five network products are a CD player, a TV, radio, doorbell and bank. Rather than integrate a display with every object, or converge many objects into one, Bishop argues for soft and hard representations to work together. For instance, the CD player is represented by a ('hard') object into which CDs are inserted but which has only three buttons (back, forward and eject). Bringing the 'soft' flat panel display to the player adds an interface with richer but less frequently used functionality. Bishop's examples also point to the different contexts in which design solutions must work, from the office to the sofa, shared spaces to private use, indoors to outdoors, seated to standing.

The Design of Everyday Things:

Donald Norman has popularised the discussion of design and human factors.

Validation:
One of the most common interactions on the Web involves validation of forms. This often includes a page refresh as the form data is sent to the server. This is disconcerting for the user as it is often unclear on the resulting page what needs to be corrected. This NatWest Bank form uses slightly comical icons to make it clear where user attention is required.

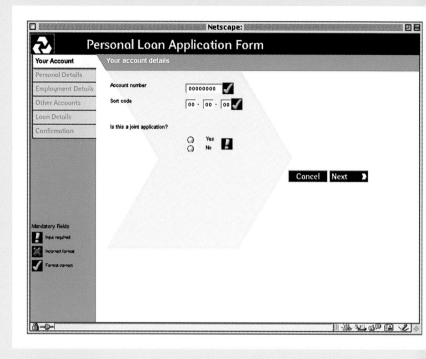

Origins of a concept:
Bill Verplank (below), a veteran of Xerox, IDEO and Interval Research, coined the term 'interaction design' with Bill Moggridge at IDTwo in the 1980s. He is a keen advocate of sketching as a creative tool.

Hypertext in context:
The Public Lettering Web site uses dynamic Web technologies to present footnotes in context by just selecting them, and without a disconcerting page refresh.

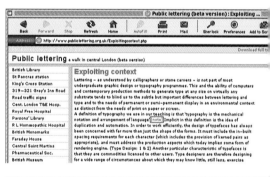

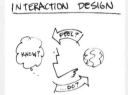

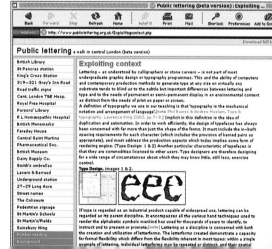

The search function on the BBC Food Web site elegantly reveals itself when selected, in a software-like fashion. This allows for more efficient use of screen space and provides a more satisfying user experience.

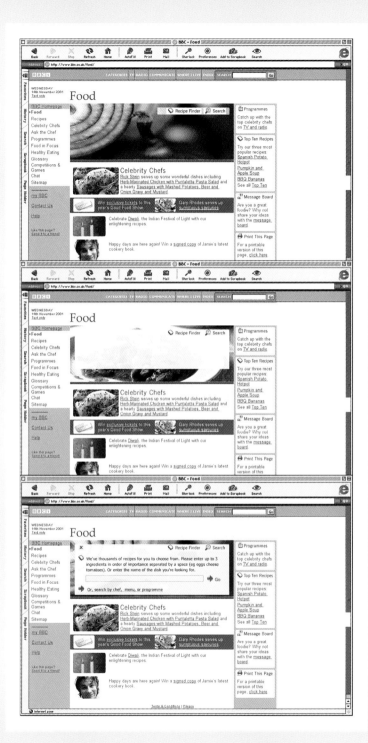

Integrating hard and soft interaction:

Handspring's Treo range of phone-PDAs (below) require tight integration of the hard and soft interface. The device supports Web access but the constrained QWERTY keypad and lack of mouse make most Web sites difficult to use. However, the screen is touch sensitive, aiding interaction with Web sites and configuring the phone's other features such as conference calling. Touch-screens can also support gesture-based input, which adds another dimension to user interaction.

Interface design

The concept of interface design is associated with software, and particularly software that exploits a 'graphical user interface' (GUI). Interface design overlaps with information architecture, interaction and information design, and the design of navigation. Its focus is communicating to users what the application or Web site they are using can do, what their options are and how they can initiate its use.

The classic interface elements (see 'GUI essentials', right) have been adopted into the Web by the creators of Web browsers and while they may not be the most appropriate interface elements for the Web they are at least familiar to users who inevitably encounter them if they are using a personal computer.

As it has tended to be more content- than task-focused than software, the Web has spawned a few new interface elements. Menus in the form of glorified lists are a significant part of many interfaces, emphasising the need to organise access to large amounts of content.

Another popular solution to this challenge is the clickable image map within which different areas are delineated for specific links.

In imitation of GUI dialogue boxes, the Web has also adopted pop-up windows to give users access to additional options or information without leaving their current screen.

The Web's content- and task-focus, and its framing within a browser and OS, present the challenge of creating enough space for the 'content' users will be seeking. Allowing pages to scroll is one solution, but sometimes being able to see all the content is valuable. Tight framing of content often leads users to focus on a small section of a Web page and ignore peripheral elements such as navigation and adverts.

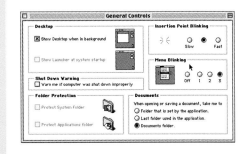

GUI essentials:
The classic interface elements (above) allow the user to select options, which may be mutually exclusive, using check boxes and radio buttons. They indicate to the user how to initiate an action using buttons. Icons represent often complex ideas and allow them to be distinguished. 'Greying out' indicates an option that is not appropriate in a given context. Text fields allow for data entry, dialogue boxes for feedback, and menus for presenting an extensive selection compactly. Many of these conventions have migrated to the Web.

GUI essentials revisited:
For its update to MacOS X (below) Apple made use of colour and interactivity that weren't supported when the original MacOS interface was created. The standard window buttons (close, minimise, maximise) are coloured and acquire icons when moused over. Items in the background are washed out but respond to a mouseover without becoming fully active.

Season Pass Manager

Press SELECT to edit a Season Pass. Use RIGHT to change the Season Pass priority (by moving it UP or DOWN in the list). A higher priority pass will be recorded if there is a conflict with a lower one.

1. Charmed (112 LIVING)
2. Sports/ Football & Manchester United
3. Dream Team (106 SKYONE)
4. Friends (106 SKYONE)
5. EastEnders (101 BBC1)

'Lean back' GUIs:
TiVo is a pioneering digital video recorder that makes the most of the television remote-control interface. Screens slide gracefully from left to right, and audio is well employed. Colour is used to create a feeling of solidity but also of relaxation. Its information design and typography are also excellent. The remote control, by IDEO, has tactile buttons that vary in size and response, uses carefully chosen colours, and sports well-considered icons.

More task-oriented Web sites often use frames, pop-up windows and Flash, to present a more 'application-like' interface, which is often appropriate. However, for content-focused sites these devices may disorient the user and make it more difficult to reference the site.

Another challenge Web interface designers have to address more than software interface designers is the creation of interfaces that can be used by novice or casual users but also by expert users. Supporting user customisation of interfaces, usually to increase efficiency, is another challenge, particularly because people will use a large number of Web sites which will tend to be inconsistent in the way they support customisation, and for most users time spent customising isn't well invested.

An additional challenge comes when an interface design is improved but users are used to the existing design. While the new interface may make them more efficient, they will initially need to invest their time to learn it and may be reluctant to do this. (See caption below, and the Bolt.com case study, pages 206–213.)

Interface updates:
When eBay decided to upgrade from its original interface it was concerned whether eBay members who use the service to make a living might find their efficiency seriously affected, at least in the short term. It resolved the problem by providing the 'classic' interface and the upgraded interface simultaneously for several months. This allowed users to continue to use the 'classic' interface for a period of time until they became familiar with the new one. Eventually, the classic interface was removed altogether.

Personalisation:
The Wall Street Journal (left) can be personalised directly from the location at which personalised stories appear.

Polite notice:
The AIGA Web site (above) pops up a custom-sized browser window with notice about supported browsers. This can be easily dismissed, leaving the user where he intended to be.

Forceful notice:
The Getty Images Web site (left) uses a JavaScript pop-up to indicate which element of a form hasn't been completed appropriately. The notice is quite well written and the field in question well flagged, but it is not clear which characters are 'invalid'.

Elements 87

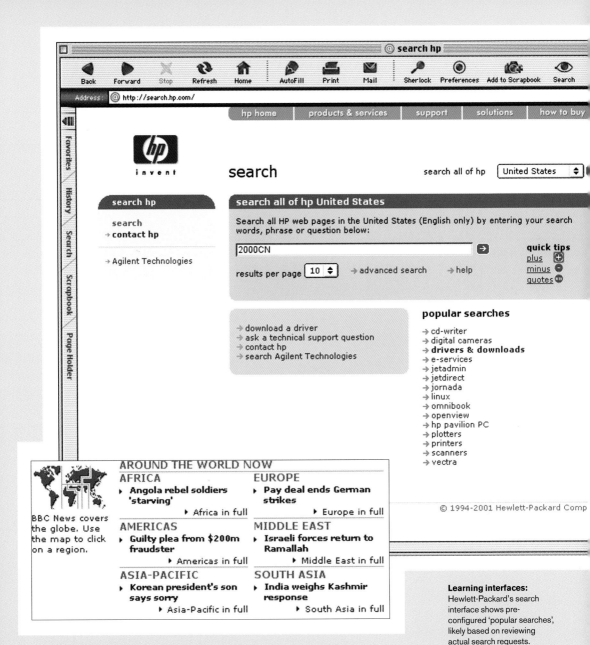

The world as interface:
An image map of the world is often used as an interface to geographically specific information or services, as in this small but clear world map used by BBC News.

Learning interfaces:
Hewlett-Packard's search interface shows pre-configured 'popular searches', likely based on reviewing actual search requests.

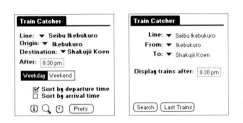

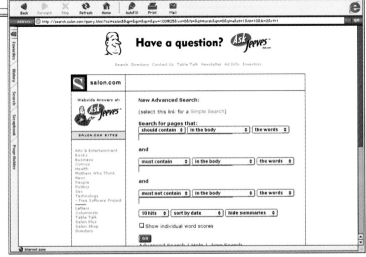

Constricted interfaces:
Mobile devices need to be light and often have mono screens, severely restricting interface solutions. The image on the left shows a first pass design of the first screen for the PalmOS-based Train Catcher application. On the left is a cleaned-up version which shows only the key choices the user needs to make, and uses defaults for other options.

Simplifying complexity
To narrow searches Boolean 'operators' are often used. *Eye* magazine (left) uses images of magazine covers in its search results to help the user work out where the article he is looking for might be. Salon.com (below) provides an easy interface to these powerful searches using drop-down menus and plain language, avoiding the need to use +, −, AND, OR, NOT and "".

Poster power:
The Italian office machinery
and computer company
Olivetti has long been a
champion of good design, in
its marketing and its products.
The power of graphic design
seen in this poster reminds us
that design is not just about
functionality. The use of
movement to direct the
reader's eye is also valuable
in editorial design for the Web,
and invaluable for the design
of forms and other tasks that
need to be completed in a
specific sequence.

Graphic design and aesthetics

On first impressions it might appear that graphic
design is the key design discipline in design for
the Web. Much of the power of graphic design
comes from a combination of visual 'movement',
balance and delineation in a layout, the dramatic
and subtle use of type, colour, space, line and
image, and high visual quality in typography and
photography. For publications, we can add their
overall structure and flow. Some artifacts exploit
elaborate paper engineering, and all benefit
from the use of high quality stock and technical
expertise in printing and finishing. It should be
apparent that many of these qualities don't
map directly to the Web, though some map to
information architecture and information design.

What we can take from graphic design is its
general approach, sensibilities and skills, along
with specific aspects of its application. (There is
much more to the effective use of graphic
design than implied by the overused term 'look
and feel'.) Much can be learned from great print
and editorial design, while taking into account
the limits of the medium, and the ways in which it
can enhance graphical presentation, particularly
exploiting use of imagery and movement.

These design skills will be even more
important in future. The initial draw of the Web,
for business and users, was its breadth, utility,
and functionality, but in future its overall quality
of experience, to which graphic design and
aesthetics are crucial, will be a key differentiator.

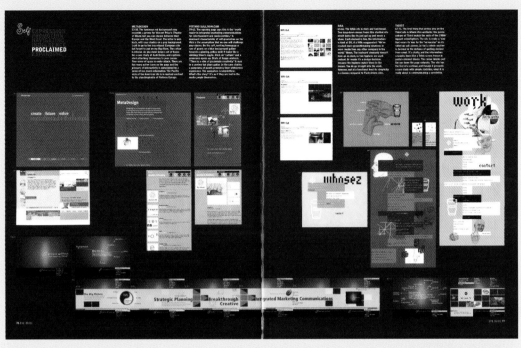

Space and movement:
The graphic design publication *Eye* combines bold but restrained typography with subtle use of a grid in which well-paced images tell a story. Colour is used richly without interfering with imagery while the typography is elegant and comfortable to read.

Low bandwidth graphics:
Boo.com (left) showed how strong graphics could work on the Web. Flat colours compress effectively, reducing file size and improving site performance. Other graphic elements include the (male/female) icons and buttons which indicate 'pressability' by their raised and tactile appearance.

Elements 91

Typography

The basic elements of good typography are legibility and readability. Legibility refers to the clarity of individual characters and is largely a function of the medium in which they are reproduced. Screens have historically been very low resolution compared to paper and for this reason legibility has also been low. Readability refers to the ease with which groups of characters – words, sentences, paragraphs and pages – can be read and is a function of character design, letter and word spacing, line length and separation, and paragraph delineation. The human eye 'reads' the shape of words and phrases, rather than focusing on individual characters. Hence the character shape also affects readability. There is some debate about how closely screen typography follows legibility and readability rules for print and the ideal typographic approach for a project may be best determined by testing.

One major way the screen differs from print is that it is luminous (light emitting) rather than reflective (light reflecting) which tends to reduce the comfort of reading. This discomfort has been ameliorated by the development of anti-aliasing, a technique (pioneered in the television industry in the early 1980s) that helps characters by introducing grey pixels at their edges, creating a viewing resolution for the eye of 300 dots per inch. Techniques such as these (see ClearType, opposite), along with affordable higher resolution displays, could bring type legibility, and readability, on screen close to that of paper.

There is a significant limit to the quality of typography the Web can currently support, which is imposed by its 'deliver and print' model. A Web server sends text with basic information about formatting to a browser, but it relies on the browser to display the text using fonts that are available from the operating system underneath it. Font display can be limited to the Courier, Times, Arial and Helvetica typefaces. Even this base set of fonts isn't standard, though font 'degradation' can be specific in the page code.

These quality issues can be partially circumvented in three ways. Elements for which a particular typographic style are required, such as navigation or headlines, can be generated and inserted into Web pages as pictures. However, apart from the difficulty of editing this 'GIF type', it increases download times, makes pages less malleable, and is not searchable or otherwise machine-readable.

A second solution is to embed the desired fonts into the Web page code where they become available to the operating system. Such models were pioneered by Bitstream and Microsoft in the late 1990s but were unsuccessful, partly because there was no standard across browsers but also because these embedded fonts required additional tools to create them. They also increase page download times and reduce browser performance, which was a not inconsiderable issue at a time when most people accessed the Internet via a modem.

A third solution is to use Flash movies to present text, as they support embedded fonts. This is one of the most successful solutions to date, but again this text cannot easily be searched, or copied, which reduces its utility.

The best solution found so far has been to create fonts designed for screen display and distribute them widely and freely, ensuring that they end up in a critical mass of operating systems. Few companies could achieve this and one of them, Microsoft, set Massachusetts-based type designer Matthew Carter the challenge. Carter created Verdana, a sans serif typeface, and Georgia, a serif typeface, that have basic characteristics to help with legibility and readability: wide characters, a large x-height and simple, open forms. These typefaces were distributed via the Web, installed with Internet Explorer, and added to the core Windows fonts. They are now fairly ubiquitous and are often specified in Web pages.

The limitations of Web typography and screen reading lead many people to print pages and read them 'offline', and even when the quality of screen typography is better, they will still do this as paper is more portable than any digital device and people tend to focus on tasks rather than passive reading when they are using a computer. For these reasons design needs to address the way that pages, and particularly type, reproduce on paper. In this medium Times New Roman, which is poor for screen reading, may well be superior to Verdana, whose screen-optimised spacing and cruder forms makes it a less pleasing font for reading.

So far we have only discussed Roman type but soon, if not now, designers will be confronted by non-Roman fonts (such as Cyrillic and Arabic), and non-character-based scripts such as some of those used in South East Asia. They will also be confronted by scripts that don't read from left to right. The implications of these challenges are enormous, though the significant move to learn English, especially in China and Japan, will reduce them for some time.

On the Web line spacing and typographic layout (important elements of readability) and other type formatting is controlled by Cascading Style Sheets (CSS). These embed in the Web page HTML and are a key tool for Web design. Although we have focused on the limits of online typography in relation to print, one major positive difference is that digital devices can display motion, and much research has been done into 'kinetic' typography and the benefits this can have for reading. Many other avenues for presentation of type, particularly display type, have been opened up including changing scale, colour and perspective and these have been investigated most extensively using Flash.

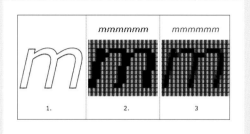

ClearType: Developed at Microsoft Typography, it uses the ability to address the three RGB sub-pixels that comprise each pixel in colour LCD displays, thus providing more control over character legibility.

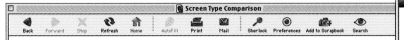

The greatest benefit of working from bitmap to outline is not felt in the bitmapped letterforms themselves but in their spacing. *Matthew Carter*

The greatest benefit of working from bitmap to outline is not felt in the bitmapped letterforms themselves but in their spacing. *Matthew Carter*

The greatest benefit of working from bitmap to outline is not f[elt] in the bitmapped letterforms themselves but in their spacing. *Matthew Carter*

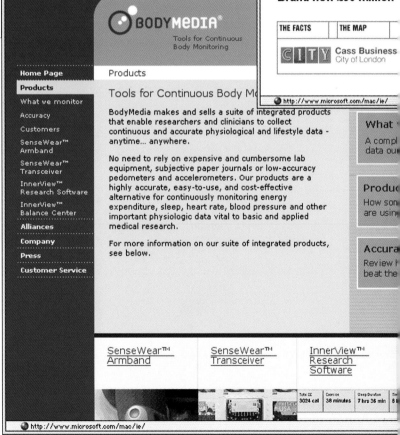

Finding the right type:
(From top left anticlockwise) Verdana, Georgia and Times presented at the same point size on the Web. The former two, designed by Matthew Carter, are optimised for the Web, and feel open and comfortable on screen compared to Times. BodyMedia chooses Verdana while Hyphen Press specifies Georgia. MSNBC Newsweek uses Times large – the only way it works well on typical monitors. Cass Business School in London employs Arial, a sans serif font which works well on the Web, although not designed for use on screen, as well as 'GIF type' for display.

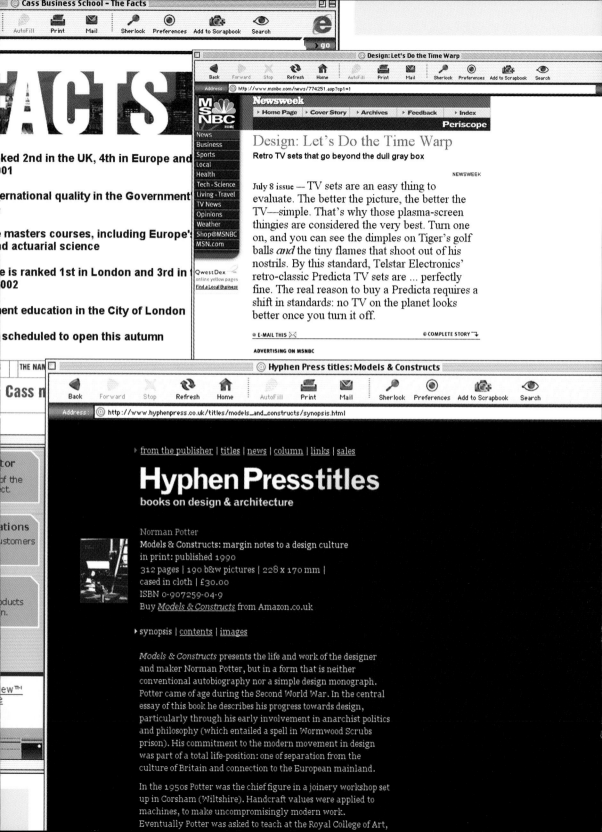

AutoFill Print Mail Sherlock Preferences Add to Scrapbook Search

FACTS

ked 2nd in the UK, 4th in Europe and
01

ernational quality in the Government'

e masters courses, including Europe'
d actuarial science

e is ranked 1st in London and 3rd in
002

ent education in the City of London

scheduled to open this autumn

THE NAM

Cass n

tor
of the
ct.

ations
ustomers

ducts
n.

ew™

Back Forward Stop Refresh Home AutoFill Print Mail Sherlock Preferences Add to Scrapbook Search

Address: http://www.msnbc.com/news/774251.asp?cp1=1

Newsweek

▸ Home Page ▸ Cover Story ▸ Archives ▸ Feedback ▸ Index

Periscope

News
Business
Sports
Local
Health
Tech - Science
Living - Travel
TV News
Opinions
Weather
Shop@MSNBC
MSN.com

QwestDex
online yellow pages
Find a Local Business

Design: Let's Do the Time Warp

Retro TV sets that go beyond the dull gray box

NEWSWEEK

July 8 issue — TV sets are an easy thing to
evaluate. The better the picture, the better the
TV—simple. That's why those plasma-screen
thingies are considered the very best. Turn one
on, and you can see the dimples on Tiger's golf
balls *and* the tiny flames that shoot out of his
nostrils. By this standard, Telstar Electronics'
retro-classic Predicta TV sets are ... perfectly
fine. The real reason to buy a Predicta requires a
shift in standards: no TV on the planet looks
better once you turn it off.

@ E-MAIL THIS ✕   @ COMPLETE STORY ➔

ADVERTISING ON MSNBC

Back Forward Stop Refresh Home AutoFill Print Mail Sherlock Preferences Add to Scrapbook Search

Address: http://www.hyphenpress.co.uk/titles/models_and_constructs/synopsis.html

▸ from the publisher | titles | news | column | links | sales

Hyphen Press titles

books on design & architecture

Norman Potter
Models & Constructs: margin notes to a design culture
in print: published 1990
312 pages | 190 b&w pictures | 228 x 170 mm |
cased in cloth | £30.00
ISBN 0-907259-04-9
Buy *Models & Constructs* from Amazon.co.uk

▸ synopsis | contents | images

Models & Constructs presents the life and work of the designer
and maker Norman Potter, but in a form that is neither
conventional autobiography nor a simple design monograph.
Potter came of age during the Second World War. In the central
essay of this book he describes his progress towards design,
particularly through his early involvement in anarchist politics
and philosophy (which entailed a spell in Wormwood Scrubs
prison). His commitment to the modern movement in design
was part of a total life-position: one of separation from the
culture of Britain and connection to the European mainland.

In the 1950s Potter was the chief figure in a joinery workshop set
up in Corsham (Wiltshire). Handcraft values were applied to
machines, to make uncompromisingly modern work.
Eventually Potter was asked to teach at the Royal College of Art,

Text and writing

Text is integral to the Web, not just the written information or prose people explicitly go in search of, but the words contextualising it (such as page titles), in help files, or in interface elements such as in navigation, buttons, error messages and dialogues – even in file and directory names.

While a designer is not typically responsible for the explicit textual content of a Web site, he should be aware of the ways that people read information on the Web and the editorial forms that best support reading in this medium. A typical behaviour is quickly scanning a page (partly because of the discomfort of screen reading), picking up on highlighted text and hypertext links, and avoiding copy that doesn't appear to be strictly informational. Designers should also be aware that a strong editorial style and, where appropriate, a text that expresses a definite opinion is more likely to draw people in.

A reader receiving an email newsletter may only see the sender, date and subject line in their in-box. A subject line that simply states the issue number or date, or is the same for each issue, won't help entice the reader into the editorial 'hidden' beneath. If he doesn't recognise the sender name he is also less likely to read on.

Where text is used in a supporting role to help the user, it is certainly the domain of design, and is addressed in information architecture, navigation design, and elsewhere. The terminology used for menus, site sections and explanatory text is critical. It is often derived from the client's organisation structure or the names of its internal processes rather than being based on users' expectations and use of classifications.

When a site is live it is often useful to review the terms users search on to get a sense of the way they categorise the kinds of information for which they are looking.

Error messages and dialogues should address users' expectations of what was about to happen and explain what *has* happened and what their options are, but avoid presenting this using system terminology.

There are many style 'standards' that can be referenced, most originally created for GUIs.

Text on the Internet is a chameleon thing. While a heading might be written for a particular article or page, it might subsequently appear in a search result, as a reference elsewhere on the site, as the title of an email, or cut and pasted by a user into a document. These situations need to be taken into account when writing online text. A general rule is to make such copy more informational and less dependent on its context.

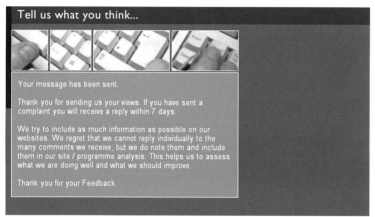

File Not Found

Try these links
- Adobe Acrobat Reader
- Adobe Products
- Customer Support
- Adobe Home Page

We're sorry! The page you were trying to view is no longer here. If you reached this page from another part of Adobe.com, please let us know so we can fix the problem.

Use our search engine to locate what you're looking for

Where to search:
- ● Entire site
- ○ Product Information only
- ○ Technical Support documents only

Enter search terms:

► SEARCH

Enter your search words, phrase or question below:

○ HP ○ Compaq ● Both

search: → help
(example: monitors +"pavilion series")

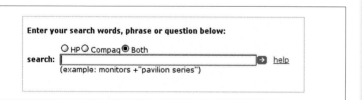

Evaluation

Because design is a problem-solving process its solutions must be evaluated, and this *will* happen when its product is finally put to use as it was intended. However, it is both possible and desirable to evaluate design solutions before they 'go live'. It is possible because aspects of the design solution can be simulated in use without having to complete the product, and it is desirable because it is cheaper and more time efficient to redirect the design and development of a product earlier in the process. It is also less demoralising for the project team.

There are a number of important aspects of evaluation. The first is working out how to present a design idea in a way that will elicit the right kind of feedback, but isn't too labour-intensive to produce or iterate. These may include pencil sketches, paper prototypes, rough interactive mock-ups in PowerPoint or Flash, HTML wireframes, or finished screens created in Photoshop linked in the sequence of a task. Other forms may be appropriate depending on what is being evaluated.

These ideas may be evaluated either by someone with design expertise who can be objective about the approach, by the client, by another stakeholder in the project or by a selection of people from the target audience who are not familiar with the project. This evaluation, particularly in the last instance, has to extract what the problems with the design would be if it were actually being used in a real situation, and must try to understand the way the user interacts with it based on his mental models and expectations of the product.

See 'Usability and usability testing', page 99, for more detail on testing with real users.

Finally, this feedback and learning needs to be translated into appropriately refined design solutions (though if the designs failed badly these may be new solutions) to be tested again.

Evaluation is not a substitute for great design thinking and problem solving. Evaluation can only identify bad design or lay the basis for making good design better. It can't turn bad design into good design.

An expert evaluation may be based on the evaluator putting himself in the situation of intended users performing tasks and looking for problems in the design solution, simply looking for problems based on their experience and knowledge, or reviewing the design according to general principles of good design, often referred to as heuristics.

Testing prototypes: Organic's MIN schematics (see pages 236–243)

Usability and usability testing

In the mantra that states that a good product should be "useful, usable, and desirable", the *raison d'être* of many Web products to date has been at best only for the first. As a result, users have been delivered frustrating products which fail to fulfil their promise because their designers didn't evaluate them for ease of use.

In some ways this was an understandable and even appropriate state of affairs. With any new technology excitement is generated by the realisation that it is now possible to do something that was previously impossible or at least impractical. At this point in the development of a product certain people will use it irrespective of its lack of usability. This was true of computing from its inception through the eras of punch cards and command line operating systems until the early 1980s and the development of the graphical user interface. During this period many people enthusiastically embraced the power of computing, grateful that it was even available. As usability researcher Jared Spool has noted about new technologies, "it's not what the horse says but that it speaks at all" that impresses people.

As a technology evolves people start to take it for granted and competing products appear that put the pioneers in perspective. At this point the ability for the intended users to use the product effectively becomes an issue. This is the domain of usability. While usability is a broad subject and overlaps with interface and interaction design, and with information architecture and writing for the Web, at its heart are two basic propositions: that the users for whom a product is designed should be able to successfully and efficiently carry out the tasks it is intended to facilitate, and that it is possible to test how well a design (and the supporting technology) achieves this.

Usability tests seek to observe users who are typical of a product's intended audience, but who aren't familiar with the proposed design solution, attempting the task it is designed to support, in a situation similar to that in which they might use the product in real life. Tests may be qualitative or quantitative (or a combination of the two), the former seeking to understand how the users are thinking while they address the task, the latter recording task completion time and other metrics. For both types of test the observer does not advise or assist the user, as he would not be on hand to advise in real life.

For qualitative tests the observer typically encourages the user to 'think out loud' about what he thinks the product offers, what is possible at each point, how he decides each action, what he thinks has happened based on how the product responds, where he is generally confused, and when he thinks he has successfully completed the task.

Tests can be done on design solutions at any stage in the process, and are typically done when there is a significant design development, or a number of design solutions have been developed and the best one can't be evaluated in any other way. While the prototype used for testing can be quite crude, it needs at least to allow the person being tested to imagine the way the design and the system are intended to work. Quantitative tests can't easily be combined with qualitative tests, as the process of thinking out loud would affect results.

For qualitative tests users' actions and comments should be recorded, along with any thoughts they have about the design and how it might be improved, while for quantitative tests timings and other metrics should be recorded. With both tests it may be appropriate to ask users to rate the design's ease of use, quality and appeal. Test results are typically distilled into a report outlining usability problems and making design recommendations. Those from users will be subjective, but they should still be evaluated and may lead to good design solutions. User ratings are again subjective, but may flag up major problems for future design development.

The results of the tests will present the designer with new challenges, which may be resolved by recommendations in the report. Observing usability tests may also suggest design solutions, and it is salutary for a designer to see how their designs work in practice. However, results need to be interpreted carefully and quick jumps to 'common sense' explanations for a user's thinking and behaviour should be avoided. Human psychology is both complex and subtle and we are often not good at interpreting our own motivations and reasoning. Acquiring a better understanding of people's use of the Web will often require more extensive and thorough-going research.

Usability testing should be part of an iterative cycle of design development and evaluation, and the earlier it is feasible to test a design, the lower will be the overheads involved in getting it right. Testing is also valuable after the launch of a site for identifying problems that were missed (or couldn't be properly tested pre-launch) and for positing issues for future site development.

Usability is a valuable tool in helping designers to identify bad ideas and refine good ones. It doesn't seek to challenge the problem as presented, and it cannot drive the design process – after all there is always more than one usable design solution. Neither can it turn bad

design into good, though it can enhance it. Like other evaluation techniques usability has its limits. It can't test for more subjective but equally important criteria such as quality of experience, yet these are aspects of usability. As Donald Norman argues: "More pleasurable things are easier to use. We should not separate pleasure and beauty from usability."

As products evolve to become usable, usability becomes less important to users, and quality of experience comes to the fore. "Usability is always secondary. It's never the most important thing about an experience," notes Norman. "I will accept poor usability if I get what I need, if the total experience is great. I will reject perfect usability if I am not rewarded with a useful, engaging experience."

Testing times:
It is often useful to photograph or video usability tests, ideally recording what is happening on-screen at the same time. Videos are time-consuming to review, but may be useful for making a case to a client or other associates. One-way mirrors (bottom) are a popular observation technique that avoids interference with the test.

Technical testing

The technology and engineering behind a site are factors that can have a profound impact on people's experience of using a Web site, and should be considered alongside design factors.

Technology is one of the constraints within which design works, and design solutions need to take into account technical performance and quality. However, this will not always be possible, and while many technical and engineering factors are not the direct province of designers they should not be ignored.

The most basic technical issue is whether a design will, in principle, work on the platforms for which it is intended, and whether the final coded version *does* work (and work quickly). The first issue depends more on what standards and features browsers support and the second on how they implement them. The key standards relate to HTML.

Although standards for HTML are well established, browser software manufacturers have tended to only pay lip service to them in the past and we have been left with hundreds of browser versions from tens of companies, which are all slightly or extremely incompatible. The advent of scripting languages and dynamic code, such as Javascript and Dynamic HTML, has further exacerbated these problems.

It would be very unusual, and expensive (if not impossible), to create HTML code that worked adequately on all browsers, and the project research should identify the key browsers that need to be supported. However, even supporting just one version of Netscape's Navigator and one of Microsoft's Internet Explorer on one version of Windows and one version of MacOS can throw up plenty of compatibility issues.

Compatibility testing (one element of a process often known as quality assurance or QA) can be time consuming, and problems are often laborious to fix. The more testing that can be carried out during the design and implementation stages, the less time will be needed at the end of the process – time which, as a result of the vagaries of Web development, always gets squeezed.

A less obvious but equally important issue is performance. Even if a user's browser does support the features of a Web site, and the HTML and other code displays and behaves as intended, site performance can still undermine the users' experience of the site.

The level of performance a site can achieve is partly determined by the client's budget and how this is allocated, and performance levels should be set at an appropriate level rather than being open-ended. Performance is one of many factors that affect user satisfaction with a Web site and should not be unduly prioritised over other factors.

One of the fundamental aspects of performance is page loading time which is affected not just by the size of the page elements but also how many (new) elements it contains. It is also affected by the amount of code in the page that requires processing on the client browser, as well as the speed of the server, how much data it has to serve, the bandwidth of the connection it is on, congestion on the Internet between it and the user, and the bandwidth of the user's own connection. Not all of these variables can be controlled by engineering, but even factors such as Internet congestion can be circumvented.

Another technical factor that affects performance is caching. This is a technique

zoowa

profile | settings

people
notes
voice/email
clubs
homepages
tagbooks
boards
e-cards
photos
quiz/polls
horoscope
free stuff

ap | chat | radio | play

customize skin

ight © 1997-2001 Bolt.
ll rights reserved

468 X 60

Gaming

Features:

5k

Game on Quiz
Take the gaming quiz and see if you are all that

go

5k

Play Multiplayer Games
Wormhole and switchout multi hours of fun

go

5k

Face Off
Take the gaming quiz and see if you are all that

go

372 X 40   9k

Gaming Clubs: more

flag   club name   members

1k   angelbabes singlepeeps only
      founder:
      if your single and have your eyes set on
      someone t...

1k   Big I Official
      founder:
      Officially the first club
      the ...

1k   big eye art
      founder:
      no crying   no crying

Gaming Boards:

Post

the greatest movie
"Too Wong Foo, Than
by:

She'll Never Be a t
"So what do you think
by:

news about caitlin
caitlin went into the h
by:

Gaming Tagbooks:

Question   Replies

If there is a Big Brother 3 should Julie Chen be t...
by:

Pick your favorite name out of these:
by:

Best looking girl?
by:

18

Poll:

Do you
camera

○ Yes,
○ No, b
○ What

Newsle

☐ Get

Total Gra

banners

Weight:
The Bolt.com design team (see pages 206–213) spec out the 'weight' of each page element in order to help determine site performance (left).

Performing for your users:
One site that was a victim of poor performance more than poor design was the sports and outdoor fashion-inspired retailer Boo.com (below). As the site launch date loomed, it was decided that it would be quicker to add site functionality on the client side. The upshot was that pages downloaded more slowly but, more importantly, processing the page code slowed the client browser considerably, and its complexity generated more errors than 'flat' HTML.

which allows the browser to reuse an element (usually an image) that it has already downloaded, on the same page or on another. This can vastly increase page loading rates but many Web pages are coded to turn caching off, for no apparent reason, and this reduces performance.

The perceived assessment of the performance of a site is also affected by the order in which page elements load. Again, this is an aspect of performance that can largely be controlled, though a client may choose to have an element, such as an advertisement, loading first.

Creativity, innovation and the big idea

While design is largely objective and can be evaluated, at its core is a problem-solving process that involves lateral thinking, making unexpected connections, creativity and inspiration, leading to an innovation or a 'big idea'. While research is needed to inform this process, and evaluation to assess its outputs, they shouldn't subsume it. "Ask forgiveness rather than permission" is Colin Burns' mantra (first proposed by computing pioneer Grace Hopper), though he also notes that "innovation shouldn't be confused with novelty".

The people who created the Xerox Star and the Macintosh innovated and created things that were the big ideas of their time. While the scale of innovation in any design project may not be as great, with a big idea or vision it will be easier to drive the project ahead, and with a great innovation a whole industry can be taken forward – with all the benefits that ensue for clients and the people who use their products.

Xerox Star:
Elements of its interface
and ease of use were still
not bettered 20 years after
its launch.

Apple iBook and iPod:
The concept of a laptop
computer was conceived as
the Dynabook by Alan Kay,
who later served as an Apple
Fellow. Although Apple didn't
launch the first commercial
laptop, its innovative use of
a rear-mounted keyboard
and trackpad has become
the industry standard. Its
innovative iPod MP3 player
integrates wonderfully with
Macintosh computers and the
excellent iTunes software. It is
also flexible and adaptable,
allowing for use as an external
hard disk and for storing and
displaying non-music data. It is
Apple's most successful ever
non-computer product.

Future possibilities and challenges

Since its inception the Web has been used to explore many future possibilities for networked products and services, from online banking and shopping to electronic newspapers and public information kiosks, many of which had been mooted in the previous decades. This experimentation has been possible for a variety of reasons: the Web built on the already well-established Internet; the browser took advantage of an installed base of personal computers; and Web publishers had digitised material to hand that had been created for electronic print publishing. Additionally, the Web markup protocols and language were not proprietary and were easy to learn and deploy.

However, the Web as we have experienced it – the PC browser on a modem-connected desktop computer – really only represents the future 'in beta'. This setup could only ever be applications, for instance around desk-bound clerical workers, researchers or scientists. Many developments within and beyond the Web are forging this 'beta' into real, useful and satisfying products.

These developments are being driven by the recognition of the value of networks in business and other organisations, and in a more organic fashion by the development of applications valued by ordinary people.

New network technologies

Some of the technical developments around the Internet and the Web include broadband and wireless networking. 'Broadband' refers to fast Internet connections, though an equally important aspect is that the connection is 'always on'. Wireless networking of devices via mobile phones has graduated from GSM connections via infrared to GPRS and 3G connections via Bluetooth, while direct connections (particularly for laptops) have built on the WiFi standard. Apart from allowing for fast transfer of data, 3G networks can also identify handset location.

Pervasive access to always-on connections makes the Internet valuable in more situations, leading to more applications, and makes it possible to show 'presence' on the network. Presence and location identification add two powerful dimensions to the network, allowing people to interact in more subtle ways and eliminating the need to input location information to make a service useful. Presence and location also make possible proactive services, which will have great value in many areas such as transportation (for instance locating a taxi cab).

New software technologies

Many developments are taking place in the realm of software. One of the most significant is the creation of the Extensible Markup Language (XML) which at its most basic level allows for presentation and content to be separated, content from various sources to be easily merged, and page elements to be combined and recombined. In principle, Web engineering is easier with XML, which will benefit designers, and complex information design can be more easily coded and changed. XML also addresses forms and form interaction which may make it easier to design forms well.

Web creator Tim Berners-Lee has led the development of the Semantic Web, an attempt to embody processes in a way that they can easily interact and be combined via the Internet to create applications. Again, this may reduce the complexity of engineering needed to create certain design solutions, but more importantly the Semantic Web itself will indirectly have an impact on people's experience of the Internet and thus presents important design challenges.

Many programming or scripting languages have been created to work with the Web, such as Microsoft's ASP and Sun's Java, the collaboratively developed PHP and semi-proprietary CURL, and the orphaned JavaScript. Aspects of these and future initiatives will be valuable for Web designers, helping to create better user experiences with less engineering.

New devices

Beyond the personal computer many devices can usefully be connected to or enabled by the Internet. Interactive television (iTV) presents many specific challenges. Displays are low resolution and viewed at a greater distance than a computer monitor. Control is typically via a hand-held remote that is severely limited compared to a keyboard and mouse. The medium is associated with relaxation so navigation should tend to be less demanding than for a typical Web site. TiVo (see 'Interface Design', page 85) represents a good example of iTV interface design.

We have already noted some of the design challenges and possibilities presented by mobile phones and PDAs (often, in fact, one device). The advent of data networks such as GPRS and 3G will bring the Web, and Web-like interfaces, to these devices. Such devices may have their own operating system, or run Java, and run third-party applications that connect to the Internet. This presents a number of design challenges, not least the need to learn the interface guidelines for a new operating system. They are likely to use non-Web protocols and languages which designers will need to understand to be able to work with effectively.

A related challenge is effectively combining hard and soft interaction, a challenge we have seen effectively taken up with Palm devices. This will inevitably lead some Web designers into the area of product design (see 'Background of Web design', page 20, and the BodyMedia case study, pages 214–219).

The other and more substantial design and engineering challenge is to create interfaces that can adapt to the device on which the service is accessed. This involves not only separating content and presentation but also abstracting interaction, to the extent that a menu list may employ a drop-down on a computer Web browser and a voice listing on a telephone.

Rather than all Internet services being delivered via a personal computer, for some services it is more appropriate that other physical devices are Internet-enabled. Such devices might include something as complex as a radio that streams audio from the Internet and requires an interface for tuning (see the Kerbango device, page 113), recording and personalisation, or as simple as a device that reflects the value of a stock market index (see the Orb, page 113).

This presents the possibility that some devices with limited displays or input methods (such as mobile phones) might be configured independently from their primary interface via a Web browser on a computer. This presents the challenge of designing this interface along with the design of the primary interface, and tying the two together effectively.

Often the best medium for people to 'consume content' distributed via the Web (particularly editorial) is in print, which leads to the design and engineering challenge of creating pages that are readable and print to an appropriate design. Technical and design issues include controlling typographic presentation, line length, text and breaks, and overall page layout.

New types of work

The development of broadband may facilitate the use of the Internet for entertainment as it will support more sensually engaging material such as video and audio (often referred to as time-based media). Network-delivered entertainment has been tried many times and its appropriate forms are elusive. In fact, that is part of the design challenge. Another area of time-based media that Web designers may explore is interactive television channel identities (see BBC Four announcement sting, page 113), adverts and public installations, which will require greater understanding of animation and moving imagery.

Games are one area of entertainment that have successfully moved on to the network with distance multi-player gaming and shared environments. It will be a long time before Web design and games design overlap extensively but understanding games design is an important challenge for Web designers.

In the corporate area more business-oriented applications are likely to become of greater importance. Such applications might span decision-making (see Compass case study, pages 200–205) and vertical markets such as healthcare (see SHS case study, pages 194–199) covering traditional intranets and encompassing tools for mobile workers in logistics, data collection and warehousing. The design challenges here will include developing a better understanding of context of use, more thorough task analysis, and a greater focus on efficiency and reliability. The products in these scenarios will tend to be most like traditional software applications and require designers to develop a better understanding of traditional GUI design.

New audiences

Audiences will expand in a number of areas, particularly novice users, people with accessibility issues and audiences from different cultures. Novice users will tend to be people who have no experience even of operating systems and the conventions they embody, or mental models for the ways in which computers and the Internet work. Unlike many office workers they won't receive any training, nor will they expect to read any support material before using the product.

Addressing accessibility issues will require a better understanding of the different limitations people with disabilities have and how these can be addressed in Web and other interfaces. It will also involve considerable engineering development such that content, display and interaction can be abstracted, making it easier for products developed for one platform to be deployed on another.

The most immediate issue with audiences from different cultures is language. Web sites will tend to be developed for multiple markets or the same Web site will need to support multiple languages. Where the use of language (for instance in navigation) needs to be carefully considered, a second language will require this exercise to be conducted again. Written languages have varying space needs, which is a particular issue where screen area is limited, and in navigation. Many languages are not written in Roman script (for instance, in South East Asia and the Middle East) and often scripts don't read from left to right, or follow the other patterns of Roman script-based languages. Beyond languages and scripts are cultural differences, which are often surprising and profound. An extreme example is the concept of hierarchies, which is fundamental to software interfaces and Web site design. This concept is intimately linked to social hierarchies, but in a tribal society might have little or no meaning, as such societies tend to be organised without significant hierarchy. Gaining more intimate local knowledge will be an important challenge for designers.

Localising a Web site involves other more specific challenges in relation to a country or culture. These include understanding how proper names work, how addresses are structured and how telephone numbers are organised, all of which have implications for everything from form validation to searching and personalisation. For e-commerce projects cultural specifics would include currency, taxation and shipping. And for many projects knowledge of local legislation is important.

New areas of use

Internet technologies are spreading beyond the office and into the home, into shops and other commercial spaces, and more generally into the built environment. There are many new challenges just in the home. Home users will tend to be novices and have higher expectations of reliability based on their experience of consumer durables. They will tend to be less focused on productivity and more on convenience and pleasure of use. They aren't desk-bound, and are not always seated. Products tend to be shared and users will have varying levels of experience and confidence with information technologies. Developing effective models for support will also be an issue, particularly considering the variety of suppliers in the product chain which may include a telephone company,

ISP, hardware and software manufacturer, Web service provider, credit provider and a logistics company.

New concepts

Many design possibilities and challenges are presented by developments not in technology *per se* but by concepts built on existing technologies. Two such concepts are reputation management and collaborative filtering. Neither is new but they do provide powerful ways of helping Web users to find and evaluate relevant information. Reputation management builds on the real-world dynamic that if someone we know and whose opinion we trust in a particular area recommends something in that area (for instance a site about Web design) we will give that recommendation greater consideration. Collaborative filtering uses the phenomenon that if, for instance, nine of our favourite songs are shared by another person, we will probably both like each other's tenth song. The kind of information these two concepts generate is both dynamic and relative to other people, and presents unique design challenges.

Artificial intelligence (AI) is another concept, albeit a more abstract one, that has important implications for Web design. AI refers to the use of computing to support or enhance human intelligence and has led to many developments which we now take for granted. One of the highest profile examples of AI in the area of computing was Microsoft's 'Clippy' helper which would offer to assist with everything from writing a letter to trouble-shooting problems in Word. Artificial intelligence has also been promoted in the form of 'agents' or 'bots' which might scour the Web with information queries or a brief to find the cheapest retailer of a particular product. It is easy to underestimate users' expectations of something that shows some kind of intelligence, as Microsoft found with Clippy, and deploying artificial intelligence effectively is both a technological and a design problem.

In the early days of the Web, sites were very self-contained and a designer had control over all their aspects. The new concept for the Web is of an interconnected soup of services where interfaces tend to intermingle. (The Semantic Web is a high-level example of this concept.) Early examples of this concept were seen in e-commerce services that allowed a vendor to add online shopping to their site, with the upshot that part of the Web site was no longer under (easy) control of the publisher or designer. This phenomenon has extended from search tools, video streaming and book selling, to uber-services such as 'network identity' provided by the Network Alliance and Microsoft's Passport. The design challenge here will be to incorporate effectively such services into a Web site, and create interfaces to services which can be incorporated into other Web sites, making the experience of the Web more of a seamless movement between nodes.

New interface concepts

While Web design developed from graphical user interface (GUI) design for software it has never wholly adopted it. This is partly due to bandwidth constraints and the nature of HTML, and also because GUIs are not suitable for all Web products. However, there is much value still to be gleaned from GUIs, which are fairly successfully used by hundreds of millions of people and have continued to evolve (though they have also adopted some interface

counterActive

Interactive commercial spaces:
For the flagship New York Prada store (above left) IDEO in collaboration with AMO and Kramdesign created the form factor and user interface. This is used to scan merchandise for inventory information and, when used in conjunction with a ubiquitous display, can also function as a remote control, allowing the salesperson to highlight sketches and catwalk video clips for the customer.

Counteractive:
At the MIT Media Lab, US, (above) the CounterACTIVE project uses an underlying array of sensors distributed throughout the kitchen to infer what events are taking place and respond before the user formulates an explicit 'command'.

New audiences:
UK-based Tesco, one of the largest online grocers, complements its main Web interface with a version that supports screen readers, and doesn't use scripting so it can be accessed by a wider variety of browsers (left).

www.tesco.com
access

Your favourites

Look through the favourites list, or select one of the following links:

How do I use this page?
Main Links
Maintain your favourites
Back to favourite department lists

There are 17 products in this list.

page 1 page 2

Add selected products to basket

Description	Price	Quantity	Notes
Cow & Gate Plus Ready To Feed Milk 200ml	£0.49		Note:
Cow & Gate Premium Ready To Feed Milk 200ml	£0.49		Note:
Cow & Gate Plus 900g	£5.57		Note:
Hipp 4 Month Organic Creamed Porridge 125g Jar	£0.54		Note:
Hipp 4 Month Organic Spring Carrot & Sweetcorn 125g	£0.54		Note:
Hipp 4 Month Organic Apple & Banana Puree 125g Jar	£0.54		Note:
Hipp 4 Month Organic Carrots And Potatoes 125g Jar	£0.54		Note:

concepts from the Web). It has become easier to develop more GUI-like interface elements and interactions since the development of Flash and Dynamic HTML, and client-side platforms such as Java (which can also run on non-computer devices including mobile phones and PDAs).

There are also good reasons why GUIs need to develop beyond the current framework, established in the early 1980s, many of which are well developed in research environments and are starting to be deployed.

Interfaces will also become more modular, assembled from ready-made elements created by designers along with the rules about how they are used and what with. This will facilitate rapid development and updating of interfaces, as well as interface design by non-designers.

Many future interface developments discussed in the context of GUIs will also be directly relevant to the Web. Speech-input is already used in some voice-driven computer applications, such as call centres, and while understanding commands is qualitatively more difficult than speech recognition, both will be important for Web interfaces. Sound output is well used in GUIs but almost unused in Web interfaces. While sound can be distracting in an office environment its lack of use in Web interfaces is also a result of bandwidth restrictions and lack of standards. Smell may even become a useful interface channel.

Organisational interfaces

The Web is just one of many 'interfaces' to organisations, which include telephone, email, forms and letters, and physical 'points of presence' such as shops. People will move from one interface to another in their dealings with organisations and there are considerable design challenges in presenting these interactions and conversations, not least so that those people and the staff with whom they interact have a clear record of information passed between them and agreements made. The Web will often be the best medium to present this, as it is dynamic and can display large amounts of information. Organisation interfaces are just one aspect of the design of services, which is facilitated by networked media and will make up a larger area of design.

Many of the challenges designers will come across depend on the further development of the technologies behind the Internet, and the continued deployment of these technologies by businesses and other organisations. While designers can't easily influence these developments, without them designers won't be able to help realise the real value of the Web and the Internet to their clients, to the people who use them and to society.

New types of work:

BBC Four (above), for which this 'sting' was designed, was one of the first digital TV channels in the UK. The merging of broadcasting and computing will lead to Web designers being more involved with time-based media.

New devices:

The Orb (left) is built on a platform that delivers information wirelessly. In this case the value of the stock market index is shown by changing colour. Although the Kerbango Internet radio (below) was a commercial failure, delivery of media via the Internet to stand-alone devices is becoming more popular and these devices support richer interface semantics, not least because they have their own physical controls, unlike Web applications.

Portable and locational:

Wireless PDAs, such as the Palm i705, present a number of challenges. Their screens are small and often mono and they are pen-driven, while being tightly integrated with hardware buttons. If such devices are GPS-enabled, they can enhance the ease and speed-of-use of applications such as Starbucks Coffee Store Locator.

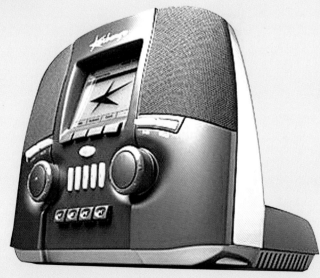

Future possibilities and challenges 113

Anatomy

A good idea is only as good as its final implementation. Getting to this point requires mastering many processes – some of which will seem to be only tangential to design.

Design projects can be initiated in many ways and come from many sources: from an external agency approached by a new client in the process of establishing their corporate identity to an internal design team working on a new feature for an established service. However, the core approach in each scenario will have much in common.

A good process enables the designer to establish what the client really wants to achieve, and what their users want to do and how. It helps create a common understanding and a good, effective working relationship with all the parties involved. It provides a means of validating ideas, making decisions and justifying those that are made. Overall, a good process should help produce the best product possible within the given constraints, efficiently and with the appropriate speed – and the least possible stress.

Here we discuss the common elements of a project. We can't be prescriptive about this process but there are some basic principles and approaches that can increase the chances of a project being a success. These approaches focus on connecting design to the project goals and restating them at the end of each stage, extensive investigation of the project landscape, understanding audiences, effective planning and proactive action, good communication and appreciation of collaborators' needs, big picture design theory and iterative practice.

Developing products for the Web and other interactive platforms is still in its infancy and the scope and complexity of a project is often difficult to determine at the outset. More than

in other areas of design, clients may be unsure about what they want to create, and unfamiliar with the medium itself. They may also be unfamiliar with the design and creative process. For this reason we recommend that you add an initial stage to a client project. In this stage you research and scope the project and use design skills to help focus discussion with the client. It may also provide an opportunity to talk to your client about the design process. At the end of this stage you and the client will be much clearer about what it is you are creating, what the resources and dependencies are and how long the project might take. You will then be in a position to quote for the overall project or, if the client has a fixed budget, to say how much of the project you can develop within that budget.

Unlike traditional software development and much Web development to date, it is also preferable for design development to lead engineering implementation. While some engineering can proceed in parallel with the research and design phases of a project, many of the product's features, and the detail of how they will work, will only be decided at the end of these phases. Hence, it is most efficient in terms of time and resources for coding implementation to begin at this point.

The BodyMedia Product Development Process Model:

Developed by Chris Pacione at BodyMedia (see case study, pages 214–219) who cites interaction designer Rob Haitani's goal of "protecting the inner tranquillity of the product". The model requires that the product must be the right thing to make, posits designers as synthesisers and indicates the relationship with users is on-going.

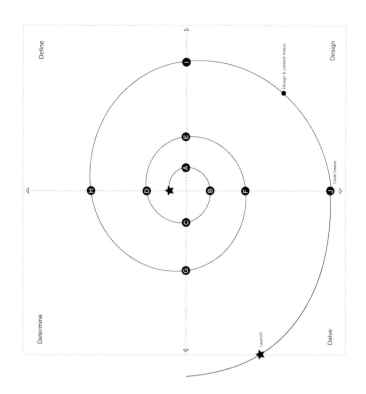

The BodyMedia Product Development Process Model is based on Dr. Barry Boehm's Spiral method and is designed to promote:

- flexibility
- parallel work
- constant and clear communication
- efficiency
- serendipity and synergy
- multiple iterations
- rapid prototyping
- smart, human centric solutions
- risk management
- predictability

★ Define - Brainstorm and Kickoff
Ⓐ Design - the Information Architecture and quick interactive prototype
Ⓑ Delve - into prototype and test the usefulness of the idea
Ⓒ Determine - the weaknesses, strengths and risks, time constraints
Ⓓ Define - new alternatives, and solutions
Ⓔ Design - update architecture, content, code and UI of interactive prototype
Ⓕ Delve - into refined solution, test for usability, and major bugs
Ⓖ Determine - solution weaknesses, strengths, risks, time constraints
Ⓗ Define - what needs to (can) change with code, UI
Ⓘ Design - Design and content freeze, all specs due. Code freeze
★ Final testing and Q&A. Launch!

More general
less specific
issues, no
details, architecture,
sketches, rough
draft of content,
quick prototypes.

Less general
more specific
issues. UI details,
code debugging,
content tweaks.

Pre-project stages

Clients can find designers in a variety of ways. They may have had personal contact with someone in the company, or the designer may have been recommended by a colleague. The client may know about the supplier from the trade press or his work with a client in their industry. They may have found the supplier's name in a directory, or put out a Request for Proposals (RFP) which the designer has seen and responded to. The designer may be brought in by another supplier, perhaps a business consultancy or engineering company, with whom the client is already working. The supplier may already have worked with the client in another area (perhaps as its advertising agency), on a previous Web project, or may have been appointed to the roster of agencies it will ask to tender for such projects. If the client has an in-house designer or design team this stage of a project will of course be less discrete.

Initial client contact

From your initial contact with the client you should try to get a broad overview of their organisation and business goals, their objectives for the specific project, how they see them being achieved, what kind of suppliers they are looking for, other parties who may be involved, the project timescale and resources, and any other major constraints on the project.

There are a number of ways a client may want to proceed. You may be the only supplier they are approaching and they may want to get you quickly involved with their organisation, and work collaboratively to research and scope the project. On the other hand, they may want you and others to respond to an RFP and to meet with or have a pitch presented by those who are short-listed.

Goal-directed design:
Created for an article in 'Gain' by Hugh Dubberly to describe Cooper's design process. For simplicity it deliberately leaves out the feedback loops and iterations that are necessary for producing good work. © 2001 Dubberly Design Office.

Goal-directed Design

User goals should be at the center of the software design process.

This diagram shows the process proceeding in steps from left to right. It reduces a complex set of feedback loops and iterations to a linear sequence of steps – in order to make the basic structure more clear.

Alan Cooper and his staff provided the framework for this diagram and much feedback in its development.

Users —— provide input to

Managers provide mandate to Designers provide spec to Programmers provide code to QA certify product for release —— Users

provide feedback on usability to

provide bug reports to

Primary responsibility: insure financial success | insure customer satisfaction | insure performance | insure reliability

Software development process

Initiate ——→ Design ——→ Code ——→ Test ——→ Ship

The goal-directed design process takes place within a larger software development process.

	Research and Analyze (focus in the first half, continuing throughout)			Opportunities, Constraints, and Context (Who will use the product? What problem will it solve for them?)			Form, Meaning, and Behavior (What is it? How will it behave for users?)			Synthesize and Refine (ongoing throughout, focus in the second half)	
Activity:	Define intent and constraints of project	Review what exists (e.g. documents)		Apply ethnographic research techniques	Define typical users	Deduce what users want	Imagine a system to help users reach goals	Tell stories about using the system	Derive components based on users	Organize the components	Refine details; describe models
Result:	**Scope**	**Audit**	**Interviews**	**Observations**	**Personas**	**Goals**	**Concept**	**Scenarios**	**Elements**	**Framework**	**Spec**
	desired outcomes time constraints financial constraints general process milestones (Scope may be loose or tight.)	business plan marketing plan branding strategy market research product plan competitors related technology	management domain experts customers partners sales channel (This step leads to a project mandate.)	use patterns potential users their activities their environments their interactions their objects (tools) (aeiou framework from Rick Robinson)	primary secondary supplemental negative served (indirectly) customer partner organizational	life end experience personal practical corporate false	problem definition vision definition design imperatives (May require changes in scope.)	day-in-the-life key-path error set-up	information objects functional objects control mechanisms	object relationships conceptual groupings patterns logic / narrative flow navigation structure	appearance language flow / behavior product character product story
Artifact:	Project Brief	Summary Insights	Tapes Transcripts Summary Insights	Tapes Transcripts Summary Insights	Notes	Notes	Formal Document Problem Statement Vision Statement	Notes Storyboards	Lists Sketches Diagrams High-level data models	Sketches Flow Diagrams	Formal Document Demonstration Prototype
Meetings:	Briefing		Interviews	Chalk talk (early findings)		Chalk talk with management	Presentation			Chalk talk with programmers	Presentation

Goals: lead to → Goals → drive*

spark inform motivate filter organize prioritize prioritize validate

Request for proposal

An RFP or pitch document states the client's business goals and the parameters of the project. It lays the basis for a contract between them and a future design supplier (perhaps you), and prepares the ground for the brief when that supplier is selected. Ideally the document should be fairly detailed at this stage, indicating that the client has thoroughly thought through the project and its relationship to their business goals. During the project the RFP should act as an external reference point that will allow all the parties to pursue the same set of ideas and objectives.

A request for proposal:

↗ enables you to glean sufficient information about the project such that you can make an offer about what you can do for the client, and

↗ enables the client to elicit from you enough information to allow them to make a judgement about your ability to usefully contribute to the project.

The client may also choose to include information about their budgets if they are asking you to indicate how much of the project you can complete within the budget allocated to your services.

An RFP is issued in the early stages of a project yet the scope and shape of the project is likely to change. In responding to an RFP it may be appropriate to question assumptions it makes, or to emphasise your general approach to design projects. If the project is complex, vaguely defined or subject to tight constraints, you should also propose a paid initial research and scoping phase which can lay the basis for properly costing the design elements. This may lay the basis for the client modifying the project scope and asking designers (including yourself) to quote on this more precise request.

If you choose to quote on the project at this stage you should make clear all the assumptions you are making and what you will require of the client and other parties involved in the project.

A client will evaluate an RFP on a number of grounds, particularly cost (though you may not have chosen to quote for the full project at this stage). More experienced clients may be impressed by a clear explanation of your approach to design, an indication that you are thinking ahead about the project beyond the design phase, or your understanding of their business goals and ability to think beyond their immediate project objectives.

Making the pitch

You may be invited to pitch based on a response to an RFP, though they may also ask you to pitch directly for the project, with no RFP stage.

There are typically two kinds of pitches: credentials and work. Credentials pitches aim to demonstrate that you have the skills, experience and resources to complete the project, and for the client to investigate whether they could work with you effectively.

For a work pitch the client asks the designer to investigate the specific design problem. It is important in this kind of pitch to communicate the 'big idea' that forms the core of your design solutions clearly, though you may communicate this in a way that the client doesn't expect. As with a response to an RFP or a credentials pitch, a work pitch may be won on the basis of your general approach rather than specific design solutions.

However, work pitches are not ideal, as the designer has little chance to understand the nature and scope of the problem they are addressing. As they are essentially an early design phase, clients should offer a fee to designers who do them. This may or may not happen, depending on the state of the industry.

In any pitch you shouldn't assume that the client has the same understanding as you have of the nature and value of design, and should look to explain its role and its value in business.

Evaluating the project

Though the RFP and pitching processes are about a client evaluating designers, you should also take the opportunity to evaluate your potential client. The criteria on which you evaluate them will reflect some of the criteria by which they evaluate you.

If they have asked many suppliers to pitch, or ask for work pitches, you may consider that they are clear about what they want, or how to evaluate design. Of course, you may consider working with them to be an interesting challenge.

You should look at the possible extent of your creative and strategic input in the project, which may be constrained by the involvement of other designers (working on branding, or elements of the project implemented in other media), or the role of engineering or marketing.

There is no such thing as a bad client though there are ill-conceived projects. There may also be clients you feel disinclined to work with, or don't feel you have the time to engage with in a discussion of design that could lay the basis for its successful application.

Negotiation and discussion

There is of course much to negotiate before and after you have been retained for a project. A major area of discussion is likely to be fees, and this is more likely to be an issue the less a client understands the role of the design. One approach to this discussion is to visually outline the roles design is playing at different stages in the project and where the dependencies lie. On this basis the client can see where the project's scope may realistically be scaled back. It is also important to discuss timescales and deadlines, particularly where other suppliers are involved, or when the client has to prepare key material for the project. Overall, it is important to set the client's expectations about the design process, how you can most effectively contribute to the project objectives, and likely outcomes and consequences of your involvement.

Contract

If your proposal (for the full project or a research and scoping phase) has been accepted you may proceed to agreeing a contract with your client. For smaller projects a letter of intent, or even a verbal agreement, often take the place of a contract, though a written contract is preferable in most situations as it forces both parties to consider scenarios which could lead to dispute.

The RFP (if there was one) and your response contain the essence of a contract, though the contract should reflect any issues that may have come up since your response to the RFP, or since your pitch. The contract gives you a reference point you can return to if needed.

Legal advice and IP

At this stage you may want to get legal advice from a contract lawyer.

You should also be aware of the status of intellectual property (IP) in design. The bottom line is that unless there is an explicit agreement the rights to designs reside with the designer if they are an external supplier (and the organisation if they are working internally). Even though this is the case you should make it clear to your client to prevent it becoming an issue later in the project.

Original pitching:
For its pitch to a financial services client (see pages 236–243) the New York office of Organic prepared a Flash movie showing a possible day in the life of a broker demonstrating how far they believed the service could develop.

Scoping and research

As we have mentioned, it is often valuable to have a separate scoping and research phase. For a designer working in-house this phase will probably not be necessary. Neither will it be necessary for a design company that works very closely with a client and should be as familiar with its business as are any of its employees.

Goals

While this phase is ostensibly to allow you to clarify what you are committing to, it also serves a number of other roles:

↗ Better understand your client's business
↗ Review any market research or business competitor analysis the client has conducted and understand their business landscape
↗ Become familiar with the roles, interests and needs of the stakeholders and other parties involved in the project
↗ Learn about the audiences for the project, their needs and the likely contexts for their use of the product
↗ Consider whether the planned product is likely to fulfil the client's project objectives
↗ Understand the scope and complexity of the project
↗ Scope any design or other project constraints and dependencies
↗ Evaluate the non-design resources, skills and inputs that will be needed
↗ Investigate what IT systems, if any, currently exist and the constraints they impose, and scope what engineering resources are available and will be needed

If your client isn't clear about their goals you won't know what problem your design is attempting to solve and it will be impossible to measure the success of the project. If you don't know where you are going it is unlikely you will get there. Although the client will incur costs for this phase, and the phase will add time to the project, it will lay a firm foundation for delivering the right product within the given time-frame and budget, and maximise the client's investment.

Techniques

Much research can be conducted and through formal and informal interviews, and workshops. Other research sources might include:

↗ Research reports on the client's industry and product sector
↗ Client information and research on the product sector and audiences
↗ Client project plans
↗ Evaluation of existing products
↗ An audit of the client's current use of design
↗ Discussions with other suppliers

Design techniques such as sketching and diagramming may be useful in helping you, your client, and other parties such as engineering, to think about and understand your findings.

Deliverables

At this stage you may feel that the client's business model has problems and choose to discuss this with them. You may even feel that the Web may not be the best medium for them to use. Assuming you feel the client is on the right track it may be appropriate to produce:

A reassessment of project scope and vision: This should identify the true scope of the project, its key elements and the measures by which its progress and success might be determined. It may also be appropriate to expand the design scope of the project if you feel your client isn't effectively addressing their goals, and to restate the strategic vision for the project in your own words.

Design concepts: These should be high-level design ideas. Your research and the way you present it may also help the client clarify their project objectives, or convince them of the value of a particular design solution. This may extend to developing a prototype 'proof of concept' for a proposed design solution.

A design brief: This should be developed in collaboration with the client, and should frame the challenge rather than propose solutions. It should be a reference point during the project.

> However, a design solution proposed in a brief can be a way of illustrating what the client is trying to communicate, and should also be evaluated on its merits.

If the client has already created a design brief this revised brief might restate it in your terms, which can help flag up misconceptions about the project (see also 'Planning a project', page132).

Supplier recommendations: If they haven't yet been appointed, you might recommend appropriate suppliers. You may already have good working relationships with such suppliers and might suggest inviting them to pitch.

A quotation for next phase: A quotation might break down the cost of independent elements of the project or, if the client has a set budget, which elements of the project could be completed within the design fee. The quotation should outline the assumptions you are making and what you will require of the client and other parties involved in the project. It should also point out areas where there may be problems and how likely they are to occur, and indicate what minimal 'critical mass' of design work will be delivered.

Next steps

If the client agrees that the scope of the project will have to be extended, or accepts that what they wanted can't be achieved within their budget or time-frame, they may decide not to take the project further. However, it is as likely that this phase will have clarified and refined the project goals and increased its chances of success. At this point you may return to negotiating fees and the contract.

Planning and managing a project

It is easy to neglect explicit project planning and management, as elements of it are inevitably thrown up by the project, or it is assumed that there is already a common perspective and implicit agreement on how it should proceed. This may be the case for internal teams or established collaborators. If not, planning and management should be explicitly considered.

Working with collaborators

Good working relationships with collaborators – from engineers to writers – are one of the keys to developing a successful project. Collaborators who are confident about their skills and abilities, and willing to share their knowledge and reasoning, will be the most valuable contributors. Taking on board and responding to collaborators' ideas with constructive suggestions, rather than negative criticism based on emotion, lays the groundwork for the best working relationship.

It is important that you try to understand the approach and ways of working of your collaborators and find out their priorities and motivations when considering how you communicate and collaborate. Give them the attention you would when considering the audiences for the product you are designing. Similarly you should make your own priorities and motivations clear to your collaborators. When making a request of someone, try to be as clear as you can. Don't expect them to know about what you do, and follow up afterwards to check your request was really understood.

While each team will have its own priorities, to secure effective collaboration it is important that the needs of the people who will use the product and the project's objectives are kept to the fore, as ultimately most issues will be resolved in relation to them. Compromise for the common good will sometimes be appropriate.

Amicable relations often turn sour for one common reason – time – which has to be carefully managed. Project overruns, changes in project objectives and technical problems all affect the quality of collaboration between teams and if not properly addressed can cause people to retreat into their own space.

Engineers, coders and systems integrators: On the surface it would appear that engineering and design are quite at odds. Engineering aims for regularity, predictability and repeatability, while the results of the design process are specific to the problem. Engineers can fall back on maths and other objective knowledge to justify their work, while designers can often only claim instinct and experience to validate their work. Engineering addresses what can be done and how to do it; design proposes what to do. In fact there is more in common between engineering and design than would first appear. Both are very focused on problem solving within known constraints. Both embrace concepts of regularity, predictability and modularity, and both build on the concept of patterns. ➔

Shared workspace:
Often it is most useful to sit with a collaborator and talk through ideas, changes and corrections. Explaining and discussing the reasons for changes will help colleagues understand what you would want in a future situation. Studio of Bolt.com.

As with usability experts, designers often see engineers as being 'nay sayers' in the creative process, and it is certainly the case that once something has been coded they are understandably reluctant to change it. However, designers often don't appreciate enough what engineering can do and don't take advantage of its insights and processes. Experienced engineers may know of ways of solving problems that designers hadn't anticipated, enabling better design solutions. And their understanding of the way a particular technology works may allow them to point out possibilities that a designer hadn't appreciated.

It is important for designers to collaborate effectively with engineers on a more basic level. Engineers can indicate what can be done within the project scope, flag up unforeseen consequences of a design solution and identify possible performance problems. They can also estimate implementation times, helping ensure a projects stays on track.

To achieve this level of collaboration designers need to communicate their approach effectively. Engineers will invariably need to make some design decisions. If this communication has been successful, they will be able to make them in the spirit of the design, or anticipate issues of concern to the designer.

This collaboration should also start early in the design process and continue throughout it, as many design decisions are made during implementation. Designers shouldn't be precious about showing design work to the engineering team, even in a rough state. Later on in the process it may be necessary for a designer and an engineer to sit together to finalise design details.

As engineers were the original users and interface designers of software products, they sometimes, understandably, consider themselves to be real users. One way of addressing this is to invite them to take part in usability testing or in the user research.

As former software programmer and author Alan Cooper has noted, "code is the best brief", that is to say, the final product is the best blueprint for a design implementation. Short of that, designers need to present engineers with all the information they need to implement a design concept, and this will involve extensive thinking through of the interactions that will take place with the systems behind the Web site. Computers are built on logic, and in general if it is possible to describe how a design works in a logical fashion it can probably be implemented.

Visualising timelines:
Gantt charts, such as this one from the eDesign project (see pages 228–235), allow project stages and sub-stages to be mapped out, showing elapsed time, resource allocation, dependencies and milestones.

Changing order:
As the software industry has matured so has the relationship between design and engineering.
Phase 1: Originally, programmers did everything, from conceiving to testing software.
Phase 2: Businesses grew, their programs became more complicated and managers were brought in. They created requirements documents, but in order to ship the product feature lists would be "cut from the back". The resulting feature sets often made little sense to users.
Phase 3: Testing became a separate step.
Phase 4: With the move from command-line to GUI designers got involved. Today design and coding tend to take place simultaneously, followed by testing and revision.
Phase 5: Alan Cooper insists that design precedes programming, with all decisions proceeding from a formal definition, created by the designer, of the user and their goals. Thus design precedes programming. Created for an article in 'Gain' by Hugh Dubberly. © 2001, Dubberly Design Office

Writers, editors and content creators:
Designers need to work with writers on elements beyond copy, such as navigation, page titles, error pages, and email announcements and acknowledgments, and the two should go hand in hand. Any substantial Web site will have a content management and publishing system, however basic, and the designer will need to collaborate with the 'users' responsible for editorial and content creation to develop the interface to the system.

Usability companies: While many design companies, and some client companies, conduct usability testing (see 'Usability and usability testing', page 99), those that don't may need to work with an external usability consultancy. You need to brief the usability testers thoroughly on the elements of the design you are interested in evaluating, and the audiences whom you intended will use them. The usability consultancy's report should be carefully considered. It may even suggest ways in which a design could be improved. This input may be very valuable, though it needs to be evaluated in the overall framework of the project.

Hosting companies and IT systems people:
There are a number of other suppliers whom you may work with whose role may have some effect on the implementation of your design work. These include IT systems people, who will play a role in enabling the client's employees to edit and update the Web site and will also facilitate setting up any collaboration tools you plan to use. The Web hosting company may control access to many of the elements of the site that affect the user experience, such as error and 'page not found' screens.

Effective communication and collaboration

It is hard to overemphasise the importance of good communication in Web projects and you should work with your client to define a strategy for how you will communicate and collaborate. Any time invested in working out how to make appropriate decisions and discussions visible and accessible will be well spent, and as professional communicators designers should take a lead in this process.

A Web product is an intangible thing, in a medium that may be relatively unfamiliar to your client, and there are likely to be more people involved in creating the product than there are in, for instance, a print design project. This makes it doubly important that you pay attention to how you communicate and collaborate with your client and the other parties involved in the development process.

While it needs to be effectively managed, good communication can ensure that problems that arise are quickly resolved, which will save time and resources and avoid stress.

It is important to be open about your design process and design work as it is developing rather than only revealing your work when it is to be presented or handed over. If you make your process open your collaborators will be able to identify problems and new requirements quickly. They will also better appreciate what you do and will be able to more effectively reflect your vision in their project deliverables.

Shared language: Early on in the process it is important to establish a common and accurate vocabulary and language for describing the project objectives, project stages, design and technical elements, and the elements of the Web site. Much ambiguity and misunderstanding can be avoided if you can stick to this vocabulary and language in communication and documentation. You will also need to develop a language to describe how the user will perceive and think about the system (see the discussion of 'Scenarios and personas', page 58).

Value of meetings: Although Web sites exist 'in the ether' this doesn't mean all collaboration has to be conducted virtually. We are far from being able to replicate the characteristics of the real-world interactions that meetings facilitate, and shouldn't be blind to their value.

Meetings are great for ensuring everyone is 'on the same page' of the project, for discussing and evaluating ideas, reviewing common visuals and creating shared artifacts, prioritising activities, planning and assigning tasks, holding people to account, identifying and addressing political issues in a project, reviewing the project vision and – in some ways most important – motivating people.

Project meetings should, if practical, be held regularly and include representatives from the primary teams involved in the project. It is also important that decisions taken and actions assigned in meetings are quickly shared with those in the meeting and other stakeholders and in a way it is easy for them to review and manage.

Conference calls are also valuable where frequent meetings are impractical, for instance with an international team. While it is difficult to discuss common artifacts on a conference call they do have many of the valuable characteristics of meetings.

With both meetings and conference calls it is important to have access to current project documentation so that when issues arise you

can review prior research and discussion, look at previous and current design ideas, and review the information and reasoning that informed previous decisions.

Direct communication: While meetings play an important role, many design issues on a project can be resolved directly between individual parties. If significant issues can be resolved and new ideas addressed promptly people's time will be spent more effectively. It is preferable to have direct access to the right people on the client side and in the other teams involved in the project, though this shouldn't be at the expense of a project manager's need to have an overview of the project and guide it accordingly.

It is worth keeping a short 'elevator speech' about current design issues or strategy to hand in case you have an impromptu audience with a client executive responsible for the project.

Sometimes it is appropriate for two team members, for instance a designer and an engineer, to sit down together and directly work through a problem.

Appropriate communication: Different forms of communication are appropriate to different messages, and you need to evaluate whether you are communicating in a way that your messages can be usefully understood. You should also be clear that your priorities and knowledge are unlikely to be shared by the people with whom you are communicating. For instance, to communicate the design rationale behind an agreed design it may be better to run a workshop than to share a document with your collaborators.

Shared workspace: Working on Web-focused projects can be very abstract and all too virtual. If you have sufficient space it is a good idea to dedicate a room, or an area of your office, to the project and use it for all meetings and informal discussions, and to display project material such as site maps, design ideas, samples of text and images, project timelines, and the like.

If client confidentiality is an issue or space is limited, mobile walls might be more appropriate.

Having such documents visible allows old ideas to be revisited quickly and makes current information easily accessible. A project space is also an effective way to present the progress of the team to others who have an interest in its success.

Shared virtual workspace: Creating a virtual workspace is a design challenge in itself and the value of doing this properly is hard to underestimate. You need to think about the type of information being shared, who will access it, what they may need to do with it and the context in which they will use it.

The site is likely to be built and tested on a private 'staging server' and while this will be maintained by engineering this is a key part of the shared workspace.

Your client may have an established strategy for collaboration and communication. If they do, you should evaluate how easy it would be for you to fit with those systems.

However you decide to collaborate, updates on the project should be regularly circulated, perhaps by the project manager, as a supplement to periodic meetings.

Design processes

In new areas of professional work such as Web design, creating and following processes is a valuable and important way of ensuring that the basis is laid for good design work. As the profession matures and all parties involved gain a better understanding of design for the Web, explicit process will become less important – in the meantime it can act as a 'hidden hand' guiding projects.

Core to design development is the idea of iteration: an idea is worked up fairly quickly, and then reflected upon, discussed and perhaps tested, at which point appropriate modifications are made and the process repeated. Iteration here is counterposed to linearity where a stage is fully worked through before being passed on to the next team in the chain (often referred to as 'throwing it over the wall').

Processes and development models should not be set in stone during a project, or from one project to the next, but if a process isn't followed at all the project is likely to suffer. To be effective processes need to be discussed and agreed with all the parties in the project, and to evolve they need to be reflected upon during and at the end of the project.

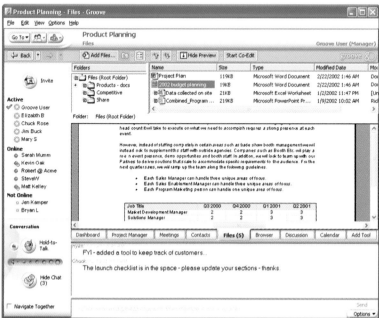

Shared workspace:
Although project documents will be in digital space, you can access them more easily, and move from one to the next, if you use physical space such as this office wall at BodyMedia (above). For a project that is location specific it can be very productive to actually do the design work in the space in which it will be used.

Shared virtual workspace:
For digital design it is appropriate that much of the collaboration be conducted electronically. Groove is a peer-to-peer workgroup environment (left) that supports email, instant messaging, document sharing and reviewing, and meeting planning.

Planning a project

Good planning is crucial to developing effective design solutions. Much of the project planning should be done with the other parties involved in the project to secure their input and ensure they are clear about the project approach and goals.

The planning should aim to:

↗ Develop the brief
↗ Clarify who is or could be involved in the project from the supplier and client sides (including partner organisations), identifying any missing roles or suppliers, and clarify the roles and responsibilities of each party, their needs and how they work
↗ Establish how the parties will communicate and collaborate, and agree a procedure for signing off work
↗ Flag up project dependencies (such as parallel or related projects, content creation or training) and establish a timetable with specific milestones
↗ Identify all work to be done, research needed and decisions to be made.

An initial project meeting should address these issues and:

↗ Begin to establish the shared language we discussed earlier
↗ Investigate the client's project goals, including how the client wants to present itself, and any specific requirements
↗ Agree and spell out project stages and deliverables
↗ Consider the profiles of the target audiences
↗ Develop an understanding of the tasks the intended audience should be able to achieve (including those mandated by law or regulation), and the functionality needed to support them
↗ Identify at the top level the site content and content types and any content creation issues
↗ Discuss potential future needs that should be considered, including scalability
↗ Discuss the design and technical issues.

Apart from the parties on the project, this team should ideally include a project manager, someone from the client side with the authority to make decisions, someone who can represent users (who could be from the design team), someone representing the people on the client's staff, and possibly those further down the supply chain who will be involved in delivering the service.

Managing a project

Web design projects tend to be complex, have many dependencies and involve a lot of people with diverse skills. Day-to-day and strategic project management is crucial and necessary on both the design and the client side.

The design project manager needs to work closely with the client, and be on the case from the moment the client signs on. He may be an information architect, or use his skills in understanding how a complex product comes together. He needs to understand the role of each team, how they work with the others, and the project dependencies. He needs to be able to communicate effectively, spot problems (particularly with the timeline), know or be able to find out how they might be resolved, and broker compromises.

The design project manager also needs to be able to manage the level of delivery on the design side – based on what the client wants and their expectations – as designers may tend to over-deliver to the detriment of the project timescale. Additionally he needs to be able to keep a perspective on the project to ensure it is still addressing its wider goals.

Deliverables

Updated design brief: One deliverable may be an updated design brief. Whoever documents the brief (and it is often the designer) should liaise with the other parties in the project team and with other stakeholders to ensure that they are happy with its final form.

Project plan: This should summarise the agreed plan and may include Gantt or other charts to illustrate the activity timeline and milestones.

Research and discovery: The areas of investigation of the research phase are close to those of the 'Scoping and research' (see page 122), though their remit is broader and their goal is to understand the scope and the subtleties of the design challenge, identify in detail the requirements and unearth more subtle potential problems. Equally importantly, the research phase also lays the basis for the creation of original design solutions.

In this phase you may also identify issues related to corporate politics that might impede overall progress towards the project goals, and the design process in particular.

In general, all research should be shared with all the parties involved, so they are clear about the insights upon which design is progressing. This includes any research conducted by the engineering team.

Research and discovery

Business research

This should start from the information that should be in the RFP (see page 118) or by eliciting this information if it wasn't in the RFP.

A lot can be learned from looking at products competing with the one you are developing, and more generally at Web sites in other areas with similar functions or that have a good quality of experience.

> Competitor analysis is an approach used in many areas of business. Be careful to identify who your client considers to be their competitors. If your client has an existing site you should include it in the analysis.

This doesn't mean that you would simply copy what other businesses do, but it does allow you to establish a baseline of quality, and find ways in which the product might differentiate itself. There may also be aspects of those sites that are so standard that you feel it would be better for your client's users if you were to adopt them.

You may also look at how similar problems are addressed in other domains, including, but not restricted to, other industries. More generally you should also determine the business rules within which the product will operate, or which it is intended to facilitate. These rules reflect the processes a business needs to go through to operate and if the product doesn't support them it will fail.

You should also build on interviews you have conducted with project stakeholders and decision-makers, and encourage your client to give you access accordingly. You should be looking to understand what is important to key client decision-makers, what they are expecting and why the project is important to them, and their criteria for judging if the project is a success. This research will also help to secure people's support for the development of the project. Also, try to identify any existing processes that will need to be supported in future.

Finally, identify any third-party stakeholders whose interests you need to understand. Typically they might be regulators or government agencies. Your client will be familiar with their concerns, but there may be particular issues that will directly impact design, such as legislation on accessibility, regulations relating to financial activities or medical practice, or data protection rules. (See SHS Orcas case study, pages 194–199.)

Taking stock:
Hugh Dubberly's analysis of the elements of a Web site audit (see page 136). © 2002, Dubberly Design Office

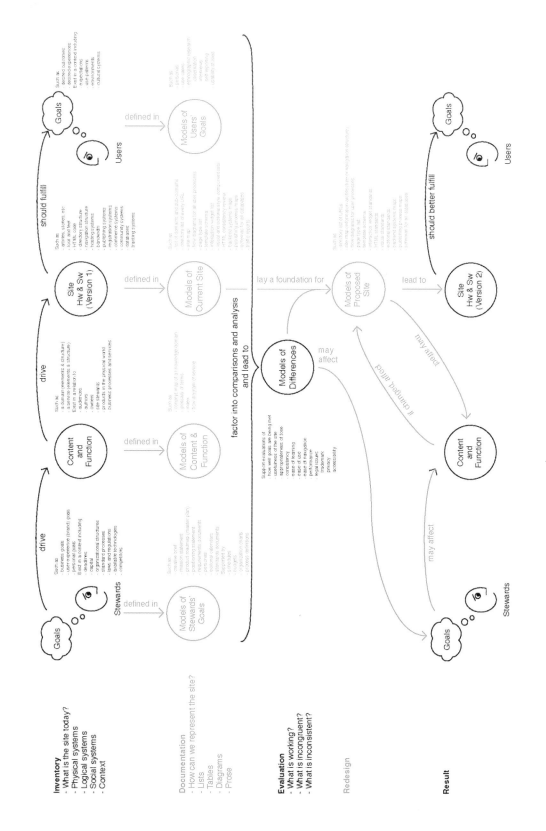

Design, engineering and production

In order to be able to understand the constraints on design and development you will need to become familiar with any existing corporate identity, design or brand guidelines that constitute part of the brief. Also look at any design implementations, including Web sites, that follow these guidelines.

It is important to audit any existing technical setup related to the project. You should look to understand its functionality, how it works, the constraints it imposes, and what it can integrate with. It is also valuable to understand what skills and capabilities the engineering team has. (If someone on the design side is familiar with engineering and the tools likely to be used he may be able to act as an effective conduit.)

If there is an existing site you should find out how it is produced and maintained. This will not only help you to think about the design of the site maintenance process, but also what the issues will be in moving to a new site design.

You should discuss with engineering what technical possibilities are likely to be available in the future and, combined with your own knowledge in this area, use this as a basis for thinking about design solutions that will work now but take advantage of these developments.

Additionally, you should find out what software and collaboration tools (such as email) the client uses, the level of training and skill of those staff who will maintain and develop the product, and their level of Internet access.

Content

To be able to develop design solutions you will need to determine all the types of content that will be used to create the site, from written text to tabular data, photographs to moving images.

Your audit should establish where the content will come from, how is it created and who needs to approve its publication. This will help you think specifically about how the content could be structured and presented, and help the engineers think about how that content will be input, managed, stored and published (which will also have design implications).

For particular design solutions you will need to make sure the required content, or content arrangement, exists or can be created considering constraints on time and resources.

It may be valuable to create a prototype Web site that can be populated with content and accessed internally or by selected users. This will help flag up missing content, and draw out the detailed issues that design, image and typographic solutions will need to address.

Content creation extends beyond prose to data, descriptions and images. Often the first time an organisation has tried to gather together all this content is for a Web project and it can be a time-consuming process that needs to be factored into the project plan. Designers need to work with those responsible for assembling this content to evaluate its quality and develop a method of classification.

Domain experts

For a specialist product another way to learn about the client problem is to talk to and work with people who are knowledgeable about the field in which the client operates – often referred to as 'domain experts'. They may well be people employed by the client but there may be external domain experts to whom it would be valuable to talk. Domain experts should be able to give insights ranging from the way users currently work all the way up to the legislative or regulatory requirements related to the audiences for which the product is intended.

Audiences

From the client's project goals you should research as fully as possible the client's target audiences, familiarising yourself with their behaviour, values and goals. Bear in mind that one 'audience' will be the people in the client organisation who will use and maintain the product from day to day. (This may, in fact, be the main audience. See the BT Group Human Resources intranet case study, page 220.)

Understanding the client's audiences may involve conducting interviews or running workshops with them, spending time observing the way they work and the context in which they might use the product, evaluating their level of experience with computers, and identifying which platforms and Internet connections they are likely to use. Research techniques (described in 'User research', page 60), are broadly quantitative and qualitative.

Quantitative techniques include looking at Web logs (often referred to as a clickstream) for an existing or related site, or compiling a survey or questionnaire.

Qualitative techniques include ethnography and informal video interviews, reviewing user feedback (if there is an existing Web site), interviewing people such as sales or technical support staff who regularly deal with your audiences, visits to interview typical users in the place where they use or may use the product, and conducting focus groups.

Researching the context in which your audiences use or may use the product is important for understanding constraints that might be put on their use which wouldn't be revealed in interviews or with tests conducted elsewhere.

Bear in mind that search engines may also be an 'audience' for the Web site. Users may read site content or search the site through a third party conduit such as Google, and search engine promotion may be part of the product marketing strategy.

Increasingly, audiences are likely to be multinational and be drawn from more diverse cultures, which will require adaptation and creation of these techniques, and will add costs to the research phase.

Deliverables

There are a number of deliverables from 'Research and discovery' that will support the design phase and focus discussion with the client and with engineering.

Scenarios and personas: You should be able to develop fairly comprehensive scenarios and personas (see page 58) that can be reviewed with your audiences and the client. Scenarios should also be developed that relate to the maintenance of the product.

Initial information architecture: This should describe the content types and their source and dependencies, and be used to focus discussions with the client on content assembly and creation, and with engineering on content management and workflow.

Initial requirements document: This should outline, prioritise and group the desired site functionality. It is important that the functionality is prioritised and grouped in ways that will make sense to users. This will help the client think in more detail about costs and the additional processes their organisation may need to support. It will also allow engineering to consider the technical issues of implementation and, where elements of the product are agreed that aren't shaped by the design process, to begin development. This document may become an informal contract between design and engineering.

Strategic review: At a more strategic level it may be appropriate to create a document summarising the project as it is now understood that can be used to discuss and verify strategy with the client. If your research has revealed information that suggests that your client's priorities or understanding of its audiences' needs are wrong, this should also be discussed with them.

Monitoring screen size:
The design of the *Newsweek* Web site anticipates readers with smaller and larger monitors and uses the part of the page that may be chopped off to present less critical stories.

Newsweek.com

The Magazine The Death Penalty on Trial **With HyperCover Links**

Wednesday, June 7, 2000

SUBSCRIBE TODAY

INTERNATIONAL EDITIONS
SPECIAL ISSUES
FOCUS
CAMPAIGN 2000
ARTSCOPE
LIVE TALK
SITE INDEX
ARCHIVE

Featured Advertiser
Planet a Cyberjoy

MARKETPLACE
Online Shopping

BUSINESS CLASSIFIEDS
Education & Services

WASHINGTONPOST.COM

BRITANNICA.COM

◄ SEARCH THE SITE

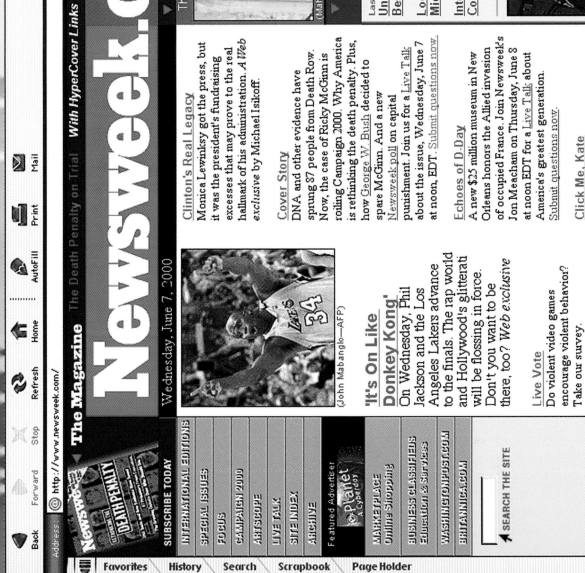

(John Mabanglo—AFP)

'It's On Like Donkey Kong'

On Wednesday, Phil Jackson and the Los Angeles Lakers advance to the finals. The rap world and Hollywood's glitterati will be flossing in force. Don't you want to be there, too? *Web exclusive*

Live Vote
Do violent video games encourage violent behavior? Take our survey.

► Photo Gallery
This Week: Young and Royal

(Maher/Attar—Corbis Sygma)

Clinton's Real Legacy
Monica Lewinksy got the press, but it was the president's fundraising excesses that may prove to the real hallmark of his administration. *A Web exclusive by Michael Isikoff.*

Cover Story
DNA and other evidence have sprung 87 people from Death Row. Now, the case of Ricky McGinn is roiling Campaign 2000. Why America is rethinking the death penalty. Plus, how George W. Bush decided to spare McGinn. And a new Newsweek poll on capital punishment. Join us for a Live Talk about the issue, Wednesday, June 7 at noon, EDT. Submit questions now.

Echoes of D-Day
A new $25 million museum in New Orleans honors the Allied invasion of occupied France. Join Newsweek's Jon Meacham on Thursday, June 8 at noon EDT for a Live Talk about America's greatest generation. Submit questions now.

Click Me, Kate
The Tonys go cyber; plus a special

► Top News washingtonpost.com
Last updated: 11:14 p.m. EDT
Unilever Agrees to Buy Bestfoods for $20.3 Billion

Looming Deadline Impels Mideast Talks to U.S.

Intel Exec Calls for E-Commerce Tax

Design

In the design phase, the information and understanding that has been gleaned from research lays the basis for developing possible solutions in the context of the overall project objectives.

You may have presented initial design ideas when you pitched for the project, or at the end of the 'Scoping and research' phase, in which case you may be building on this work.

Bear in mind that not everything that needs designing will appear on the Web. Among other things, you will need to consider the design of email communications, possibly including registration and feedback acknowledgements, newsletters, and responses from customers or technical support. These design requirements should come out of the scenarios and user journeys you develop.

While the design-driven development of the product concept leads engineering work (see diagram, page 127), some development of the site can be produced in parallel with the design process; for example, database development or the developing content management and workflow tools. Other parallel activities will include setting up Web space and any services that will run on the server (such as e-commerce software).

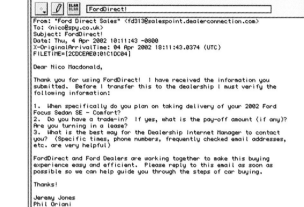

FordDirect!

```
From: "Ford Direct Sales" <fd313@salespoint.dealerconnection.com>
To: <nico@spy.co.uk>
Subject: FordDirect!
Date: Thu, 4 Apr 2002 10:11:43 -0800
X-OriginalArrivalTime: 04 Apr 2002 18:11:43.0374 (UTC)
FILETIME=[2CDCEAE0:01C1DC04]

Dear Nico Macdonald,

Thank you for using FordDirect!  I have received the information you
submitted.  Before I transfer this to the dealership I must verify the
following information:

1.  When specifically do you plan on taking delivery of your 2002 Ford
Focus Sedan SE - Comfort?
2.  Do you have a trade-in?  If yes, what is the pay-off amount (if any)?
Are you turning in a lease?
3.  What is the best way for the Dealership Internet Manager to contact
you?  (Specific times, phone numbers, frequently checked email addresses,
etc. are very helpful)

FordDirect and Ford Dealers are working together to make this buying
experience easy and efficient.  Please reply to this email as soon as
possible so we can help guide you through the steps of car buying.

Thanks!

Jeremy Jones
Phil Oriani
FordDirect.com
1-800-810-4356

FordDirect is here to help you purchase a vehicle from a Ford dealership.
If you are not planning to purchase a vehicle within the next 3 months
then please let us know and we may be able assist you with any information
you might need.

The FordDirect price does not include any rebates (IF AVAILABLE).  The
price also does not include tax, registration, title, and dealer
aftermarket add-ons.
```

Non-Web design:
(above) At FordDirect.com (see pages 168–177) if a visitor specifies a model and contacts a specific dealer about purchasing he will receive an email asking him to confirm his request and for any additional information that is needed before the request is passed on.

MAIN
DETAILS
PAGE

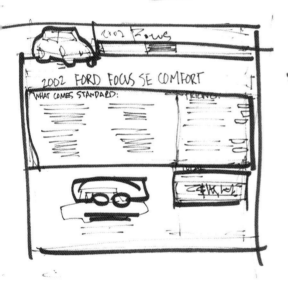

2002 FORD FOCUS SE COMFORT
WHAT COMES STANDARD:

selected vehicle image

YOUR WINDOW STICKER

WHAT COMES STD

BASE PRICE $19

OPTIONS:

YOUR TOTAL $19

Sketchy idea:
Design concepts for
FordDirect.com (see
pages 168–177) often start
out as marker pen roughs.
Sketching in another medium
avoids design ideas being
automatically constrained
by the digital environment.

VEHICLE IMAGE (SELECT

FORD DIRECT

WELCOME TO

FORD DIRECT

Next

BUILD + PRICE

SEARCH

QUICK QUOTE

STANDARD FOOTER ELEMENTS

FMC B
(STAND

→ FOCUSES PAGE ON VEHICLE SELELTION
GROUPS THE ZIP CODE ENTRY WITH PA
ALLOWS FOR SEVERAL SUB-TASKS TO B
BELOW THE MAIN TASK SELTION.

RELOADS?(OR PASSD IN -HARD-CODED)

(?) CAN THE IMAGE RELOAD ON SELECTION?
IMAGE FLOATS ABOVE EVERYTHING ELSE

LARGE FD BRANDING
(SET OFF IN WHITE SPACE FOR MAX EFFECT)

ZIP CODE SELECTION

3 MAIN PATH SELECTIONS

(?) HOW TO GET VSISR TO
ENTER ZIP CODE BEFORE
CLICKING A PATH? ERROR
CASE?

SECONDARY OPTIONS:
- HOW IT WORKS
- PRE-OWNED INVENTORY

(?) HOW TO DOWN PLAY
THE PRE-OWNED BUT
SO MUCH THAT IT IS IGNORED

ARKS
)

ND

ELECTION

SITIONED

OPTION 1: VERTICAL

Developing concepts

The development of design concepts tends to work best if it is initially open-ended and can approach the challenge from a number of directions using a variety of techniques, while reflecting on the context of the problem. Creating a 'big idea' which can give coherence to a solution is important, while feedback from and discussion with other parties in the project allows for possible issues to be identified.

Investigating the problem: Many tools and techniques support analysing and developing solutions to design problems. These include:

↗ *Sketching:* Pen or pencil sketching on a whiteboard or on paper is quick (avoiding commitment to an idea) and can be conducted almost anywhere. Sketches are good for communicating abstract concepts and relationships between things, and their crudeness can help avoid people (especially clients) focusing on detail rather than concept.
↗ *Post-It Notes:* A valuable tool for organising and reorganising Web site content, navigation and functions, Post-Its can be written or drawn on and stuck to a vertical or horizontal surface. As they can be grouped and spaced, they help people to conceptualise a multidimensional product such as a Web site.
↗ *Wireframes:* These are interactive representations of a Web site best used to investigate navigation structure, and page content and structure. They are typically developed in HTML though they can be created in other applications such as PowerPoint.
↗ *Click-through sketches:* These are mocked-up screens representing a sequence of actions, and which click through to the next screen.

↗ *Interactive demos:* Similar to click-through sketches (though often less finished), they allow for top-level browsing through the design.
↗ *Maps and diagrams:* These are visuals typically used to show site structure and flow. They can be printed out large and stuck to a wall to be commented on and critiqued by an individual or group. As they are on paper they are easy to annotate and make or change connections.
↗ *Prototypes:* This refers to any kind of design solution mock-up that allows some aspect of it to be investigated. Prototypes may be created and used on screen or printed out, or created using paper elements.
↗ *Look and feel:* These are more finished treatments of design elements (such as navigation, a form, use of imagery) that may be used for testing but are as likely to be used to solicit client feedback or initiate a discussion with engineering.
↗ *Type treatments:* These may be experiments with typefaces, sizes, styles and typographic layout used to investigate aesthetics and feel, and to test for legibility and readability (see 'Typography', page 92).
↗ *Mood boards:* These are visual associations of imagery, typography and colour samples generally culled from sources of cultural references such as magazines and adverts. They are used to investigate how a product might communicate at an aesthetic and sensual level.

Sketchy-Thingy:
Developed by Chris Edwards at ATG, Sketchy-Thingy uses hand-drawn and -coloured imagery assembled and made interactive in Director. This technique is often referred to as card sorting.

Analysing the problem: You should initially 'walk around' the problem, using the tools listed, to get a feel for it in its entirety, based on the research you have done, your understanding of its overall context and the project goals.

You will need to be particularly aware of the constraints on the project and those imposed by the context of use of your audiences, including the platforms from which they will access the product. However, you should begin by considering what would be the best or ideal product and then constrain the realistic solution along that path. This will ensure that the product vision is retained, and that decisions aren't made which would make it harder for the product to evolve towards that vision.

It may be appropriate and valuable to include representatives from the engineering and other teams at this and subsequent stages. Domain experts may be particularly valuable for giving substantive feedback on the problem analysis and proposed solutions.

Developing ideas: This is the 'secret sauce' of the design process when lateral thinking and inspiration meet sound understanding and analysis (see 'Creativity, innovation and the big idea', page 105). This 'big idea' should inform and serve as a reference point for much of the subsequent design development. It should also cohere the overall product development and provide a reference point for evaluating other ideas and decisions.

A big idea should encompass a conceptual model that should help users understand the product and the way it works. It should also capture the way in which the company wants to present itself, and the product in particular (in effect, one aspect of its branding).

Just as there is no recipe for this kind of thinking, neither is it predictable when ideas will come to you. It is unlikely to be when you are sitting at your desk, or even in a design meeting. Of course, you may and should ideally have a number of big ideas and evaluate them accordingly, which may include informal presentations to your client.

When you have settled on a big idea and its associated conceptual model, you can develop more specific design solutions for the site. For a complex project you should consider how your design solutions can be related to the project goals in a way that can easily be audited, and determine that each goal has been addressed.

Right:
Prototypes should be quick to develop and change, and focus discussion on the appropriate issues. This example is a 'high-level sketch', created in PowerPoint, from the SHS Orcas case study, see pages 194–199.

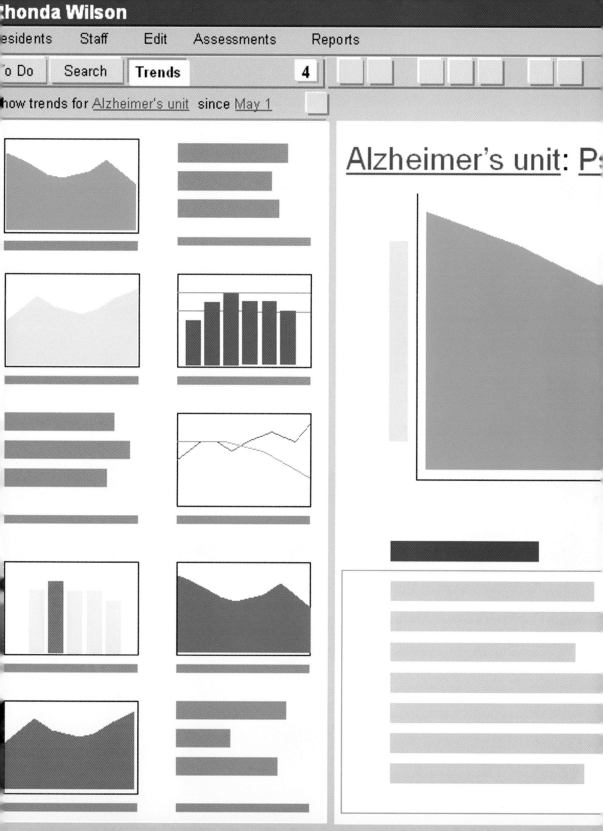

Your design solutions might include:

↗ *Content model:* This captures the types and uses of text and images (content) for the site for each of the user types defined in the brief. It describes how, when and under what circumstances different types of content will be used to achieve a specific goal (see 'Content and writing for the Web', page 96).
↗ *Navigation model:* The navigation model combines with the conceptual and content models to inform the creation of the site map or, for more software-like products, an interaction diagram (see 'Navigation', page 70).
↗ *Site map or interaction diagram:* A site map will typically include all the site pages, or page types; the functionality and key types of content on each page or page type; the links between those pages, and the hierarchy in which they sit; and areas of the site which the user can only access if he has completed a certain task (such as logging in). It should help ensure that the site will serve your audiences, identify where technical elements will fit, flag up features or information that haven't yet been identified, and consider how the site might be maintained (see 'Information architecture', page 66).
↗ *Interaction model:* This shows how the elements of the site with which the user interacts behave; for example rollovers, forms, and dynamic interface elements (see 'Interaction design', page 80 and 'Interface design', page 84).
↗ *Information design and typographic approach:* This indicates how best to display complex information that is clear, contextualised

and understandable, and present structured and running text in a clear and readable way (see 'Information design and visualisation', page 74 and 'Typography', page 92).
↗ *Visual treatments:* These illustrate the graphical treatments for the various elements of the site, including navigation, page headers, treatments of pictures and graphics (see 'Graphic design and aesthetics', page 90).

With the more substantial and conceptual elements of the design, it is easy to spend a lot of time working through ideas, considering constraints, scenarios and users' needs. If this process works well you will relatively quickly get to a point where everything seems to hang together. The return on further time spent will tend to decrease and you should consider moving on to tasks where your time can be better utilised, or to evaluating your idea. Even if things don't feel quite right, at some point a good enough solution will come up against a project deadline and bigger issues will come into play.

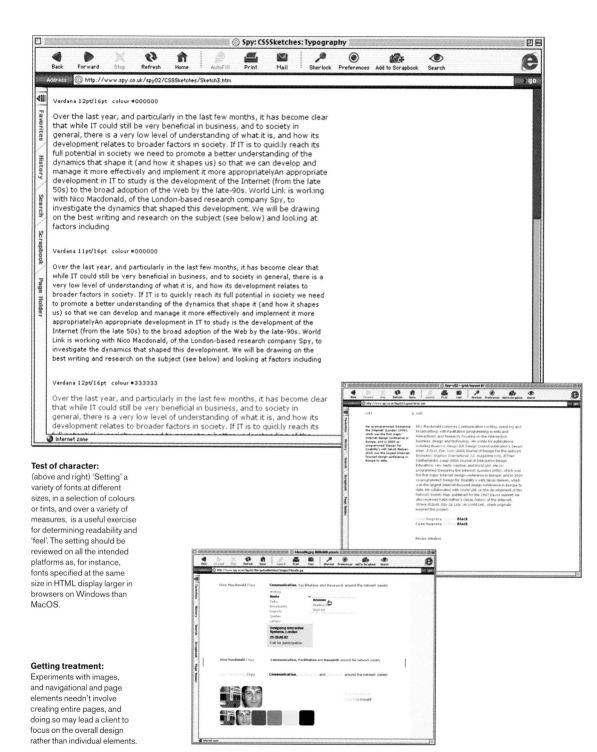

Spy: CSSSketches: Typography

http://www.spy.co.uk/spy02/CSSSketches/Sketch3.htm

Verdana 12pt/16pt colour #000000

Over the last year, and particularly in the last few months, it has become clear that while IT could still be very beneficial in business, and to society in general, there is a very low level of understanding of what it is, and how its development relates to broader factors in society. If IT is to quickly reach its full potential in society we need to promote a better understanding of the dynamics that shape it (and how it shapes us) so that we can develop and manage it more effectively and implement it more appropriatelyAn appropriate development in IT to study is the development of the Internet (from the late 50s) to the broad adoption of the Web by the late-90s. World Link is working with Nico Macdonald, of the London-based research company Spy, to investigate the dynamics that shaped this development. We will be drawing on the best writing and research on the subject (see below) and looking at factors including

Verdana 11pt/16pt colour #000000

Over the last year, and particularly in the last few months, it has become clear that while IT could still be very beneficial in business, and to society in general, there is a very low level of understanding of what it is, and how its development relates to broader factors in society. If IT is to quickly reach its full potential in society we need to promote a better understanding of the dynamics that shape it (and how it shapes us) so that we can develop and manage it more effectively and implement it more appropriatelyAn appropriate development in IT to study is the development of the Internet (from the late 50s) to the broad adoption of the Web by the late-90s. World Link is working with Nico Macdonald, of the London-based research company Spy, to investigate the dynamics that shaped this development. We will be drawing on the best writing and research on the subject (see below) and looking at factors including

Verdana 12pt/16pt colour #333333

Over the last year, and particularly in the last few months, it has become clear that while IT could still be very beneficial in business, and to society in general, there is a very low level of understanding of what it is, and how its development relates to broader factors in society. If IT is to quickly reach its

Test of character:
(above and right) 'Setting' a variety of fonts at different sizes, in a selection of colours or tints, and over a variety of measures, is a useful exercise for determining readability and 'feel'. The setting should be reviewed on all the intended platforms as, for instance, fonts specified at the same size in HTML display larger in browsers on Windows than MacOS.

Getting treatment:
Experiments with images, and navigational and page elements needn't involve creating entire pages, and doing so may lead a client to focus on the overall design rather than individual elements.

Feedback and discussion: As we have emphasised elsewhere, it is vital at this stage to have a dynamic conversation with other parties in the project, particularly with the engineering team. This discussion is particularly important for any elements of the product being developed that will need design input. The engineering development may also influence the design solutions or, more directly, the engineering team may suggest possible design solutions.

Deliverables: The deliverables at this stage are primarily for discussion with other parties (perhaps including the client) and for testing. They could be any of the artifacts identified in *Investigating the problem,* (page 144). Brought together they will constitute a 'blueprint' for the site design and functionality (see 'Deliverables', page 154).

Testing concepts

Testing is not a discrete or linear element of the design and product development process and it may be appropriate at any point to evaluate a design idea or solution. (The principle models are discussed in 'Evaluation', page 98).

Testing of design ideas is a part of the design process and one way of identifying solutions that might work. Problems are rarely solved at the first attempt and you shouldn't be too precious about abandoning or modifying design ideas that don't work.

When testing or discussing a design solution, you need to be clear about the aspects of the design on which you want to focus. This should partly determine the form in which you present your design ideas.

While evaluating ideas you need to keep in mind the client's project goals, and these will also be part of the approval process discussion with the client (see 'Approval processes', page 152). You may, of course, present design ideas to the client before looking for design approval and you may also find it useful to have one of your team play the role of the client.

Expert testing: This kind of testing may be conducted by someone on your team who is able to be detached about the project and the design solutions (perhaps yourself). It should be based on the heuristics of good Web design and that person's own instincts about what works and what creates a good quality of experience. Reviewing by domain experts may also be appropriate.

Testing against scenarios and with personas: These methods can be used most effectively as design ideas come up, and are also useful for communicating with other parties about whether a design idea may or may not work. They can also be combined to consider a user journey through a proposed design solution (see 'Scenarios and personas', page 58).

Testing with users: Testing with the intended audiences for the product is the most common type of evaluation. Usability testing (see 'Usability and usability testing', page 98) is likely to be more useful in refining design concepts, and post-launch. Depending on the project and your client's disposition, you may favour quantitative over qualitative testing. Tests with relatively few users, which may be all that time and budget allow, are still likely to be useful, though on some projects (such as complex tools for which users may need training) extensive usability testing may be less useful as users will receive training. You may also find it helps to support your design decisions if your client and someone from the engineering team observe the tests. It may also be useful to run a focus group, do an online survey on your design solutions or ask users for more informal feedback (particularly if you are redesigning an established product).

Testing with engineering and other project stakeholders: Discussion of design solutions with engineering should be a regular activity and be very iterative. Not least it is important that engineering assess the performance implications of possible design solutions, perhaps by coding mock-ups and testing them in a realistic context.

While reviewing and testing concepts with engineering, you should make sure you explain how your design approach and thinking has informed your design solutions. The more engineering understands and is sympathetic to the solution, the more closely they will be able to implement it as intended, and where design decisions need to be made during implementation (as they inevitably will be), the more appropriate will be their decisions.

It is important to evaluate ideas with other project stakeholders. Where possible get face-to-face feedback. Make sure you are clear about what aspects of the design you are discussing, and record and share feedback you receive.

Approval processes

Getting positive client approval is critical to moving on to implementation. If the decision-makers on the client side have clearly understood the design solution and its implications you should be able to avoid extensive design adjustments later on. Although there are major presentations of design solutions it is appropriate to show solutions to the client at other points, which may also help narrow the scope of the design investigation.

For major presentations you should offer a number of design solutions. This will facilitate discussion of the scope of the project and contrast the possible solutions.

With each presentation, you should make it clear to your client which elements of the design brief you are addressing, why you have chosen to present your design ideas in a particular form and what you are asking them to respond to or decide upon. Using real text, data and calculations in a presentation will avoid them becoming a focus of discussion.

Bear in mind that your immediate client contact may not be the only audience for your presentation and they may find it valuable to present to their colleagues and other stakeholders. If this is the case they will need to be able to tell the design story effectively too. Your client's feedback and decisions may, on occasion, be frustrating and reveal what you consider to be a lack of understanding, but it is the job of the designer to explain the design solution to the client clearly in terms that are understandable and meaningful to them.

Other client decisions may be rationalised in broader terms. You may have created the best design solution but if the costs or the time implications are considerable, the client will have to make a business decision about the design. It may also be the case that the project goals and user needs don't entirely map.

To help your client make these business decisions it may be useful to create a dependency and requirements document showing what the removal of particular pieces of the product will affect. Similarly, a client may want to change or add to the product and you may need to use a similar technique to make the implications of these decisions clear to them.

At this stage it is also appropriate to confirm that the scenarios and personas are still correct and representative, and to check that all aspects of the product specification map directly or indirectly to the project goals. This process should also involve engineering and may need to involve other parties.

This is also the point to discuss any concerns you have about project implementation, and make sure that you and your client are clear about what you are going to deliver. The challenge here is to get everyone to engage and think ahead to see where there might be a problem, rather than blithely acknowledging possible scenarios. It is also appropriate at this stage to review any project dependencies or other company activities that may affect the product development and launch.

Exploring possibilities:
For The Ocean Conservancy project (see pages 186–193), MetaDesign developed a number of page treatments, focusing on three aspects of the client identity: inspiration; its scientific nature; and its participatory nature.

Printable pages:
Many editorial Web sites have a 'printable page' option but there is more to this than formatting for print rather than screen. The *Wall Street Journal* Web site (right) makes any links explicit, as underlined text is no longer 'clickable' on paper, even if it *is* blue.

Deliverables

When your client has signed off the project specification and design, this needs to be documented for implementation.

Functional and technical specification: Sometimes known as 'requirements documents', these are typically created by the engineering team, but should be based on the design solutions developed by the design team.

The functional specification describes 'what the site does'. These functions should be grouped such that they make sense to users, and that if during implementation some need to be held over they can be 'cut from the back', leaving the product still making sense. The functional specification should also describe the elements that make up each page and outline all the interactive elements of the site, describing the options a user will have, what he will see for all the permutations of actions he could perform (including those where there is an error), how pages load and what happens subsequently to any data generated.

The technical specification needs to describe any existing systems that the Web site will be built on, specify the client platforms on which it is intended to work, indicate how it should perform and describe any systems with which the Web site will need to integrate.

At this point the specification of the site is frozen, though amendments to both documents should be allowed so they accurately reflect decisions made during implementation.

New features and design elements should ideally be noted for the next phase of the site development. If the project runs late during implementation, those that have already been agreed may also be moved to the next phase.

Content specifications: The content specification should be created in collaboration with engineering and will be used by them, but will also be relevant to the people responsible for assembling and creating the site content.

For a typical site the specification will include page title and heading levels. It should also include typical examples of each different type of content, which might encompass: text with subheads; lists; catalogue entries or database records; tables; and forms (including validation and response text). Non-Web elements should also be addressed (including such ephemera as subject lines and sender names).

Blueprints: On the design side you should develop detailed specifications to describe all aspects of the way the site design will work. While it doesn't need to show a design for every page, if standard design elements and treatments are presented the blueprint can be thought of as a working dummy of the site. This should be supported by additional written and visual documentation and interactive 'demos' to help engineering understand how the design, and particularly the interactions, work.

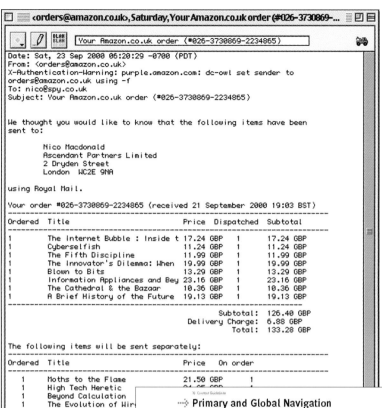

```
┌────────────────────────────────────────────────────────────────────┐
│ ☐ ▤  <orders@amazon.co.uk, Saturday, Your Amazon.co.uk order (#026-3730869-...  ▤ ▣ ▤ │
├────────────────────────────────────────────────────────────────────┤
│ ◇  ✎  BLAH│ Your Amazon.co.uk order (#026-3730869-2234865)           🚚 │
│         BLAH                                                          │
├────────────────────────────────────────────────────────────────────┤
```

Date: Sat, 23 Sep 2000 06:20:29 -0700 (PDT)
From: <orders@amazon.co.uk>
X-Authentication-Warning: purple.amazon.com: dc-owl set sender to
orders@amazon.co.uk using -f
To: nico@spy.co.uk
Subject: Your Amazon.co.uk order (#026-3730869-2234865)

We thought you would like to know that the following items have been
sent to:

        Nico Macdonald
        Ascendant Partners Limited
        2 Dryden Street
        London   WC2E 9NA

using Royal Mail.

Your order #026-3730869-2234865 (received 21 September 2000 19:03 BST)

Ordered Title   Price Dispatched Subtotal
----
1   The Internet Bubble : Inside t 17.24 GBP   1   17.24 GBP
1   Cyberselfish   11.24 GBP   1   11.24 GBP
1   The Fifth Discipline   11.99 GBP   1   11.99 GBP
1   The Innovator's Dilemma: When 19.99 GBP   1   19.99 GBP
1   Blown to Bits   13.29 GBP   1   13.29 GBP
1   Information Appliances and Bey 23.16 GBP   1   23.16 GBP
1   The Cathedral & the Bazaar   10.36 GBP   1   10.36 GBP
1   A Brief History of the Future 19.13 GBP   1   19.13 GBP

                            Subtotal: 126.40 GBP
                     Delivery Charge: 6.88 GBP
                               Total: 133.28 GBP

The following items will be sent separately:

Ordered Title   Price On order
----
    1   Moths to the Flame   21.50 GBP   1
    1   High Tech Heretic
    1   Beyond Calculation
    1   The Evolution of Wir

Payment in other currencies m
rates and to charges made by

In an attempt to give you the
this partial shipment. The t
will of course remain the sam

If you have any questions, pl
(orders@amazon.co.uk), Fax (0
For international customers F
phone (+44 20 8636 9451).

The joys of ASCII:
Designing email is often considered unglamorous as "it is only ASCII," but it is precisely because it is so limited that it is an interesting design exercise. The designer can use all capitals, letter spacing, indenting, underlining, rules (that you can invent as you go), line spaces, bulleted lists and hanging paragraphs. For many, the most important element of a mailing is how to get off the list and this 'unsubscribe' information needs to be unambiguous.

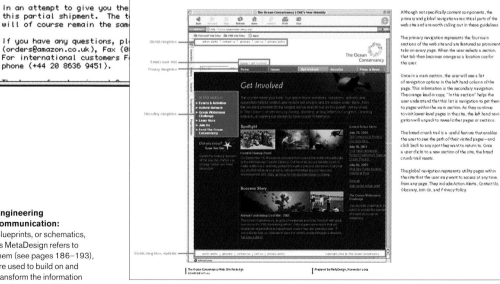

···❖ Primary and Global Navigation

Although not specifically content components, the primary and global navigation are critical parts of the web site and are worth calling out in these guidelines.

The primary navigation represents the four main sections of the web site and are featured as prominent tabs on every page. When the user selects a section, that tab then becomes orange as a location cue for the user.

Once in a main section, the user will see a list of navigation options in the left hand column of the page. This information is the secondary navigation. The orange lead-in copy, "In this section" helps the user understand that this list is navigation to get them to pages within the main section. As they continue to visit lower-level pages in the site, the left hand navigation will unpack to reveal lower pages or sections.

The bread crumb trail is a useful feature that enables the user to see the path of their visited pages—and click back to any spot they want to return to. Once a user clicks to a new section of the site, the bread crumb trail resets.

The global navigation represents utility pages within the site that the user may want to access at any time, from any page. They include Action Alerts, Contact Us, Glossary, Join Us, and Privacy Policy.

Engineering communication:
Blueprints, or schematics, as MetaDesign refers to them (see pages 186–193), are used to build on and transform the information architecture into Web pages.

Implementation

This phase is largely driven by engineering but will also be very interactive as the engineering team clarifies elements of the design about which it is unclear. Although most technical and design implementation problems should have been ironed out during the design phase, there will invariably be further compromises that need to be made, some of which will simply be a result of time and resource constraints.

If engineering understands your design approach and solutions well enough, they will be able to take the initiative when they have a design-related question and, where some design specification may have been omitted, should be able to work through and apply an existing design approach.

Of course, there will be aspects of the implementation of the design that are incorrect and you will need to have a clear way of indicating corrections to engineering. This is much more difficult with Web projects than with print design, as the artifact is both digital and interactive. It will often be valuable and appropriate for a designer and engineer to sit together to work through an aspect of the design implementation, or at least for the designer to explain the principles clearly so the engineer can investigate how best to address it.

It may be valuable to ask client representatives to use the product during implementation, to familiarise themselves with it, and allow them to get a sense of what it will really be like to use.

There is much more that may need to be done at this phase of the project. Engineering will have further back-end integration, configuring and testing to do and you should be aware of these activities in case they reveal any design issues that you hadn't considered.

Content creation should also be continuing, and if you are redesigning or developing an existing product, content migration should also be in progress. Both of these processes will throw up design issues that you will need to address.

This may also be an appropriate time to be working with the people who will maintain, run and develop the site to explain your design approach further, and look at the design-related decisions they will need to make in their role.

Deliverables

The main deliverables at this stage will be clarifications of design elements that aren't clear from the blueprint, adjustments to the design that are required for implementation and design specifications for any site elements that weren't identified during the design phase.

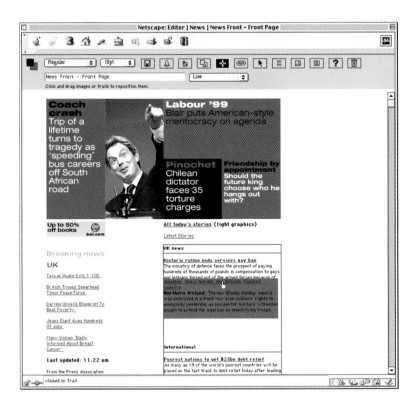

Design for the back room:
The audience for a Web site is generally imagined as the people who will use it rather than those who will maintain and develop it. Editorial Web sites, for instance, have extensive content publishing systems which writers and editors will use all day, and for whom the quality of the design is critical. The London *Guardian* newspaper created its own interface to its system that allowed for direct editing of page elements by simply selecting them.

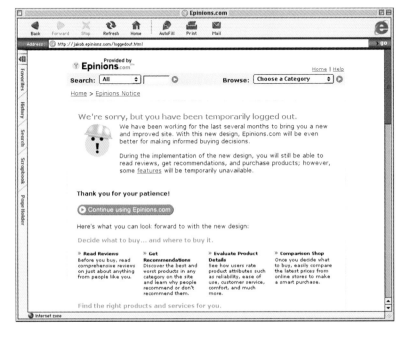

Anticipating updates:
Epinions does a better job when anticipating a site update, using a humourous image to reassure, no doubt, irritated users. This design requirement should have come out of the product scenarios.

Testing

Once the product has been developed to specification and the design has been satisfactorily implemented, the site is ready for testing. Tests need to address content, whether the product does what it is intended to do and whether it performs well and reliably. There will be fewer surprises here if some testing was done during earlier phases. Some testing at this stage may be appropriate to determine whether design changes, or the performance of the implementation, have any impact on usability.

Checking and proofing

As Web products are often content-driven, testing needs to consider whether the site content (text, images, data) appears in the appropriate places, is presented in the correct way and loads in the right order. All text (including text in buttons, page titles, navigational elements and alt tags) needs to be checked for spelling, style, formatting and consistency in use of terms and structure of page titles. Alt tags should also be checked to ensure they have been used where they were specified. These tests may be carried out by the site content creator along with the design team.

Beta testing

This stage involves testing the site against the specification to see that it functions and behaves as planned. Beta testing of much of the site can take place before the design is finalised or implemented, particularly for elements that are developed in parallel with the design. These tests are usually done by engineering.

Performance

Site performance may have been part of the design brief or the product specification and is therefore appropriate to beta test. However, it is best to consider it separately since performance issues on the Web often have serious implications for user experience. Performance testing is typically done by engineering but design can also be involved, and should certainly be aware of what needs to be tested.

Performance is affected by many factors that are under the control of the client, including the amount of code in the page, the number of page elements and the size of each one, the complexity of rendering the page code, code which 'executes' on the browser side, 'calls' to the server (including form validation and automatic page refreshing), and server speed and load. There are a number of performance criteria that should be considered:

↗ Are pages slow to load? Do page elements load in the right order? Do they load completely? Do the pages look and behave as expected?
↗ Is the text readable and are images clear?
↗ Do menus and other navigation elements work as expected?
↗ Are forms slow to submit?
↗ Are any errors displayed?
↗ Is server-generated information accurate?

Testing should also be done for scenarios that might have been missed in the design brief or product specification. For instance, how does the site and design respond when the browser window is re-sized, and how do they perform with a browser's back and forward buttons?

These tests are usually done by engineering. If there are serious performance problems, you will need to meet with them and the client to discuss what can be done to rectify them.

Quality assurance (QA)

Quality assurance considers whether a site performs consistently over time and on the platforms and over the bandwidths on which it was intended to work. In software development and large Web projects it may be conducted by a separate team but could also be conducted by the design or engineering teams.

Soft and hard launching

A soft launch allows you to control who sees the nearly finished version of your site. It is an opportunity for your client, their clients, friends, suppliers and staff to review the near-complete project – available at its final URL. A soft launch is useful for soliciting their response to the product, and may reveal problems that may have been missed in the testing process.

There will invariably be final changes to be made but you and your client will have to decide about what is feasible to incorporate before the hard launch. The only changes that should be considered at this stage are those that will seriously affect the performance of the site for the users or for the client's staff. Minor changes should be held back to the next phase of the product development.

If the product is replacing an existing one that is heavily used (very likely if it is a product used internally) there may be a period of 'piloting' where both are used side by side to ensure that the new product is sufficiently reliable to start using for real. Some external Web sites are publicly piloted alongside the old version, often to a select group of users.

For a project such as Compass, Visual I|O (see pages 200–205) usually conduct a piloting phase where the new system is used alongside the one that is being phased out.

A hard launch is no different from a soft launch in that the product is public and at its final URL.

However, at this point it will be publicised to its intended audiences, 'real' people will use it – and its performance will be publicly tested. At this point your client will need to have in place the organisational mechanisms to support the site, and provision for backup and site failure.

Deliverables

The main deliverables at this stage will be adjustments to the design blueprints to take account of unanticipated design or technical problems, or performance issues. Images and code may also be optimised for size and to improve page-rendering speed. This may be done by engineering in conjunction with design.

Post-launch

Post-launch evaluation

The hard launch should only be the end of the beginning of the project. When the product is out there in the world it starts to become more real and your design thinking will have even more tangible material to work on.

Measuring success

At the beginning of the project your client will have defined project objectives which included metrics for success. These may have included increasing profits, sales or numbers of users for their services, or greater efficiency for their staff if the product is used internally. Being able to determine how successful (or not) the project was lays the basis for evaluating how effective your design approach has been and measuring the effectiveness of any future changes you make – though, of course, design is only one factor in a product's success.

Web log analysis

It is only after launch that you will be able to analyse the logs from the client's Web site effectively, including the patterns of purchasing (if the site is used for commerce) and how the site is being used.

Analysing this Web log information can provide invaluable insights about where your design is working well and where it can be improved, and you should review the logs on a regular basis.

Logs can indicate which parts of the site are badly flagged in the navigation, are slow to load or have a confusing interface. They can also give you information about the client's customers: those who simply look at the home page and those who spend more time on the site.

Indicators that the site is not working may include customers not getting through to specific pages, uncompleted payment transactions, forms that are accessed but not submitted and pages that no one visits. These will all be discernable from the Web logs.

Usability testing and focus groups

Usability testing can and should be an ongoing process. It can help evaluate how features that still aren't easy to use could be changed and suggest to you features that might be added. The client may also wish to consider using focus groups at this stage, although they tend to provide fewer insights than usability testing.

User feedback

User feedback can be very helpful in understanding which aspects of your design are working and which aren't. It may lead you to new design ideas or alternative solutions, and may even help your client generate new business ideas.

These evaluation techniques are broadly reactive and while they will help you make the site design work better they are not a substitute for the design innovation during the next phase of the project. If design involvement does continue it is important that the tactical nature of this involvement (working on fixes and making slight improvements) doesn't blind you to the bigger issues and developments that will really take the product forward.

Live learning:
The search engine Google is so highly used that Google's designers can tell how well a design change is working within hours of rolling it out on just one of its many Web servers.

Training and documentation

Documenting the design guidelines is important for staff working on the site and for anyone who will be developing the site design in the future (including people in your own team).

Documentation doesn't have to be complex or involved, and can be built on the material that you presented during the design process and the design blueprint prepared for engineering – incorporating the inevitable last-minute design tweaks made during and post implementation. This documentation will also be useful for any new client staff or engineers who get involved in the project in the future. Additionally it will be helpful for any of your own staff who are brought in to work on later phases of the project.

The documentation may also cover the design development process, which is particularly valuable for communicating the value of the design input to project stakeholders who were directly involved.

Creating good documentation is also a design challenge. The traditional 'thick binder' type of design documentation may not be the best way to communicate with your users, and is unlikely to support their context of use.

Design training with the people who are maintaining and developing the new product should be initiated, or concluded if it was initiated pre-launch. As they will be intensely involved with the product, an emphasis should be placed on educating these people to identify design problems and communicate them effectively to you.

On the BT Group Human Resources intranet (see case study, pages 220–227) post-launch changes to the design were made by the engineering team.

Future phases

By the end of a project you will have deliberately, or of necessity, created a considerable list of features and design ideas to be evaluated for development in the next phase. Managing this nascent specification effectively so it is a coherent, living document is a considerable challenge and requires a well-defined process.

Post-project reflection

While your client may get the best from your input if you are involved long term, the project may end at this point. Repeat involvement with a client or a project is usually more rewarding than continually starting over, and if you like working with them you should try to maintain a relationship with your client. This might involve making proactive suggestions about new site features or proposing new design models that may be appropriate for future phases of the site.

You will benefit tremendously from reflecting on the way the project developed. This reflection should ideally be conducted with the client and other parties who were involved in the project to see what went well and badly, and to see how such a project could be better designed in future. This isn't an excuse for recrimination but for thoughtful learning. You should also reflect on your own design approaches and processes, and project and client management, and consider where they can be improved.

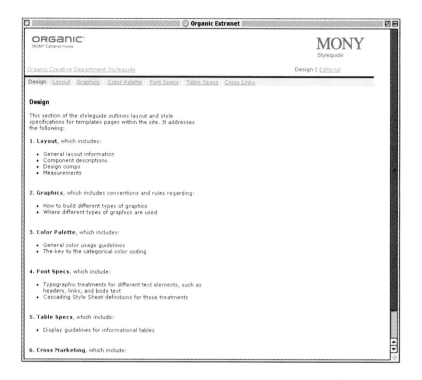

Documentary evidence:
For the MONY Independent Network project (see page 236) Organic developed online documentation detailing how each element of the site was constructed. MetaDesign creates a 'Red Book' (below) for each project and this is used to present the design issue and approach – including usability research findings, process and methodology architecture, and visual design – to the client and others.

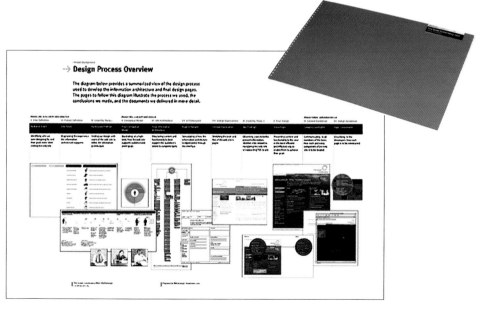

Web design project workflow

Workflow diagram:
(right) This diagram maps to the project stages previously discussed in the Anatomy section, indicating deliverables and points where iteration is needed. It is presented as a basis for discussing the planning and execution of a project with the parties who are directly involved. Although the duration of each phase is only approximate, the period prescribed for implementation and testing is infringed up at the peril of the project. Elsewhere in Anatomy we present some alternative and complementary diagrams from BodyMedia (see page 115), Cooper (see pages 117 and 127), Hugh Dubberly (page 135) and MetaDesign, North America (page 163). A digital version of this diagram can be found at www.whatiswebdesign.com

Web design tools and deliverables:
(below) The core Web design disciplines overlap, as do the tools and deliverables they deploy. These tools and deliverables are discussed more extensively in the Anatomy section. Some, such as usability testing, are useful at many points in the workflow while others, such as competitor analysis, tend to be used on a particular point.

See 'Pre-project stages' (page 116) and 'Scoping and research' (page 122)
A client's business goals lead to a project with specific objectives. Based on this the client may create an RFP or a simple design brief, or ask the designer for tenders. To ensure the designer knows what they are being asked for they should research the organisation and business area, audit the available resources, and scope the project, ideally for a fee. The tender should make clear the designer's assumptions and not raise expectations unduly. It should indicate what minimal 'critical mass' of design work will be delivered. An initial technical specification and design brief will flow from the RFP.

See 'Planning and managing a project' (page 124) and 'Research and discovery' (page 134)
Establishing a framework for communication and collaboration is critical to project success. Research with project stakeholders to establish their roles, interests and requirements, and help map the problem area. Audiences include staff who will use the product. Auditing the text, images and data to be used will reveal issues. Ask 'domain experts' and the client about the business rules and associated processes the Web site must support.

See 'Design' (page 140)
Design should collaboratively lead the engineering process to ensure that what is built has been considered and tested so it is less likely to need costly and time-consuming revision (see page 124). A number of engineering tasks can take place in parallel with design including setting up servers and other infrastructure, and the evaluation of performance issues for design solutions can happen at this stage. The design solution should begin with a 'big idea' (see pages 105 and 119) before being evaluated and tested. Reviewing possible solutions against scenarios and personas that were developed is a quick and effective method and is easy to discuss.

See 'Implementation' (page 156)
At this point the functional and technical specification should be frozen, and any new features requested should be noted for future phases of site development. The design and specification documentation should be updated to reflect any 'tweaks' made to the systems set-up. This stage is led by engineering with the designer clarifying his documentation and specifying any elements that have been omitted or were unforeseen. This may involve the designer and engineer working closely together.

See 'Testing' (page 158)
Design documentation should be created in tandem with any digital deliverables (including source files) the client will need to continue running and developing the product. Where appropriate, training of client staff could take place at this stage. New ideas for future phases of design and technical development can be consolidated.

See 'Post-launch' (see page 160)
Further training of client staff may be appropriate, particularly around aspects of the design that only came into play after launch (for instance content publishing or the creation of email newsletters). The live site will furnish the designer with information that will enable him to reflect on the success of the design solution, particularly in relation to the project goals. It is also valuable for him to reflect with his client and collaborators on the success of the process.

Branding and Corporate Identity
- Focus groups
- Brand maps
- Mood boards
- Typographic investigations

Interface Design
- Look and feel studies
- Function grouping
- Metaphors
- Sketches

Information Architecture
- Card sorting
- Wireframes
- Reference documents
- Style guides
- Functional specifications
- Taxonomy development
- Log analysis
- Content analysis
- Tables and matrices
- Site maps and diagrams
- Schematics

Interaction Design
- Report and recommendation documents
- Scenarios and personas
- Prototypes
- Usability testing
- Expert and heuristic testing
- Competitor analysis
- Interactive demos
- Storyboards

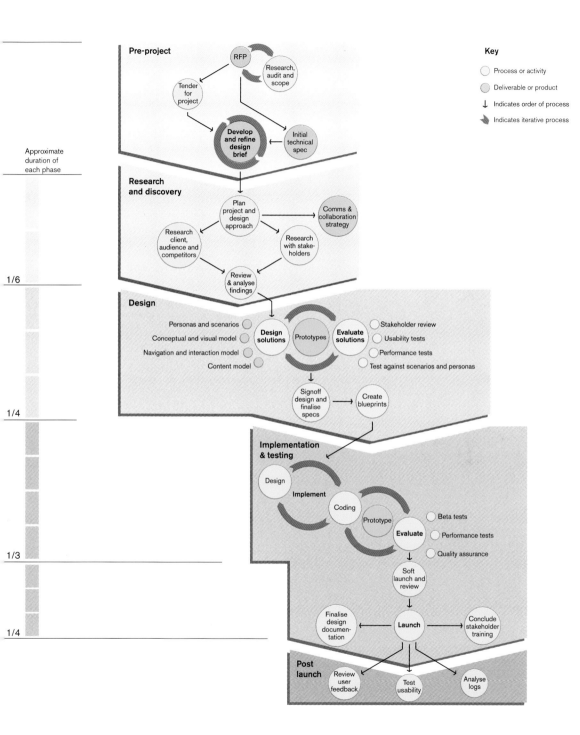

Pre-project

RFP

Research, audit and scope

Tender for project

Develop and refine design brief

Initial technical spec

Research and discovery

Plan project and design approach

Comms & collaboration strategy

Research client, audience and competitors

Research with stake-holders

Review & analyse findings

Design

Personas and scenarios
Conceptual and visual model
Navigation and interaction model
Content model

Design solutions

Prototypes

Evaluate solutions

Stakeholder review
Usability tests
Performance tests
Test against scenarios and personas

Signoff design and finalise specs → Create blueprints

Implementation & testing

Design

Implement

Coding

Prototype

Evaluate

Beta tests
Performance tests
Quality assurance

Soft launch and review

Finalise design documentation ← Launch → Conclude stakeholder training

Post launch

Review user feedback

Test usability

Analyse logs

Key

○ Process or activity

◯ Deliverable or product

↓ Indicates order of process

➤ Indicates iterative process

Approximate duration of each phase

1/6

1/4

1/3

1/4

Practice

The Anatomy section is intended to give you an overview of the issues in Web design development, and present a good working process. However, no project will ever conform exactly to this. There are many types of client, from manufacturing to retail and services, not-for-profits to government, large and small, established and startup. Designers may be working in-house, independently, as part of a large consultancy or as an adjunct to a professional services company. Products developed may be for internal access, a membership audience, or for public use, aimed at a small group of skilled users or a mass of people new to the Web. They may be lightweight Web sites or complex Internet-enabled applications, standalone or integrated into another service, PC-based or accessed via a mobile phone or interactive television. Teams may be small (perhaps just yourself) or large and spread across multiple locations. Products may be new, being extended, or being reworked to address design problems or new possibilities.

The case studies show how some of the conceptual and practical issues we discussed in Anatomy work out in reality, by reviewing projects that range across the axes we have defined. The ten case studies that follow were identified from personal knowledge and colleagues' recommendations. It was assumed that projects from designers who had a history of executing good work, and reflecting on their practice, would showcase smart and imaginative design thinking and intelligent practice. These case studies are intended to be informative rather than critical.

In order to present a rounded rather than a design-focused perspective on the design process interviews for the case studies were also undertaken with the people involved in commissioning and implementing the products, as well as the designers, and they attempt to draw out the dynamics of the working relationships, looking at how collaboration and compromise are achieved.

No design solution starts with a blank sheet of paper and without limitations, and the success of any solution needs to be judged in context. The case studies attempt to present the brief along with the constraints on the projects. These constraints encompass budget and resources, timescale, existing design implementations, the interests of secondary and tertiary stakeholders, delivery platforms, engineering limitations and legacy systems. They also look at problems that were encountered, and how these and the already known constraints were addressed.

The artifacts presented in the case studies range well beyond the finished 'Photoshopped' screens which are commonly used to represent the material of Web design. They range from pencil sketches and marker visuals to illustrations used to explain concepts, from requirements documents and card sorting exercises to wireframes and prototypes, from photos of collaboration spaces and usability testing in action to site maps and storyboards, and from screen descriptions and 'pulled out' interfaces to engineering diagrams and specifications.

It is almost impossible to judge a design solution without pursuing at least some elements of this approach. Design practice is complex and multi-faceted and can't be casually critiqued and we should be wary of cursory judgements made on Web design solutions from one individual's brief use of a site. Of course, we can comment on the heuristic aspects of a Web site without knowing its background, and this kind of teaching by examples has considerable value when combined with other forms of design education.

Well-researched and properly considered case studies are a valuable tool for designers learning about the Web, but also for helping non-designers learn about design. They are particularly valuable with clients as the case study form is central to any management training.

In the early years of the development of Web design practice there wasn't enough attention paid to documenting work and sharing lessons in the form of case studies. However, this is changing and any designer who is serious about reflecting on the successes (and failures) of his work should actively document his projects – including the factors outlined above, his process and thinking, the artifacts he created along the way, and the end result, the latter reflecting the way the product interacts in use.

Of course, many designers produce excellent documentation for their clients, and this could form the basis for a case study, a show and tell, or, more ambitiously, a piece of research or a paper based on the project. To achieve this it will be necessary to have the cooperation of the client, and although many will be wary of exposing some aspects of a project others will see the value of sharing their learning and demonstrating their successful application of design.

Tying design goals to business goals

Client: FordDirect www.FordDirect.com
Designers: Trilogy www.trilogy.com

FordDirect was established in 2000 to help Ford dealers sell via the Internet. FordDirect is owned by the dealers, and the Ford Motor Company is a major investor. The service allows people to search the inventory at their local dealer, build and price a new car, and search the dealers' pre-owned inventory. "FordDirect.com had two goals," reports Vice President of Technology and Product Development Jared Rowe. To "provide the customer a more realistic view of the world" – considering what inventory options were possible and whether dealers actually had them in stock – and to bring to dealers buyers who are more serious "because they know there is a car with the options they want sitting on a lot somewhere".

Trilogy, based in Austin, Texas, makes e-business software applications that deal with complex business rules in configuration, pricing, compensation and engineering systems. Trilogy has provided the back-end for FordDirect.com from the outset. It had created a pioneering online vehicle retailer, CarOrder.com, in the 1990s and from this understood the ins and outs of online configuration and transaction, and the value of getting regular feedback from customers.

Many of FordDirect's 25 staff have worked at other online vehicle retailers and already had considerable experience with design and Web development, though agencies they had worked with tended to be kept at arm's length and only brought in on a project basis. "FordDirect wanted to work with a partner who specialised in interactive web projects," notes Director of Technology and Products Development Tim Pulliam. From experience, FordDirect staff were wary of design companies who didn't share their methodology, which included carrying out clickstream analysis and user testing.

There was no formal creation of a brief. "Instead," reports Rowe, "we brought them inside and let them look around our business," noting that "they are as familiar with our business as anyone who works here".

FordDirect has to satisfy three parties: Ford dealers; Ford Motor Company; and the customers who use the site. As they had an existing site, much was already known about this latter audience. They are leisurely, coming to FordDirect.com early in their shopping cycle and leaving early or late in the process, that latter behaviour indicating that they are gathering data to use offline. Much site activity is at midday, indicating they are at work. They tend to be middle-aged, with some computer experience, and use an AOL browser.

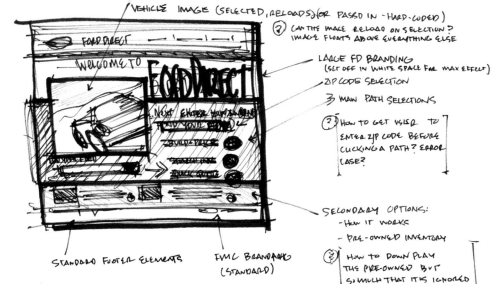

FOCUSES PAGE ON VEHICLE SELECTION AND GROUPS THE ZIP CODE ENTRY WITH PATH SELECTION ALLOWS FOR SEVERAL SUB-TASKS TO BE POSITIONED BELOW THE MAIN TASK SELECTION.

OPTION I: VERTICAL

Sketching

Lead designer Drew Miller investigated design ideas using sketching techniques. This sketch and the one shown on page 171 are for the version of the front page also shown there.

Is it usable?

Usability testing is a key aspect of Trilogy's process, and plays an important role in their client interaction.

Testing takes place at each stage of the design process. It is typically conducted one person at a time in a usability lab equipped with a one-way mirror through to an observation room and a video camera. Initial tests may be broad, across every area of a site and address general features such as the submission process. Subsequently testing will address a particular site feature being developed on which the team want early feedback. Screenshots of a user journey are employed, along with wireframes and paper prototypes.

Users are asked to make observations and for their expectations (such as what they expect to see if they perform a certain action). The observers record what they say, their behaviour, whether they completed the task and, where appropriate, how long they took to complete each task. Reports on the usability test sessions are written and sent, along with video tapes, to the client. Finally a debrief is conducted on a conference call.

Front page

Top: The initial front-page design emphasised marketing and the explanation of why dealers were building this site over explaining what FordDirect was and how the site worked. The Zip code field needed more explanation, while continuity with a separate Ford vehicle-marketing site (www.fordvehicles.com) was poor and colour use weak.

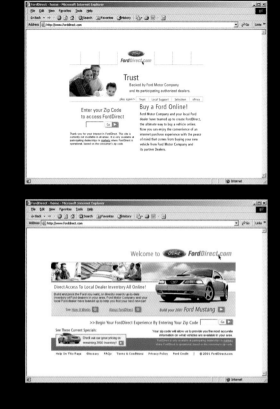

Centre: A large, attractive image was added, emphasising the site was about selling cars. The images to the left show the process visually, supported by a one-line 'sell' and shorter text below. The Zip code entry box indicates the main action on the page with the word 'Experience' replacing the more prohibitive 'Access', and text was added to explain why it is important to ask for personal information such as a Zip code. For visitors from the Ford Vehicles site the 'Build your...' image is now determined by what they were looking at, and 'Help on this page' is contextual. Tertiary level links to standard site elements appear at the bottom of the screen.

Right: After the site was more closely integrated with the Ford Vehicles and Dealer Connection sites it was customised further. The top navigation only appears if a visitor comes straight to the site. Visitors from the two sites see a different header, and a footer that refers to the specific site. 'How it works' is broken down to offer a clearer explanation. The 'Your selected model' menu replaces a picture-based selection as customers coming from the two sites would know what car they wanted. If they come from a specific vehicle page the image of that vehicle appears above the menu and the menu entry is hard-coded to the vehicle. If they also entered a Zip code they may bypass this page entirely, so it can't be too critical.

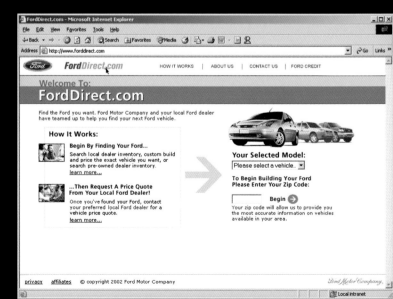

FORD DIRECT OR FORD VEHICLE HEADER

BIG FD WELCOME BRANDING

VEHICLE SELECTION AND ZIP CODE ENTRY ARE GROUPED CLOSELY TOGETHER WITH VEHICLE PICTURE, AND IN-BETWEEN BRANDING AND PAGE SELECTION OPTIONS.

WOULD STEPS BE NUMBERED OR WOULD THE STANDARD "NEXT" ARROWS BE USED TO DIFFERENTIATE?

SECONDARY ACTIONS LOCATED BELOW MAIN TASKS. USES A MORE NEUTRAL COLOR TO ALLOW MAIN SECTION ABOVE TO STAND OUT.

STANDARD FOOTER / STANDARD FMC BRANDING

POSSIBLY MORE SUCCESSFUL THAN THE VERTICAL APPROACH AS IT BRACKETS THE ZIP CODE REQUEST IN BETWEEN THE VEHICLE SELECTION/DISPLAY AND THE ACTIONS TO LEAVE THE PAGE.

OPTION 2: HORIZONTAL

WOULD LIKE VEHICLE IMAGE TO REFRESH IF VEHICLE IS SELECTED

Left: To reduce the number of clicks required by the user the front page was subsequently redesigned to combine its existing features (vehicle selection and Zip code entry) with those from the path selection page.

FordDirect business owners and the engineering team before they fully commit to the project and create a complete specification document.

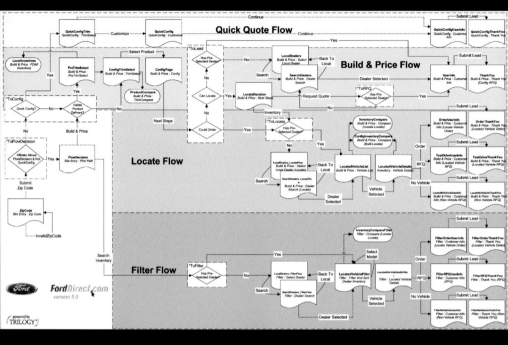

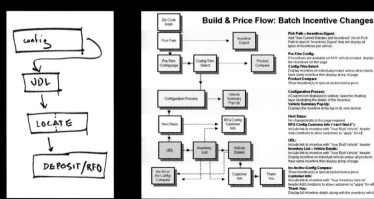

Above: A detailed process flow created in Viso showing the options and interactions at the system level. Loops in the system typically represent validation of user submissions. This diagram also reflects the business logic behind the site.
Right: A high-level sketch showing the site process flow. (UDL refers to the Universal Dealer Locator functionality.)
Far right: Specification of incentive-related changes that need to be made by engineering to the 'Build and Price' flow.

Right: The initial design used vehicle images plus rollovers, which required downloading 30 images and reduced site performance.

Below right: Previous models were moved to another page and only up-to-date models displayed. An image map replaced the 30 images, using a DHTML-created selection box as a rollover, thus requiring only one rollover image. Steps 1, 2 and 3 were added at the top, each with a sub-menu, with each stage explained in 'How it works' at the bottom.

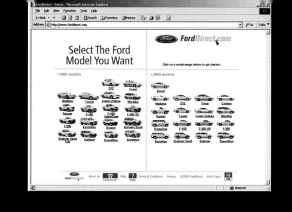

Below: If the visitor had selected a vehicle on the Ford Vehicles site and entered his Zip code there would be no need to select the vehicle again. The previously selected vehicle is presented with 'Quick Glance' information and pop-ups, allowing the visitor to see more about the model. The three options under 'Select your next steps' are separate so that 'Pre-Owned' can be removed if necessary, while 'Search local dealer inventory' appears first at the client's request. The Zip code request field is being moved away from the start of the process, as some visitors consider it an invasion of privacy. In general, requests are being moved to where that information is actually needed, at which point it can be explained to visitors why it is needed.

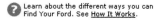

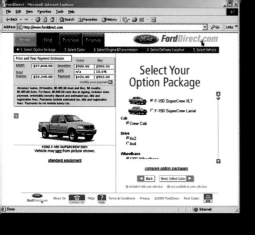

Build and Price

Above: In the initial design customers weren't sure what element of the process 'Home' and 'Finance' represented. Space on the right was poorly used and the 'Select Your Option Package' didn't make it clear what each package was. The button to confirm product selection wasn't significant enough and its supporting text made it look like it was for selecting colour.

Above right: 'Locate' and 'Purchase' were shown as the next stages in the process, which is how customers thought about it. Vehicle specifications were organised into columns with a standard slider control, though this didn't work well for more than three models. It also presented the challenge of delineating entries that took up two lines, and showing the difference between products when there are more than two.

Right: A two-column, vertical arrangement of cars made better use of space, particularly when there was considerable variation in the standard equipment on models. While the vehicle selection was made on the previous page, characteristics could be modified on this page using the 'Modify Your Selected Vehicle Preferences' menus. 'View colours or options' on the left allowed customers to see what selections would be available later in the process.

74 FordDirect

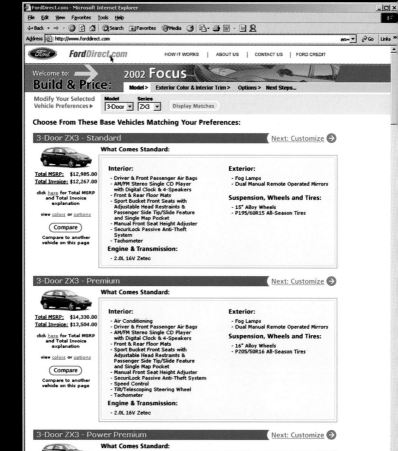

Design development
Miller's designs typically begin as sketches which are progressively developed, discussed with the engineering team and the client, and usability tested. Other sketches from the project can be seen on pages 141–143.

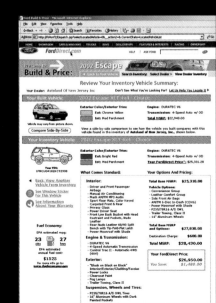

Locate

Right: The initial design didn't show the customer's build specification, so they couldn't easily compare it to the 'finds', and the characteristics of the 'found' vehicles were difficult to scan. It was also unclear whether the elements in the top navigation were sequential steps – and they also appeared to 'run out'.

Far right: The customer's build specification was shown at the top as 'Your built vehicle' along with a button for 'Didn't find what you want?'. The wording for the 'Select' button became 'Next: See vehicle summary', considered to be more inviting.

Centre: The presentation of 'Your built vehicle' was improved, using the same abbreviated language as is used in the inventory list, with interior and exterior colourway displayed. Greyscale model images with colour swatches illustrated the vehicle style presented. Pricing was stacked, making it easy to compare. The compare functionality option allows comparison between any of the vehicles displayed.

Below left: To show the stock held by a particular dealer, the dynamic 'filter flow' interface was developed. Changing a menu selection automatically updates the page, with the 'Matches found' number reducing as the selection is filtered.

Below right: In order to be able to filter dynamically the page contains all the relevant data, so is very large. When customers move to the page, the page is greyed out and a modal dialogue appears to reassure customers that something is happening.

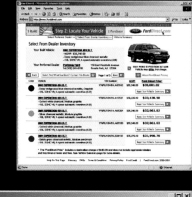

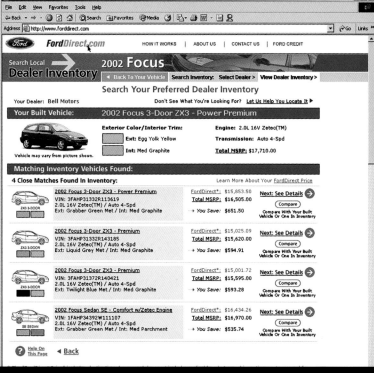

Conclusion

"Trilogy's interface design work has met the client's objectives," Rowe says. FordDirect reported a several-fold leap in requests for vehicle price quotes, and Forrester Research rated FordDirect as one of the best auto sites they have reviewed.

"The closer the design team is to you and your business and what your business is about the more success you will have," notes Rowe, adding that Trilogy "doesn't design for the sake of design but for our business goals". Miller backs this up. "It feels like their goals are our goals," he says, commenting that they haven't had a client who is so accessible on previous projects. "We can just call them up and show ideas and get feedback," he continues. "They value our experience and expertise and know it is worth their time to think about it."

Morkes adds that FordDirect "has faith in our design abilities and that we will be usability testing design concepts. This is invaluable to our process. Where there is some debate we put it through usability testing." Pulliam endorses the value of usability testing, pointing out that it "validates proposed changes and let's us build a business case for new ideas".

The collaboration between design and engineering at Trilogy also works well. Miller observes that Web designers "solve design problems for customers that engineering can implement".

Jay Kamm, who manages technical delivery at Trilogy for the FordDirect.com project, observes that the designers and engineers have worked together for some time and as a result can anticipate what one another might say. He advocates good expectation management, noting that Miller knows which design ideas may present technical problems and need to be discussed with engineering. Similarly, for FordDirect.com he says: "We would always make time to talk to Drew, even if we were busy, as we knew it might save us some time." Finally, he champions iterative development, rather than 'throwing things over the fence'. "Have something on the table, resolve it and move on." Where problems were difficult to resolve he observes that it is necessary to look to the business owner to make the call.

The collaboration between FordDirect and Trilogy isn't clearly delineated. Pulliam notes that FordDirect passes on ideas on how they could create or improve the designs in ways that might help reach their business goals (and "we are not afraid to tell them that a design stinks"). Trilogy "are clear with us about business ideas that they don't think will work".

Designing with a big idea

Client: Manchester United www.manutd.com
Designers: Dimension Data www.didata.com

Manchester United plc is one of the UK's major soccer clubs, and the best known outside the country. Twenty-one per cent of ticket sales are already made online. "We have moved beyond football to how we create, interact with and commercialise our global fan community," notes Director of Business Development Ben Hatton, "and we are limited with respect to the physical markets we can be in." The primary goal of Manchester United's Web site redevelopment was to overcome this limit and create a stadium for 56 million people.

The design team at Dimension Data characterise their approach as creating innovative solutions to meet customers' and clients' needs while innovating around technological limitations. "We start from brand values and customer needs," says Creative Director Bill Galloway. "At this stage we feel that technical limitations can hamper the creative process and they are largely ignored. We feel comfortable doing this only because we are very good at applying creative solutions in a technically restricting medium." Galloway's approach draws on advertising's conceptual 'big idea'. Although clients like this approach, he admits that it can be difficult to translate to online design without the relevant experience.

Manchester United wrote a brief based on their objectives and allowed the companies who were pitching two weeks to respond.

"Create the best fan-focused site" and "getting your football fix" were key concepts in the brief and desired characteristics for the site included: contemporary; global; and heritage. From their experience of other online clubs, Manchester United indicated that they "didn't want the site to be like 'downtown Tokyo'".

The Club's objectives included increasing page impressions, unique visitors and site registrations. The intended audience was Manchester United fans. (They concluded there were plenty of other Web sites people looking for general soccer information could use.)

The brief also addressed more technical issues such as browser version and computer platforms to be supported, maximum bandwidths and page weights, and the need to integrate with the club's existing content management system.

Manchester United also gave the companies open access to the stadium, their people, to matches and fans. Once pitches had been developed TWI Interactive, the site developers, spent time with each organisation in order that they could confirm that the design pitches conformed to the technical requirements.

In evaluating the pitches Hatton and the Manchester United team were looking for a point of difference: simplicity and cleanliness; ease of navigation; ease of commercialisation and ease of integrating content. Costs were considered for the final shortlist, although the final decision wasn't made on cost.

The major research undertaken by Dimension Data consisted of qualitative interviews with around 40 Manchester United fans, conducted around their Old Trafford stadium, and also video-recorded. Fans were asked questions such as "If Manchester United could give you anything in the world, what would it be?" to which the most common answer was "The treble!" (winning the league competition, and the FA and European cups), and no one person answered outside the scope of football. The insider knowledge we gained here was invaluable," says Anthony Webster, and is what led to our creative solution." In addition, the design team conducted extensive competitor analysis on soccer Web sites, partly to understand what 'downtown Tokyo' meant in design terms.

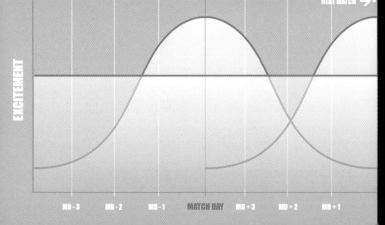

Analysing the fan relationship

The design team observed that there were overlapping 'Bell Curves' of supporter excitement centred on the match days. Wanting the Web site to be able to react to whatever emotion a fan had when they visited, led the team to conceive of the site with complementary sections: 'Football Now' focused around the build-up during and after the game and the competition between the teams; 'Theatre of Dreams' focused around the stadium and the Club history; 'Shop@MU' was the third section of the site.

Sketching and planning user journeys

Right: The site architecture began with three boxes: 'Football Now'; 'Theatre of Dreams'; 'Merchandise and Services'. This was developed by mapping the business requirements and user needs (what *has* to be there), and brainstorming to produce a matrix of elements. This was then turned into a site map.
Below: Wireframes and screens were then developed to show user journeys including this short registration process.

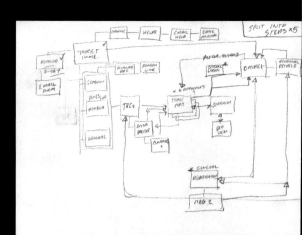

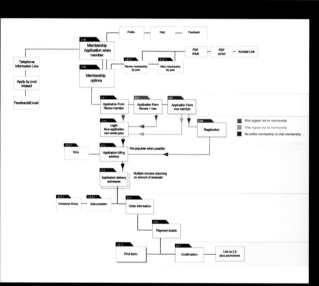

Prototyping match tools

Right: The Match Tracker is part of the Match Tools that allows fans to follow match progress. It was originally conceived by TWI Interactive. "We had brought it a long way and there was a lot of heated debate about how we took it forward," notes Aubrey-Batchelor. "Once Dimension Data had seen it and found it interesting, we were able to work together." The interface was prototyped using PowerPoint and developed in Photoshop (see top of next page).

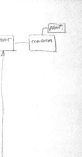

Brand development
To investigate the brand experience the team mapped the characteristics of Nike, Coca-Cola and Mercedes Benz. "We set ourselves a plateau to try to reach through the design by thinking about the things that inspire us," remarks Webster. "Unless you have a train of thought you can lose direction."

The design team initially developed a brand progression board showing the development of the brand values into detailed design and functionality.

Design elements and colour
Right: The site architecture is indicated in the top level navigation, where merchandise has become 'Megastore'. The idea for the match countdown feature came out of the short usability tests, and was made larger after reviewing feedback from subsequent tests.

The whole site reacts to the colour of the kit the team will be wearing for the next match, and all photographs show players in the same colour kit (see above and right). 'Theatre of Dreams' (previous spread) is always red as it is the home colour for the team.

Prioritising information

Screens showing paths users would take were placed in a browser frame and stuck on the wall so the team could "tear them apart". For the ticketing and membership 'journeys' this exercise was conducted four times. Next the team developed the design in Photoshop focusing on how information would be prioritised. These designs were then reviewed, though less formally, by the design and technical teams.

Right: The application form for the paid membership of the site.

Below: A pop-up window for Web registration that allows limited access to ManUtd.com services.

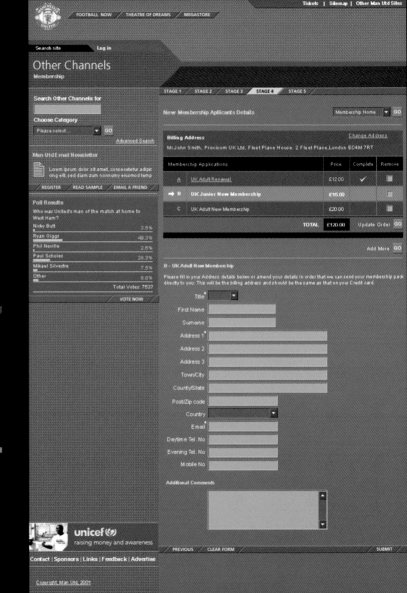

Briefing engineering
When the design work was complete Dimension Data provided TWI Interactive with about 60 Photoshop files and wireframes showing navigation and page structure for the template pages. When they had been coded Dimension Data moved on to the design of the particular screens.

A strict file naming and page numbering system was used in conjunction with an extranet and a version control system. Not only did this help with asset and content management, but it could also be used to relate business requirements to elements of the site.

Specification
Global navigation and buttons were documented, showing rollover states and typographic details. Colour palettes were specified for menus and pages, indicating the HTML values for each colour.

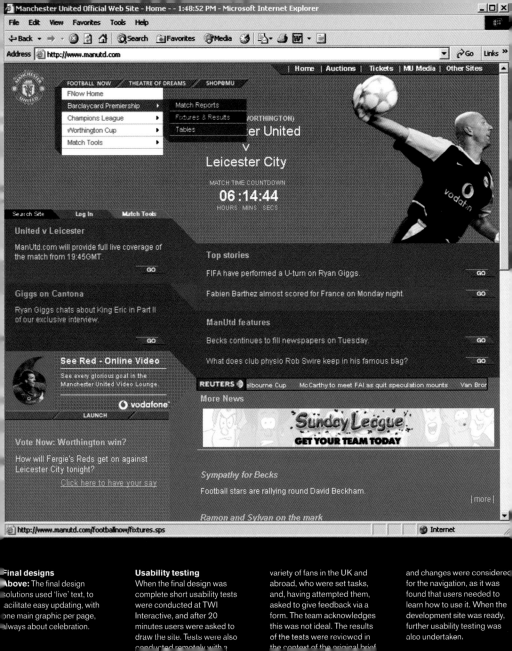

Final designs
Above: The final design solutions used 'live' text, to facilitate easy updating, with one main graphic per page, always about celebration.

Usability testing
When the final design was complete short usability tests were conducted at TWI Interactive, and after 20 minutes users were asked to draw the site. Tests were also conducted remotely with a

variety of fans in the UK and abroad, who were set tasks, and, having attempted them, asked to give feedback via a form. The team acknowledges this was not ideal. The results of the tests were reviewed in the context of the original brief

and changes were considered for the navigation, as it was found that users needed to learn how to use it. When the development site was ready, further usability testing was also undertaken.

Conclusion

The new site was soft launched, just linked from the home page of the existing site, and generated 3,000 broadly positive emails from fans in the first week.

Having appointed Dimension Data the Manchester United team had tended to be hands-off. "We let them do what they were good at and didn't try to second guess them," notes Hatton, adding, "we worked quite hard to create an environment for the designers that wasn't filled with obstacles, as we didn't want to constrain them".

"We have done something that hasn't been done before," says Galloway, who claims they have achieved more than "just improving a bit on other football sites" as they "refused to accept their limitations because we didn't think they worked for the fans". The key challenge was creating design solutions that would integrate with the existing content management system, while working to a very tight deadline.

The design team found some innovative ways of using the existing page templates and developing new ones. Having reviewed some design solutions the TWI Interactive team would sometimes say "that is not achievable". "We would sometimes come up with a better design as a result of being challenged," comments Webster. "If you have a good core idea you can go away and redesign if necessary."

Aubrey-Batchelor notes that the working relationship was quite difficult to manage initially as the design team was pushing the envelope of what was technically feasible. This tension was resolved by running weekly project meetings to air Dimension Data's ideas, outline how TWI Interactive worked and discuss what couldn't be done. Bigger decisions about prioritising features, design and engineering were the appropriate domain for the client.

According to the Dimension Data team one aspect of the project in which there needed to be more clarity was their level of input into the site build. Should the design work be handed over after creating Photoshop files or having built templates or a template site, or should they sit with the TWI Interactive team and oversee them building the site? For the project all these solutions were used in some form. As Dimension Data are used to doing design and integration this confusion may have been exacerbated.

Overall, the design concepts were creatively and user-led rather than technically led. "We would like to say we have forums and so on, but in reality we base what we do on previous experience and knowledge, and on the clients' customer audits," notes Galloway. "We put ourselves in the heads of customers."

Hatton feels Manchester United now has "a great looking site, that works, is clean, attracts sponsors, and was delivered on time with a minimum of fuss". "Everything they delivered went beyond our expectations," he adds. "You expect things to overrun on budget and timing and it didn't."

Justifying the solution from beginning to end

Client: The Ocean Conservancy
www.oceanconservancy.org
Designers: MetaDesign, North America
www.metadesign.com

When Stephanie Drea, a former executive vice president at a public relations company, joined the 30-year-old Center for Marine Conservation in Washington DC as Vice President of Communications and Marketing, she recognised that the organisation had made significant gains on behalf of ocean conservation with the legislative and executive branches of government in Washington DC. At the same time it had not built understanding and support for its oceans policies among the broader US public. "I knew from when I walked in the door that we needed to use the Web as a cornerstone to reach and educate new audiences about the value of and condition of our oceans," she comments. "And to do so we needed to rethink and redesign our Web site." She put together a fairly traditional but detailed RFP, issued it nationwide and short-listed three respondents, one of which was eliminated on cost. She visited the other two in San Francisco, one of which was MetaDesign, North America, a long-established design firm which had been well known for information design and branding before developing skills in interaction design for the Web.

She met with David Peters, a Senior Strategic Consultant, who "already understood the branding concept" and the need to extend the design brief beyond the Web. As she wanted all the design work to be undertaken by one firm that understood 'the big picture' Drea appointed MetaDesign.

They began by "taking ten steps back" and embarking on a design strategy and rebranding process led by Peters that paralleled the organisation's identity change process that ultimately resulted in the 'Ocean Conservancy' name. Two teams took up the assignment: one focusing on user research, conceptual architecture and interaction design and the other on the visual identity and screen design. They analysed who their audiences were, what relationship they wanted with each, why and how they were trying to reach them and what they wanted them to do when they got to the Web site.

The audiences they identified were their 120,000-plus members, policy makers, students and other stakeholders including divers, surfers, beach goers and fishers, while their research found that people really cared about 'issues' rather than 'learning'.

MetaDesign had responded to the RFP along with Steve Knox, owner of the Washington State-based engineering company IS[2] (www.is2inc.com), who they had worked with on other projects. They both conducted a design and engineering research and scoping phase on which they could base project costs.

Back | Forward | Stop | Refresh | Home | AutoFill | Print | Mail | Sherlock | Preferences | Add to Scrapbook | Search

Address: @ http://www.theoceanconservancy.org/ → go

action alerts | contact us | glossary | join us | privacy policy

The Ocean Conservancy

| Home | Issues | Get Involved | About Us | Press & News |

Advocates for Wild, Healthy Oceans

We envision a world of healthy, protected oceans with wild and flourishing ecosystems, free of pollution and filled with diverse and abundant marine wildlife.

Top Ocean Issues ▲▼

Regional Offices

Our Regional Offices ▲▼

Visit our regional offices pages to learn about local ocean issues in your region.

Action Alerts

You can help save the oceans! Action Alerts notify you of critical issues that need attention now. (Signup and we'll send you the

Issues

▶ **Hawaiian Monk Seals**

Hawaiian monk seals have called the remote northwestern Hawaiian Island chain home for millions of years. Now listed as endangered, there are less than 1,500 alive today—learn what you can do to help ensure their survival.

Get Involved

▶ **Join Our Activist Network**

People just like you are the most powerful force for protecting the oceans. Our Activist Network can give you the tools you need—learn when and how to use your voice to influence key decision makers. Together, we can make a difference.

▶ **Join The Ocean Conservancy**

▶ **Make a donation to The Ocean Conservancy**

▶ **Support our Campaign for the Oceans**

Internet zone

Scenarios and Cases

MetaDesign developed preliminary scenarios to illustrate how the conceptual model they had developed worked, to tell stories about the experience they wanted the site to support, and to generate design concepts.

Coastal Area Resident
Situation: Through the radio, Amy, a graduate student, hears about a beach cleanup event organized by some local organization. She participates in the event with a friend. During the event, Amy learns about TOC's involvement and affiliation with the event.

Outcome: Amy is interested in volunteering for a non-profit that is ocean conservation-focused. She finds information about TOC's mission, programs and benefits from its site.

Commercial Industry
Situation: Jack is a commercial tuna fisherman who, via his union newsletter, found out about TOC's new proposal to restrict tuna fishing from his fishing territory.

Outcome: Jack uses TOC's web site as a place to learn about fishing laws and policies. He becomes more involved with TOC through the discussion forum where he can voice his concerns.

Hobbyist/Recreationist
Situation: Susan is a novice diver who is looking into joining a community of divers. She is referred to TOC's website by someone in the dive shop.

Outcome: Susan meets other divers through TOC's web site and becomes actively involved in its program.

Interested Organization
Situation: Emily is a Girl Scouts of America local leader from Berkeley. She is looking for an activity that she can do with her group around the topic of the ocean.

Outcome: Emily becomes interested in working closely with TOC after finding valuable information on its web site.

Legislator/Policy Maker
Situation: Rebecca is a congresswoman who just received a signed petition (from concerned citizens in her district) asking for a development restriction on a nearby coastal town. Because she lives in an important coastal district, Rebecca is targeted by TOC.

Outcome: Rebecca uses TOC's web site as means to connect with her constituents regarding issues in which she is involved.

Lifestyler
Situation: A Miami-based company is looking for end of year gifts for its employees. It decides to get calendars from TOC that features Florida's ocean wildlife. The calendar contains marked dates for TOC's scheduled events.

Outcome: The company is attracted to becoming a corporate member.

Scientist
Situation: Nicole is a scientist who is working on a research paper. She needs to find some detailed facts about a particular form of marine life as part of her continuing research.

Outcome: Nicole finds useful data, event announcements, and community links related to her research through TOC's website.

Student
Situation: Tommy is an eighth grader who is given an assignment to write a report about coastal ecosystems. He is referred to TOC's website by his teacher.

Outcome: Tommy not only finds research information for his paper, but also discovers events and activities in which he can participate.

We would eventually write a scenario for:

Press/Media

The Public

Research and analysis

Below: The conceptual model for the site was transformed into the next version of the information architecture by reviewing numerous documents related to the site redesign and conducting several work sessions. Information was gathered from competitor analysis, the client's project plan, and scenarios and use cases developed by design, engineering and the client. This information, written on Post-It Notes, was analysed and clustered. The resulting groupings helped to distinguish content that would become a section, a page, or data that would populate a page.

Revised conceptual model

Right: Influenced by insights gleaned from work sessions, the preliminary conceptual model was revised to represent more completely how the site would support the audience's primary goals (which are a synthesised view of all of their goals, and TOC's goals).

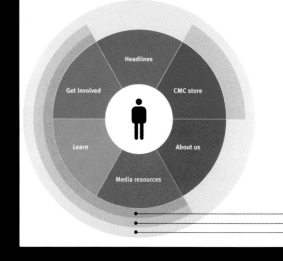

User research

Right: Two user research sessions were conducted. The first, during the architectural development, used paper prototypes with zones indicating the different sections of the site. Three one-on-one tests were conducted with 12 people over two days. MetaDesign recruited participants from a list of local members provided by The Ocean Conservancy, and several non-designers from among their own staff.

Participants were presented with a task and asked to 'click' on the category label under which they would expect to accomplish their task. Following this selection, the participant was presented with another page that would have the next layer of navigation and content available. This flow continued until the participant was able to complete the task. Alternative routes through the site were available and comments participants made regarding these were noted.

Refine

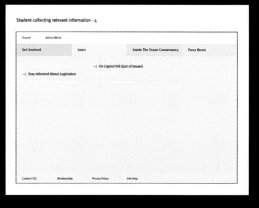

Balancing the Audiences' Primary Goals and TOC's Goals

The conceptual model illustrates the sections of the web site and the relationships that exist between the sections, the audiences' primary goals, and The Ocean Conservancy's goals.

The model as a whole supports the audiences' primary goals and The Ocean Conservancy's goals. In this model, however, we have highlighted the individual sections that most strongly support the audiences' primary goals and The Ocean Conservancy's goals.

Audiences' Primary Goals

"I want to be informed about ocean conservation." ● ● ●
"I want to promote ocean conservation." ● ●
"I want to participate in ocean conservation." ●

TOC's Goals

Expand activism, advocacy, and volunteering
Grow its membership community
More effectively communicate its mission and programs

Revised and final information architecture

The revised information architecture builds upon the final conceptual model along with numerous discussions, explorations and work sessions. The architecture, which comprises four sections – Get Involved, Issues, About Us, and Press and News, along with a global resources component – aims to support both the users' and TOC's goals, giving users multiple points of access. MetaDesign devised three 'use flows' which would increase volunteering while educating its audience, increase membership and its community of concerned citizens, and raise the public's awareness of ocean conservation.

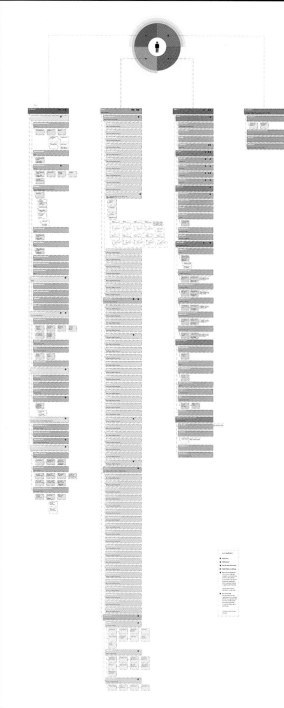

action alerts | glossary | contact us | join us | privacy policy

The Ocean Conservancy

home » issues » threats to our oceans » marine debris » 2001 data

| Search ▶ | Home | Issues | Get Involved | About Us | Press & News |

2001 Data

▶ Threats to our oceans
 » Aquaculture
 » Artificial Reefs
 » Beach Water Quality
 » Bycatch
 » Coastal Development
 » Cruis Ships
 » Destructive Fishing
  Practices
 » Entanglements
 » Global Climate Change
 » Invasive Species
 » Marine Debris
  » Sources of Debris
  » Composition
  » 2001 Data
   » Sources of Debris
   » Composition
   »» 2001 Data
 » Mixing Zones
 » Oil & Gas Development
 » Overfishing
 » Pollution
 » Sound in the Ocean
 » Storm water
 » Whaling
▶ Fish & Wildlife
▶ Ocean Places
▶ Law & Policy

The United States has been divided into nine regions with 20 survey sites within each region. Volunteers sample each site monthly for a period of five years, measuring the status and trends of 30 specific debris items (see Sample Data Card).

2001 Data Regions

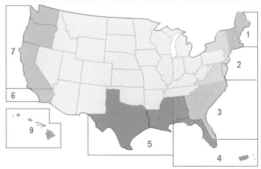

Click on a region and select a beach study site to see a summary of our findings.

1 U.S. - Canada border to Provincetown, MA
2 South of Cape Cod, MA to Beaufort, NC
3 Morehead City, NC to Port Everglades, FL
4 Northern jetty of Port Everglades, FL, Puerto Rico U.S. Virgin Islands to Gulf Shores, AL
5 Dauphin Islands, AL to U.S.-Mexico Border

6 U.S.-Mexico border to Pt.Conception, CA
7 North of Pt. Conception, CA to U.S. Canada border
8 Alaska (Southern Coast & Aleutian Islands)
9 Hawaiian Islands

final designs

The final visual design aims to "evoke a feeling of being immersed in ocean wildlife while at the same time offering an information-rich resource for all things related to ocean conservation". The home page reveals the content available within Issues and Get Involved, the most important sections of the site.

Below: The Data page provides the research findings from the 20 survey sites for each of the nine regions into which TOC divides the US.

The Ocean Conservancy

| Search | GO | Home | Issues | Get Involved | About Us | Press & News |

Advocates for Wild, Healthy Oceans

We envision a world of healthy, protected oceans with wild and flourishing ecosystems, free of pollution and filled with diverse and abundant marine wildlife.

Top 10 ocean issues ▼

Regional Offices

Headquarters ▼

Our regional offices help restore and protect ocean environments across North America. Get involved with an office near you.

Action Alerts

These announcements call attention to critical activities that protect the earth's oceans.

July 25, 2001
Tell Congress to Protect Our Beaches!

July 16, 2001
Your Help Needed to Protect California's Special Ocean Places!

July 06, 2001
Vital Sea Turtle Nesting

Issues

▶ **Threats To Our Oceans**
Red snapper like these have been overfished since 1988. Recent council action means the population will not rebuild until 2033.

▶ **Fish & Wildlife**
The Marine Wildlife program and its issues protects all creatures and plants of the sea.

▶ **Ocean Places**
This program focuses on the conservation of our ocean places across the globe.

▶ **Law & Policy**
The Clean Oceans program and its issues are committed to the preservation of our oceans and shores.

Get Involved

▶ **Events & Activities: ICC**
On September 15, thousands of people – all volunteers – from around the world will participate in the International Coastal Cleanup. Each volunteer will take hands-on action to clean the ocean and shores of our planet.

▶ **Join Us**

▶ **Fund The Ocean Conservancy**

▶ **Campaign for the Oceans**

Campaigns

▶ **The Ocean Wilderness Challenge**
Our goal is to secure permanent protection for special places in the ocean, places that we protect to the highest standard because it's right, because we want there to be some places in the sea that are natural, unchanged by humans, protected for our children and for their children.

Copyright 2001 © The Ocean Conservancy

The Ocean Conservancy

home > get involved

| Search | GO | Home | Issues | Get Involved | About Us | Press & News |

Get Involved

In this section:
▶ **Events & Activities**
▶ **Activist Network**
▶ **Ocean Wilderness Challenge**
▶ **Learn More**
▶ **Join Us**
▶ **Fund The Ocean Conservancy**

Did you know?
Sugar Sea Star

Called the walking stomach of the sea, the starfish can change his/her sex when necessary.

The oceans need your help. Our one million+ members, volunteers, activists and supporters help to protect and restore our oceans and the wildlife under them, from the smallest plankton to the largest animal ever to live on this planet. Get involved in The Ocean Conservancy by joining, donating, writing letters to Congress, cleaning a beach, or signing our pledge to save Ocean Wilderness.

Spotlight

Coastal Cleanup Event
On September 15, thousands of people from around the world will participate in the International Coastal Cleanup. You can get involved to help to clean and protect the oceans and shores of our planet.

Sign up for the beach cleanup
Pictures of past events

Success Story

Annual Fundraising Goal Met - 2001
The Ocean Conservancy, in spite of weakened economy, has met with great success in it's 2001 fundraising efforts. Critical gains were made that will enable the organization to impact more issues than any previous year.

Join us
Become a donor

Current Action Alerts

July 25, 2001
Tell Congress to Protect Our Beaches!

July 16, 2001
Your Help Needed to Protect California's Special Ocean Places!

July 06, 2001
Vital Sea Turtle Nesting Habitat at Risk

View all
Sign-up for action alert

The Ocean Wilderness Challenge

Join our bold challenge to the nation to protect five percent of America's ocean as wilderness.

Copyright 2001 © The Ocean Conservancy

Design guidelines

MetaDesign created guidelines specifying to the developers how each page component should be built, and helping them understand why elements worked in the way they did. For the TOC project these were static presentations created in Photoshop showing the stages of each interaction. On (which they also refer to as visual wireframes), which can also be usability tested.

This guide was also very useful for the content writing team (e.g. What is the purpose of this element, how big should it be and why for usability reasons?). Throughout the project IS² had access to graphics and models of interaction from

**Documentation:
the 'Red Book'**

MetaDesign creates a
'Red Book' for each project
and this is used to present the
design issue and approach –
including usability research
findings, process and
methodology, architecture,
visual design – to the client
and others. In the case of
TOC this included its board
of directors, who weren't very
design savvy and were also
very busy.

Giving the documentation
a formality and consistency
helped the client, who knew
what to expect when they
received new material. This
kind of documentation also
helps keep project continuity
as TOC staff change, and it is
also used to educate new
MetaDesign team members.

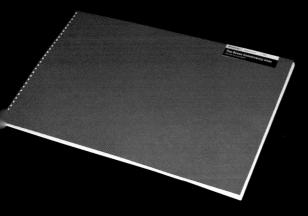

Conclusion

The TOC Web site design is considered to
be a success. Of the site look and feel Drea is
pleased to report that "we have recognition of
the strong statement we are trying to make".

Commenting on the general approach to
such a project she recommends to clients:
"Don't just jump into things but understand what
you are trying to accomplish and why, which will
give you a framework and a context, and you will
always have something to refer back to." This
context for the TOC project came from "working
closely on initial analysis of audience, how we
served them, what we wanted them to do, what
we wanted them to get from the Web site".

Drea liked the fact that with design ideas
MetaDesign always gave them two choices and
explained what they were trying to accomplish,
but didn't express their preference for a solution.

The engineering side of the project also
worked well. MetaDesign and IS[2] talked from
the beginning, and brought up problems quickly
and early, which meant they didn't get any
surprises or have to change things that were
already in development.

The two companies tended to work
iteratively as a team, rather than around the
next deliverable. "They let us see designs as
work-in-progress and don't get defensive,
as they know we won't hold them to something,"
Knox reflects. "If you won't let someone see
something in development you may get it
perfect but end up with something that
doesn't work."

Personas and scenarios

Client: Shared Healthcare Systems
www.shs.com
Designers: Cooper www.cooper.com

Shared Healthcare Systems (SHS), based in Anacortes, Washington, an hour north of Seattle, provides software for the long-term healthcare industry, encompassing nursing homes and assisted living. SHS was looking to develop a next-generation product, which would be known as Orcas, that would manage clinical, financial and case management documentation and workflow.

Orcas would allow long-term care facilities to manage resident accounts, track occupied and unoccupied beds and quality of care metrics in real time, maintain complete electronic patient records and help balance care costs appropriately with the level of care. The system also needed to be easy to learn by the nursing staff with minimal training and technical support.

David West, the then development manager for the Orcas Project, who also acted as senior software engineer, had previously worked on a project with Alan Cooper, who had gone on to develop a consultancy, Cooper, based in Palo Alto, California. "I knew I wanted to get some outside help in designing," he comments, and Cooper was invited to discuss working on the project. There was no formal RFP process.

Cooper claims to be the first company that focused on interaction design as a primary service. Fundamental to its work is the belief that the behaviour of the product is key and the form, while important, is a reflection of this. "Defining the way a software product behaves is to define (and design) the entire product," says Director of Design R&D Robert Reimann.

The design brief and the functionality were fairly open-ended. "We knew we needed some clinical features and to do billing, but it was not more detailed than that," notes West. "Cooper helped somewhat, but more importantly provided a conceptual approach." SHS provided Cooper with stacks of documentation, such as billing forms, and also took Cooper staff along to facility visits where they were able to interview staff. "Being able to observe users in their natural environment was critical to the design process," says Reimann. SHS also sent some legal, medical and technical 'domain experts' to work with Cooper and help them understand the industry in detail.

For the activities Orcas was intended to manage there was a lot of information and many ways to access it. One information and interaction design challenge was to support the needs of multiple-user types while providing visual consistency across interfaces that were tailored to different users, without hobbling users by requiring excessive navigation. (The existing SHS product had an antiquated 'green screen' interface which required users to access a number of screens for most tasks.) The product also had to meet Federal regulations. And it had to appeal to the people who purchased such products, who weren't the people who would use it day to day.

Cooper staff were also able to visit a nursing home that used a competing product. "We saw the frustrations people had with those products," reports Reimann. "They weren't organised with the mental models of users in mind. They didn't make things that had to be done on a regular basis easier to get to and do and people experienced lots of 'navigational trauma'.

Cooper's approach is to understand who the users are, and what their goals are, and "systematically translate this crisp understanding into design solutions," says Reimann. They describe their method as 'goal directed', using the goals of users to drive design decisions through the use of narrative techniques including scenarios and role-playing. To translate user needs into interaction and interface structures, they employ a set of interaction principles and design patterns developed in the course of their practice. Tools such as infinity diagrams and concept maps are seldom used.

Cooper began by developing user models, called personas: detailed, composite user archetypes based on the ethnographic interviews and other research they had conducted. "Personas capture motivations in addition to task requirements," claims Reimann, "permitting the design of interfaces that truly meet user goals."

Then, walking the personas through context scenarios, the designers were able to build up a set of functional and data needs which could then be organised and laid out as interfaces by applying principles and patterns, and employing a combination of top-down and bottom-up approaches.

These were presented to the SHS stakeholders and developers and their feedback was integrated during the interface detailing. For the Cooper team's own evaluations personas were used as the primary means of judging a design.

Once the interactions were fleshed out the main screen for each interface was developed using accurate content and applying the client's visual branding, along with additional drawings showing state changes and important secondary screens. Final screens were rendered in Adobe Photoshop.

Usability testing was employed by SHS towards the end of the process to 'sand off the rough edges' of the design. "Usability is good at optimising a given design. It can sand a rough chair into a smooth one, but it can't sand a table into a chair," comments Reimann.

The Cooper team created a detailed form and behaviour specification document, which laid the basis for the functional specification developed by SHS. "We asked new hires to read through Cooper's design documents," comments West, "and they also served as a good introduction to the industry." Once the product had been coded, it was tested.

Personas

Cooper began by developing user models, or 'personas', based on the research and interviews they had conducted. (The persona documents, which are drawn from another project are fully described on page 58.)

Primary personas for clinical, administrative, financial, point-of-care, and case management and admissions roles were developed and a secondary persona was developed for the administrative assistant's role. Cooper's approach is that if they can make the primary personas happy they will satisfy most of the other personas.

For the financial persona, Georgia Myers, the lack of connectedness of systems would cause her a lot of grief. She had no good tools to help her with billing, and no easy way of managing overdue bills.

The point-of-care persona, Carla Olivares, had a number of jobs and spoke English as a second language. During the day she would write notes on pieces of paper and put them in her pocket, giving these scraps to the nurse at the end of the day.

Opposite: Conceptual design work on the Orcas interface was begun on a whiteboard and on paper. "At the whiteboard we looked at the wireframe stage and perhaps the next level of details," explains Reimann. They asked "What is the shape of the application?" and investigated its primary flows and transitions, looking at each state of the system and each screen, while focusing on the primary interface. They also walked through personas ('a day in the life' for each user) looking at what state the system would be in when the user touched it, and what functions, data and behaviours needed to be available.

This activity continued to a point where "everything seemed to hang together," says Reimann. Usability testing was used towards the end of the process to "sand off the edges".

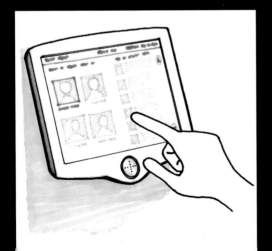

Wall-mounted touchscreen

For nursing assistants to enter the critical data they gather, the data entry must take place at the point of care, and it can't be a clumsy hand-held device that will get in their way. Cooper proposed a wall-mounted touchscreen on which simple numeric and checkbox entries would be made using oversize touch-screen widgets. A barcode scanner would allow for easy scanning of medical supplies and medications, and biometric log-in would avoid the need to remember and enter a password. This device may be implemented in a future phase of Orcas development.

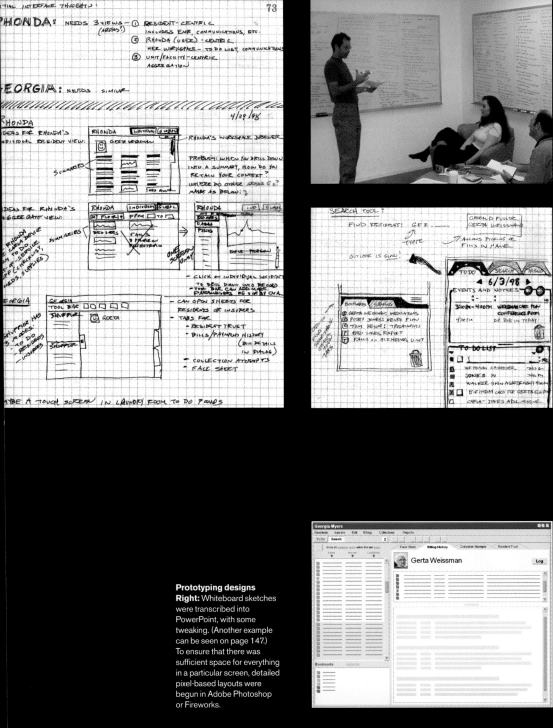

Prototyping designs
Right: Whiteboard sketches were transcribed into PowerPoint, with some tweaking. (Another example can be seen on page 147.) To ensure that there was sufficient space for everything in a particular screen, detailed pixel-based layouts were begun in Adobe Photoshop or Fireworks.

Developing screens:

Keeping track of tasks

Georgia tends to look at high-level billing information but may need to look in detail at a bill. To support this, details can be expanded and collapsed. She is frequently interrupted, so a bookmark area was designed to allow her to keep track of unfinished tasks or frequently used records. She can click anywhere in a record and drag to this area, then click on the bookmark later to return to the same spot.

Showing trends

The organiser trend view contains thumbnails of key clinical trends. The thumbnails contain current data for the facility. Rhonda can view the thumbnails for a quick overview of trends, or she can load them into the workspace to take a closer look with the trend tool. A natural language sentence above the graph controls what is displayed while the area below the graph shows details about the point in time, selected with the vertical slider.

Visualising information

As the care plan is set up for a prospective resident, the Cost Prediction meter shows whether the facility will make or lose money. The Resources widgets allow Sandra, the case manager, to allocate therapy time to different therapy disciplines and practitioners, so she can find the most cost-effective way to meet the patient's therapy needs.

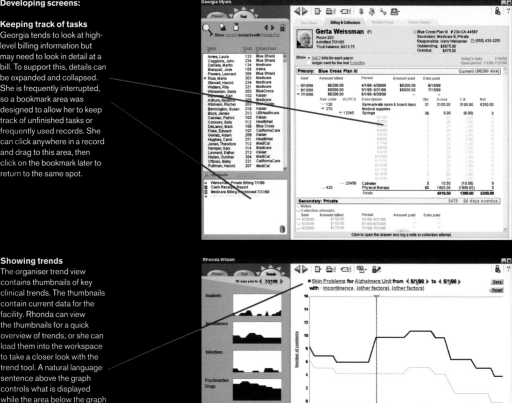

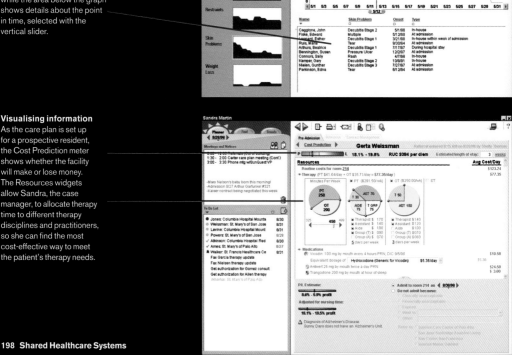

198 Shared Healthcare Systems

Conclusion

During the development stage SHS decided to move Orcas from being a Windows application to being a browser-delivered service. Because the design specification described everything to the letter the development team didn't require further design specification and were able to keep the project on course.

The SHS engineering team was largely hired after Cooper was engaged and the design solution it developed also helped recruitment according to West. The development groups at SHS were, in fact, organised along the lines of the personas, following a user rather than technology model.

When briefing the engineering team the Cooper team would discuss why the design worked in a certain way in terms of meeting the goals of a specific persona. "If you give engineers a reason why something is being done they evaluate it against the challenges in development," observes Reimann, adding that "it is important to keep in touch with engineers to make sure something is possible."

Orcas has been a great success for SHS. Shortly after its introduction, the company had sold the product to more than 400 facilities. "People absolutely love this product," reports West. "They see it and within minutes they are in the palm of our hand," he adds, noting the contribution made by the design. From early on it was clear that technical support and training needs were also lower. The persona approach was new and novel for West but he notes that it has helped with the SHS sales process at the corporate level.

Cooper's design approach also won over the engineers. "Many developers when we hired said 'Why can't we do this'," reports West. "Then they saw the Cooper design and said 'This is a whole new level of design'."

However, West observes of the collaboration with Cooper that "we could have benefited from more handholding, so that our designer could get more steeped in the process they went through. They only scratched the surface as far as designing the full complement of screens we needed."

Reimann concurs. "If there was anything that I would have done differently it would have been to check in with them more during implementation. If we had been able to review the design decisions that had been made they would have had less thrashing around." If the project were starting over "we would focus on getting it out there and wasting less time," says West. "We were going for pixel-perfect faithfulness of the designs, but if you don't get the product to market you will go out of business."

Client: Un-named pharmaceutical research organisation
Designer: Visual I|O www.visual-io.com

Massachusetts-based Visual I|O started life in 1993 developing data-driven applications for business and now considers itself to be in the field of "data visualisation for enterprise applications". Staff are skilled in information architecture, visualisation design, time-based media development, research and systems architecture.

One of the areas that Visual I|O addresses is the phenomenon that companies have a lot of data but can't use it effectively. Visual I|O's data visualisations seek to connect data to business questions using visual 'pictures' to help generate new insights for users and decision makers.

Visual I|O was engaged by a consulting firm to work with one of its client companies which was engaged in the clinical development in pharmaceuticals. The organisation wanted to know how decisions they made on product research and development were arrived at, as they were some of the most important decisions the organisation took. The president felt he had no comprehensive 'picture' and no way to 'see' the whole operation, including the risk and opportunity areas in which it operated. Managers – used to having a stack of reports land on their desk each month – weren't able to maintain sufficient resources for high priority projects as they didn't have appropriate visibility.

The Compass (COst Management – Portfolio Assessment Support System) project was intended to allow them to interact with data in real time to see problems and interrogate data further without having to ask for more reports. It would also allow them to modify the metrics that generated the visualisations based on their past experience, intuition, and outside knowledge of a situation.

Implementation of the design was undertaken by a team at the Belgian office of SPS Infoquest led by Christine Vander Vorst.

Visual I|O's approach is to bring a picture to the earliest client meetings to direct conversation, moving on to create better and better sketches (see page 202). Monthly design reviews were conducted with the client as well as frequent brainstorms about the 'concept' and the functionality required of each module of the system. This led to intensive design sessions which aimed to bring the visual metaphor in line with the expectations for the product's functionality and use, and the overall organisational goals.

To get the client to look at the overall concepts they send them a series of questions , mocking up designs to make them feel more real, and showing a number of alternative approaches. They then make prototypes with hyperlinked GIFs and observe people clicking through and using them.

Mapping visual interactions

Visual I|O's approach is to design interfaces around a train of thought. Their process begins by looking at the decisions the decision-makers have to make and their decision-making processes, the kinds of qualitative and quantitative data on which they base them, and the hierarchy of information. They then consider what kind of metaphor or mental picture may be appropriate, asking how the data could be put together in interesting or unusual ways that might produce new insights. They follow a number of design rules. The colour palette must be kept to a strict minimum with hot colours used to highlight critical issues or problems. There should be no gratuitous pictures. Every piece of the screen has to contain something that is informative, and attention should be paid to how time can be represented. If the user squints at the screen they should see a shape which communicates the most important story the data has to tell. (A corollary of this is that navigation or screen elements must not create distinctive shapes.) The display should tell the user intuitively how to get to more detail about something of interest to him and navigation should be as natural as possible. And it should allow users to see the data from many angles and present data in a 'fuzzy' way.

Mapping decision processes

Top: At the start of projects Visual I|O likes to create a number of time-based maps of the information coming into and going out of the decision process. Points at which information 'clumps' appear (1 and 2) flag up parts of the process that can be assisted visually. These maps also help to establish that Visual I|O has the same perspective as the client, and assist in determining a workflow for the interface.

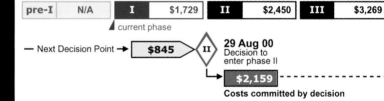

Milestone View

Above: Visual I|O then built a proof-of-concept system which the finance department used for one budgeting cycle in 1999. This system used a single visual diagram which detailed the key events for each compound in development and the cost associated with each of these events over the life of the project.

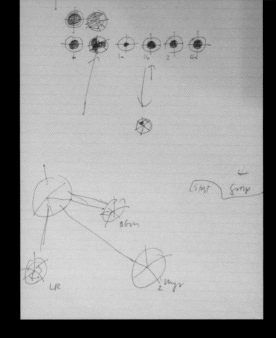

Selling the approach with baseball

Right: Having presented their initial findings the client suggested Visual I|O first develop non-pharmaceutical examples as a proof-of-concept to demonstrate the value of their approaches to the drug discovery and R&D groups. They chose to develop this using the baseball example of deciding whether to pull a pitcher, as it articulated a way of approaching data for a specific kind of decision ('go'/'no go') where each criterion can be discussed on its own merit, and a snapshot of the situation could be presented that could also reveal its underlying complexity.

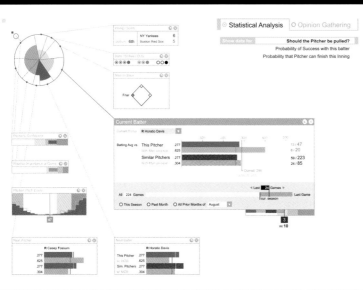

Statistical analysis

Left: The base data for the example is drawn from game statistics. The central element of the interface is a circular diagram which shows an aggregate 'finding' of whether the pitcher should be removed from the game in this circumstance. Each 'slice' of the circle represents the data from one of the criteria. The size of the slice represents its weighting, and the radius shows the value of that factor.

The criteria are grouped into shades of grey and there is a median represented by the light blue transparency. Yellow is used to indicate that a tranche is being edited. The more filled the circle, the stronger the suggestion that the pitcher should be pulled.

Opinion gathering

Right: A dynamic 'opinion gathering' interface allows users to adjust weightings manually, using direct manipulation. This demonstration tool, which was created in Flash, can be found at www.manifesto9.com/baseball

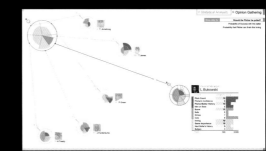

Using matrices for information analysis

Visual I|O created a number of matrices in Excel which they used to map the data available to decision-makers to processes, milestones and decision points. From this they were able to cull relationships, trends and patterns in the information, distil it into key, resonant categories, and discern groupings that might be visible on initial inspection. "We are big on matrices," notes Schindler. "We like to come to data from many different angles, as you would with architectural drawings – every bit of data has a lot of contexts."

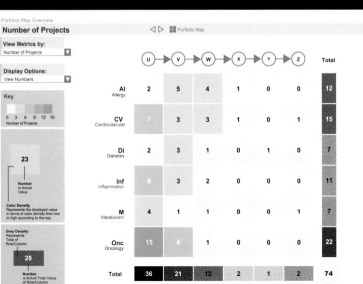

Above: The design was developed iteratively, beginning with napkin sketches, that were translated by the graphic designer into something that could be presented to the client. This is an initial sketch for the matrix map view (see page 204).

Portfolio tool

Left: This tool maps progressive levels of drug development (U–Z) to the various fields of research. Areas of greater density or value are represented by darker colour hues, used here to show project density. This matrix also functions as a portal. Any development phase (U–Z), research field (for instance, immuno-suppression) or individual square can be accessed for further detail. If it is updated on a regular basis this will present a comprehensive picture of the R&D portfolio.

Portfolio Map Overview

Number of Projects

◁ ▷ ▦ Portfolio Map

View Metrics by:
Number of Projects ▼

Display Options:
View Numbers ▼

Key

0 3 6 9 12 15
Number of Projects

23
Number is Actual Value

Color Density
Represents the displayed value in terms of color density from low to high according to the key

Gray Density
Represents Total of Row/Column

28
Number is Actual Total Value of Row/Column

	U	V	W	X	Y	Z	Total
AI Allergy	2	5	4	1	0	0	12
CV Cardiovascular	7	3	3	1	0	1	15
Di Diabetes	2	3	1	0	1	0	7
Inf Inflammation	6	3	2	0	0	0	11
M Metabolism	4	1	1	0	0	1	7
Onc Oncology	15	6	1	0	0	0	22
Total	36	21	12	2	1	2	74

Portfolio viewbox

Right: This matrix map is a step further in development from the portfolio tools (see page 203), which, while comprehensive, did not allow for dynamic change over time, and didn't include any reference to future predictions or events. This tool depicts individual projects (represented as small banded circles) in the pipeline. Developmental phases are shown along the top and specific research fields vertically. Colour saturation indicates density. Projects that are delayed, overdue or seriously over budget are in red. The bar chart below the matrix shows cost and employee hours. Any project in the pipeline can be selected to retrieve in-depth information.

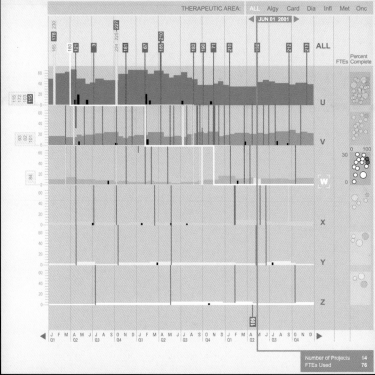

Alternative pipeline view

Left: In this alternate pipeline view, time is indicated on the horizontal axis. The progression of phases is represented along the vertical axis, descending from Phase U to Phase Z. Each project is represented by a single line and labelled by its number. The height of the horizontal bars is proportional to the number of projects in that particular phase, while raised blocks indicate project cancellations. The time slider, similar to that in the Portfolio Viewbox, highlights in yellow projects that are active at that point in time, showing their phase location in the blocks at the right.

Conclusion

Visual I|O was given great latitude by its client to explore ideas, and were able to work in an iterative fashion. An evaluation cycle was carried out each time a solution was deployed, though this was an informal process, involving interviews and focus sessions with users. "We don't get too scientific about usability tests," notes Schindler, as their typical projects have smaller user groups and lots of people who can act as user representatives. Visual I|O typically run a piloting phase where the new system is used alongside the one that is being phased out.

The first-generation Compass tool has yet to be deployed, due to a major re-evaluation of the information technology and application development across the parent organisation, so its success can't be measured.

Schindler concludes that the project has been an exciting challenge for Visual I|O's techniques of information visualisation, with multiple perspectives and opinions, multiple decision criteria seen side by side, the ability to model multiple scenarios, and the 'sense' of the algorithm-generating data and how changes affect those calculations.

Schindler believes that sponsorship of the project was lost as people moved roles. He believes that such projects need sponsorship at a senior level, but also from people at the ground level who, if they aren't brought in, may effectively undermine the project. "To make these tools truly useful," says Schindler, "we believe they must be tightly integrated to the systems in place – the people, the processes, and the priorities."

Data quality, architecture and availability were major issues, and Visual I|O did anticipate them, aware that the credibility of visualisation tools require that the data is reliable. They note the importance of knowing how the data they need gets from place to place, pointing out that you "have to talk to someone early about this because that data may not exist".

Vander Vorst believes that one of the keys to success for these projects is close collaboration, with a lot of communication between teams starting at an early stage. She observes that the designs were almost finished when they first met with Visual I|O and that they could have avoided changing things later on if they had been in contact earlier.

Schindler would have liked to have pushed the design more, particularly making the site shallower to reduce the number of jumps needed to see more detail.

The project became very well known throughout the client organisation and there was disappointment that the original application was not deployed. However, although they were never rolled out, the Compass prototype and application have had an extended life within the company, leading to the development of advanced portfolio and project tracking approaches in several areas of the R&D organisation.

Designing for stakeholders and loyal users

Client: Bolt.com www.bolt.com
Designers: Internal team

Bolt is a Web and wireless platform for 15- to 24-year-olds that provides communications tools to enable its audience to interact in online environments they create. Membership currently stands at around seven million. It began life as an initiative by New York-based Internet consulting firm Concrete Media and was spun off in late 1998. As a result, the management had a lot of experience with Web development.

Bolt's business model is based around creating a critical mass of members whose profiles and activity is of interest to marketers. Bolt also allows clients to effectively target product marketing to people who are making their first brand-loyalty decisions, and it has a 500,000-strong teen panel which marketers and advertisers can tap for feedback. "Teens have tonnes to say and no one to listen to them," says Executive Vice President of Product Development Jane Mount. "They actually like to have someone ask for their opinions."

Bolt's approach is very clear, emphasising function before form, and site performance before design. "We find beauty in the fact that the site is simple and clear," explains Vice President of Design Hafeez Raji.

Their design approach is also ruthlessly logical and member-focused. "Everything has to respond to a client need or a member need, or something that would affect us," notes Thalia Kamarga, who heads up Product Architecture. "The primary focus of what we do is 'What is the value to the member?'," says Vice President of Technology Tom Plunkett. "Something may be cool but it has to have value to our members."

Raji acknowledges that "though our process allows you to justify every decision you have made, at times you need to go with your instincts". Most of the team also have their own Web sites which helps them experiment with design ideas.

Bolt decided that the home-page design was no longer fulfiling their needs as it had become too busy. There was "nowhere for your eye to go, as everything was at the same level," says Mount. They were also keen to increase the number of advert sizes without overwhelming the page with adverts, and to find ways to drive traffic to advertisers who 'lived' in the drop-down menus rather than appearing directly on the home page. Other objectives included increasing the 'conversion rate' (of visitors becoming members) by making the site more of a draw, and allowing members to customise the page background colour.

While addressing these issues the design team thought it was important that visitors should be able to quickly understand 'What is this site about?', while older members should still be able to use the site easily, and it should be broadly accessible. (With its huge membership Bolt members access the site over connections of every possible speed.)

Research for Bolt design projects is relatively easy as the service is well established. Bolt staff receive a lot of feedback from members by email and via 'Bolt Notes' sent to them while they are online (they maintain a high profile on the site), and some feedback is specifically about design or functionality. Bolt also has member-feedback discussion boards including 'Why Bolt Sucks', and 'Tech Suggestions', as well as a 'Pre-launch Posse' club for loyal or particularly active members.

While there are effective ways of getting explicit input on usability, Mount notes that Bolt "can track any activity on the site and see people's aggregate behaviour, which is often better than asking someone what they would do when shown a screen".

The Bolt teams collaborate closely on projects. Everyone, including the content and sales teams, is involved from the beginning, which allows for obstacles to be dealt with as they appear. Much discussion of design takes place in face-to-face meetings where screenshots are reviewed. Meetings are facilitated by a project manager "to make sure we don't go too far", explains Raji. Project managers set up meetings, document the discussions, define the milestones and note what changes are to be made. Raji notes that "they are the key source for everything".

Bolt has a distinct role of product architecture, which combines information design and information architecture. Product architects, such as Kamarga, work separately from design so they can focus effectively on their role.

"A lot of the collaboration is driven by the product architect," notes Plunkett. "They work with the community, context, design, technical and sales teams and also communicate with sales to define a list of requirements." The technical and design teams then sit down with the product architect to estimate how long each element might take, on a scale of one to five, and outline the dependencies. For the home page redesign the team avoided additions that would involve any new technical developments.

Following the creation of the functional spec the product architect talks to the design and technical teams separately – "so that groups don't talk each other out of things," explains Plunkett – then they meet as a group with the project manager to develop a real timeline from the earlier estimates. The team has to agree if it is proposed that a feature be delayed, though this isn't often the case. "We have become incredibly adept at estimating timings for projects we are working on," says Plunkett.

Bolt previews designs to its 'mod spotters' research group and on one occasion has worked with a research company which conducted usability tests with screen mock-ups created in Photoshop. "We have to be careful to understand what they are saying and what they are trying to say," comments Raji.

Analysing requirements

All the requirements for the site are presented in a spreadsheet matrix. Initially, causes of concern relating to the home page were listed and the desired achievements outlined. Requirements were distilled from the research ("often with member feedback – we have to look beyond what they are suggesting to understand the underlying issues," notes Raji) and from the other teams and the (in-house) client. They were then narrowed down.

A functional spec, created in Visio, was then circulated by the product architect on which the design and technical teams gave feedback, particularly on elements that might be especially demanding.

Right: The existing front page was considered to be too busy, with nowhere for the eye to go.

Right: Colour explorations of the buttons and channel sections.

Below right: One of the specific challenges of the home page redesign was the designers' concept for rotating 'touts' (small advert-cum-sells). Although there were no particular time dependencies on the project the engineering of this element had to be left until after the agreed launch date for the new home page, as it required technical development of the site publishing system.

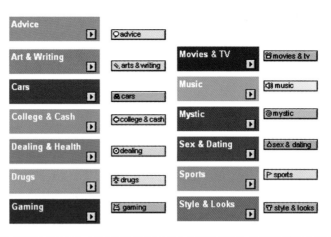

Channels for Launch

Advice · ◯ advice
Art & Writing · ✎ arts & writing
Cars · 🚗 cars
College & Cash · ◯ college & cash
Dealing & Health · ◯ dealing
Drugs · ☘ drugs
Gaming · 🎮 gaming
Movies & TV · 🎬 movies & tv
Music · 🎵 music
Mystic · ☺ mystic
Sex & Dating · △ sex & dating
Sports · ⚑ sports
Style & Looks · ♈ style & looks

Design explorations

Polls are a strong element on the home page and could move to the left, using the right (where people tend to move the cursor) for adverts. This front page treatment has a tinted chrome 'skin' applied.

Conceptual diagrams

Blueprints of the design solutions were prepared for the engineering team, highlighting the elements and their dimensions, and referencing further specifications.

Right: A blueprint for the front-page design shown on the previous page.

Below: Specification for the Member of the Day feature from the front page, referenced in the front page blueprint (right).

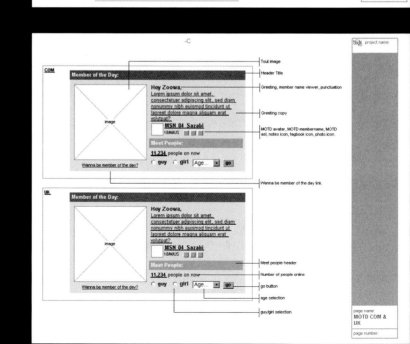

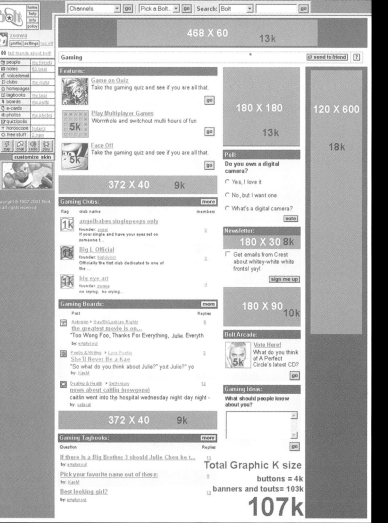

Evaluating performance

The 'weight' of each page element is specified to help determine how the front page will perform when loading.

Performance is a major issue for the engineering team though the design team does pay attention to this issue and works within certain constraints, such as file size. "They came up with good designs based on those technical limits," says Plunkett noting that, although the technical team want to have a nicely designed front page, they "sometimes have to push back, as the performance of the product would be very slow". In general, they try to avoid "getting too fancy" but for performance issues they do use frames, as the left hand navigation gets updated every minute and the whole page would have to be refreshed if they weren't used

Live designs
Design ideas are sent to the
Bolt 'mod spotters' research
group, and posted to the
'Pre-launch Posse' board,
partly for feedback and also
to seed the value of the
new design.
Right: The final design.
Below: The live site.

Conclusion

Along with the technical constraints, balancing the needs of new users (who often have problems navigating the site), established 'loyalist' users (who want member services) and 'third-party' clients (who need to promote adverts) were other substantial challenges. However, Raji observes: "Clients do understand that if people are going to click on an ad you have to keep them happy."

Not everything is project-focused. "We often sit down and talk about ideas, not necessarily leading to anything particular," notes Plunkett. A typical discussion might address the implications for particular pages of using a different technology.

Plunkett believes that there are a number of keys to success for Bolt. One is understanding who you are building the product for. Another is being good at listening "so you can understand where the people you are working with are coming from", and not responding with emotion to other people's ideas (" 'that's not a good idea' is not a constructive suggestion," he observes). He also advocates trying to do more thinking through a project using storyboards, and considering scenarios of use.

Bolt is one of the few stories of Internet startup success in New York's Silicon Alley and its approach to design is no small part of that.

Client: BodyMedia Inc. www.bodymedia.com
Designers: Internal team

Pittsburgh-based BodyMedia was incorporated in 1999 and makes wireless hardware and software for continuous body monitoring, for a variety of healthcare markets. BodyMedia's products and services are focused on its SenseWear Armband which uses multiple sensors and algorithms to continuously monitor physiological data (such as energy expenditure) and contextual data (such as the user's position or activity level).

The Armband collects data, but for researchers to be able to retrieve and preview it BodyMedia developed the InnerView Research Software (IRS). It had originally developed Web-based software to allow ordinary people to monitor their wellness, and tried to combine this with IRS as one piece of Web software. However, one application couldn't support both scenarios – researchers complained about problems with slow uploads that were, in fact, Internet-related – and IRS was instead developed as a separate client-side application, with Web 'hooks' that allow users to easily send and retrieve shared files.

The user interface to IRS was developed in-house by Vice President of Interaction Design Chris Pacione and Shelley Moertel, whose expertise is in information architecture and data visualisation. Considering his influences Pacione cites Alan Cooper on best practice "for which he has the order basically right" (see pages 117 and 127), and Barry Boehn's spiral model for coordination and timing of different disciplines (see his interpretation on page 115). "Don't put the engineering before the design," he says, though he notes that "you have to be flexible in your process". BodyMedia's approach is to ideate first, then iterate – "fail early and often" is his motto. He points out that you can't iterate with hardware. "On the software side there is code, on the hardware side there is steel and assembly lines," he observes wryly.

In order to understand users' needs research for the development of IRS was carried out using email surveys and interviews with potential users. Competitor analysis was conducted focusing on four products that competed with SenseWear. The software was also given to the client to use, and BodyMedia staff would visit those based locally who were having problems. They also received feedback from BodyMedia sales staff who were in touch with clients. "The sales team were my eyeballs," recalls Pacione.

When the design went into production there was a daily 'build' of the software on which people gave feedback, which Pacione and engineering lead Eric Hsuing would work through and address. Pacione describes this process as being "like building a play: you rehearse, modify it, and try something out".

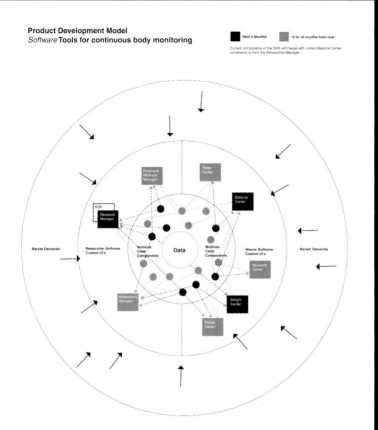

Product Development Model
Software Tools for continuous body monitoring

Next 6 Months ▪ 12 to 18 months from now

Current components of the SDK will merge with current Balance Center components to form the Researcher Manager

SenseWear armband

For the design of the armband, which was led by VP of Industrial and Mechanical Design Chris Kasabach, the team asked: "What is it we want to collect?" Then: "What sensors are required?" and "Where do we need to put these on the body?". The device also had to be forgettable and comfortable. It had to be water-resistant and the external material hypo-allergenic. They did a conceptual sweep, coming up with a whole array of product ideas which they tried out on people's bodies while also investigating technology costs. It appeared that people were willing to wear an unobtrusive armband, and they found a form that was comfortable over time and fitted a variety of body sizes.

Design development
Initial design development for IRS began with ideation, which Pacione describes as "the process of suggesting different visual and logical solutions for a design or interaction, in order to exhaust as many possible use-scenarios and thus quickly expose interaction obstacles inherent in each design path taken". Development moved on to the creation of flow charts and computer-based sketching. Many of the user-interface elements chosen were defaults that are common in applications. "You can assume that people know what a tab is right now," says Pacione.

In the requirements documents for IRS each page described what each screen was for, what it was supposed to do, outlined the screen design and specified RGB values, which elements were buttons, and how elements such as text boxes would scale.

Right: The product flow (or map) was then created in Visio in order to "put the whole landscape of interaction in context". The map illustrates interactions such as what happens when the user clicks a particular button or if he was to disconnect the armband, and flags up other requirements such as where an error screen is needed.

Far right: The team iterated on the product flow and on the screen designs by pinning them to walls in the public areas of their office for annotation. Pacione comments on this process that "it is like doing a painting; more comes into focus every day". (An additional image appears on page 131.)

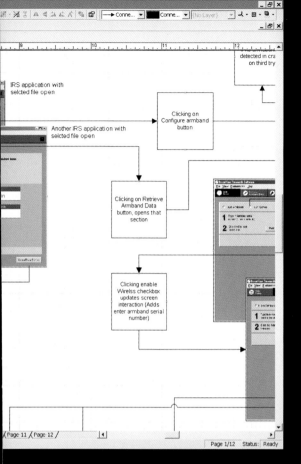

Below: Presentation

Prototype user-interface screens, stepping through the data-retrieve and -preview processes, were created in Photoshop and presented to a marketing meeting using PowerPoint.

Implementation

The application was created using Java Swing (a Web application that runs on the client side) and due to time constraints was developed concurrently with the design.

The engineering team tried to reduce the need for multiple button clicks to achieve certain common operations, but some interactions with the armband required the interface to be adjusted. One example was retrieval of the armband configuration which slowed data retrieval; it had to be engineered, and thus presented, as a separate process.

Bugs in the software and the user interface were tracked using StarTeam. Considerable time was allowed for beta and performance testing, and quality assurance (QA), which were conducted by the engineering team.

Final designs

Right: The View Summary screen gives users a quick overview of the collected data, including the data collection period and associated derived measures such as sleep duration and energy expenditure. The time selector module allows for visual ('direct') manipulation of the time parameters using sliders. Blue lines represent timestamps made by the wearer, and periods for which the Armband was off the body are indicated with stripes. The summary data to the right updates automatically as the sliders are moved.
Below right: The View Details screen allows researchers to create a customised preview graph. The time period is delineated in the same manner as in the View Summary screen, but can also be defined by the timestamps, which are listed in the drop-down menu. The user selects check boxes to indicate the Lifestyle and Physiologic Data in which they are interested.
Bottom: Clicking the 'Preview Graph' button launches the time-series view of the data.

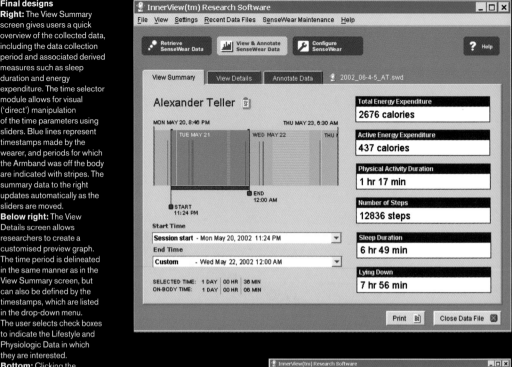

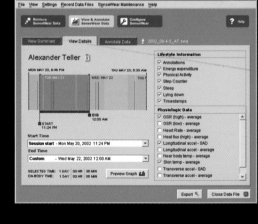

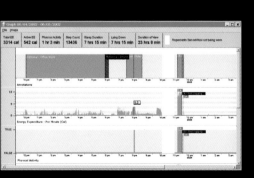

Conclusion

BodyMedia's evaluation process for IRS reflected its nature as a product used intensively by a niche audience. "We don't have a usability group," notes Pacione. "Instead we rely on technical support and sales people to help here. I would love to be able to video people but we don't have the resources to do that." Building on the value of this direct customer interaction BodyMedia is planning to have designers play the role of customer support for a day. "When you have lived that life you become very aware of the decisions you have made," Pacione reflects. He is pragmatic in his approach to getting the best design. "I realised that at some point good interaction was good enough," he comments. "Nice interaction things are nice, but you don't really know until you get something out there."

The engineering team collaborated closely with the design team. Pacione emphasises the importance of working this way as "the engineering lead is the person who will say 'this is how long this will take'," noting that he was also amenable to 'push back' from engineering where appropriate.

The quality of this engineering–design collaboration is one of the keys to BodyMedia's success. This begins from Hsuing's observation that "developers enjoy mastering difficult things and have to appreciate that they are not typical users".

He notes that there is an understanding that there will be compromises on both sides but adds that "developers tend to be reluctant to change things that are up and working". He concludes that there "needs to be some level of trust that the design is something the users will benefit from".

Pacione sees design sitting between engineers who say "we only have so many resources" and marketing people who say "I can't live without this", but adds, in the spirit of failing early and often, that "there is nothing like an irate customer screaming at you to set your priorities". This is a practical approach where a product's user base is numbered in the tens.

"Designers often have a tactical, not a strategic big picture in the company," he concludes. "It's not about good design as we define it in our magazines – it is about design supporting good business. Sometimes those decisions don't look good in those magazines."

Making information visible

Client: BT Group Human Resources Intranet
Designers: Xymbio www.xymbio.com

BT Group plc is a major provider of communications services and solutions in the UK and Europe. Its Human Resources department provides the framework for HR policies and procedures, and much of its communication with its 104,000 employees is handled via the company intranet.

At the point in early 2000 that it was decided to initiate a redesign of the BT Group Human Resources intranet site it was made up of 20,000 pages, with a further 4,000 associated documents. "The Web site was huge and had become difficult to manage," comments BT project initiator Phil Edwards, adding that "users didn't find it particularly easy to find material". He arranged for a survey of users which gave him the evidence he needed to commission the redesign.

The major project goal was to improve usability and to get people to use the site for day-to-day tasks, thus reducing the level of phone calls the HR team were dealing with. Edwards' design criteria included developing a consistent look and feel and making it easier to update documents – "to make it so easy to use that there could be no excuses for not using it".

There were minimal existing guidelines, which included having the navigation bar on the right, and a review date and owner information on each page. The site was also to be built on the BroadVision content publishing system.

Edwards was keen to keep the site as "flat" as possible, so BT people would be within three clicks of any information they needed, and would know exactly where particular information would be. "Don't make people wade through 19 pages of an HR policy to get to information on page 20," he requested.

A tender was put out to three design companies and Xymbio (then known as Mahony Associates) won based on their design approach which Edwards reports was uncluttered and minimalistic. "They had a better understanding of what we wanted to do," he comments.

Their first step was to consult with users by conducting interviews and setting up three workshops, which were run by Xymbio consultant Ruth Miller. They involved all the BT Group Human Resources stakeholders including employees, technical people and the HR department (including policy people and the HR director).

One workshop activity was a Post-It Note exercise designed to identify which intranet pages (apart from the BT share price, BT Today Newsdesk, and jobs site) employees used most, and how they grouped or linked the various types of content. This helped to inform the creation of a revised site architecture and design. Project manager and technical liaison Kath Stynes, who conducted the workshops, notes that this "was a good way of getting people involved at the start of a workshop".

"People said again and again that they wanted a fast and easy way to access HR information – to get in and out as quickly as possible," notes designer Nick Loat. This indicated to Xymbio that they should make the site a portal and maximise the number of links on the home page. The Xymbio team also conducted a site audit on the use of colour, linking strategies and other aspects of the existing BT Group HR site, finding, according to Loat, "a multitude of interfaces, all as different as could be".

Stynes analysed and collated the findings of the audit and workshops, compiling a report which helped define the site's structure and formed the basis for initial design sketches. When this had been signed off, the information architecture was developed further, with particular emphasis on reducing the number of clicks between information elements.

As well as creating the information architecture and a new look and feel for the site, Xymbio also reviewed the site content structure with a view to ways in which usability might be improved, and easy updating facilitated for people beyond the HR team.

The Xymbio team devised a set of page styles which dictated look and feel, and specified how navigation would work at each level. These were built as HTML templates and Stynes liaised with the BroadVision engineers to ensure they were effectively "converted into 'BroadVision speak'".

Liaison with the developers was conducted early on in the project, and audio conferencing was used for meetings and reviews, with attendees able to review designs online.

Specific design solutions were presented to BT and to the developers as flat Photoshop files, with interactions shown over a number of screens in which the cursor was displayed to show the user's action. Once development was underway, the Xymbio team spent time answering questions from the developers with the aid of marked-up printouts of screens.

Xymbio also rewrote some sample intranet pages to illustrate clear writing style and appropriate tone of voice for BT Group Human Resources, to complement the clear design. As the content publishing system would give more BT people authority to publish on the intranet, Miller held a training workshop towards the end of the project on 'Writing for the intranet' to which writers, editors and managers were invited. This helped ensure that they would be able to maintain the clarity and consistency of the pages for which they were responsible.

Analysing the existing product

One characteristic of the existing intranet was the mismatch between what managers wanted to communicate and the information employees wanted to find, the former sometimes obscuring the latter.

Pitching the concept

Top left: The designs were intended to keep things clean. The 'Home|Search|Feedback| Help' menu was required as it was standard BT navigation.

Top right: The colour of the main navigation changes on mouse-over to the section colour, visually linking to section-specific news stories at the left.

Bottom left: The home page navigation is referenced above the sub-navigation. Anticipating that it will be fixed the second-level navigation uses GIF images.

Bottom right: Third-level navigation uses text for easy updating, with second-level navigation accessed via a drop-down menu in order to use screen space efficiently.

Far left: Another navigation treatment presented second-level navigation as the user moused-over the main navigation. A banner device was added to give the BT brand elements more prominence and the interface design more structure.

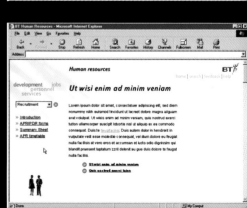

Developing the design
Right: Experiments with typography including using GIF type for headings and subheadings (right) and HTML text (centre right).
Below: Imagery was developed to help users identify specific site sections by association. An image for the 'About HR' section is shown.

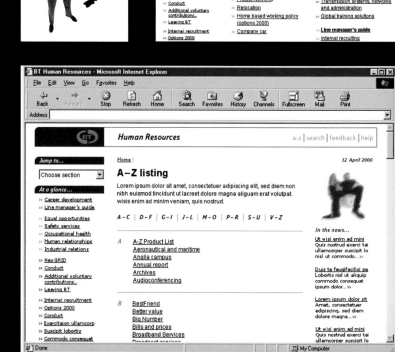

Navigation conventions
The A–Z navigation solution was closest to the existing intranet navigation. It was adopted to provide continuity with and aid migration from the old site, though the design team felt it was not intuitive and didn't map to the structure of the new site. A breadcrumb trail was also introduced above the main heading.

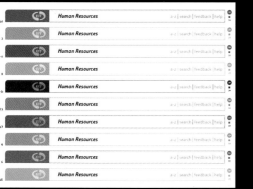

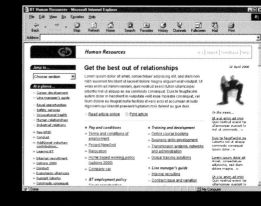

Using colour
Above: A proposed colour palette applied to site sections.

Tweaking the design
Above right: It was decided for ease of editing that page headings should be in HTML text. A 'print article' link and icon were developed and the new Web version of the BT Web logo (design by another company) was incorporated.

Solving search
The workshops revealed that employees weren't using the complex features of search.
Left: Sketching out search specification and behaviour.
Below left: The design aimed to be clean and simple, with search tips explicitly stated.
Below right: Results restate the search query and the total number of items found. The location of each item is indicated, as well as its owner and last review date (information used to ensure that documents are accurate and up to date).

Conclusion

Designer Nick Loat considers that the project was a success. "Solid information architecture and sound usability in response to the needs of the site's users made what was a chaotic mass of information into a streamlined, ordered, quick and easily accessible resource," he reports.

"People took to the system whole-heartedly," says Edwards, noting that since launch "a number of BT intranet sites are becoming more designed, rather than 'put together'".

Measures of success for the three different stakeholder groups included reducing the number of queries and negative feedback received by HR. Reduced reliance on the A–Z navigation tool would also indicate that the general navigation was working more effectively.

A year after launch, the BT Group intranet was audited for usability by Giga Information Group, as part of an annual BT exercise. Auditing was conducted against Giga's intranet scorecard, which measures seven categories they consider to be important, including HR support. BT equalled or exceeded the highest recorded scores in most of the categories assessed, one of which was HR support. "This reinforces what we have already known based on all the previous evidence gathered as part of our day-to-day practices," comments Edwards.

He considers that Xymbio "did their homework and showed a clear understanding of what we were trying to do" and brought to BT's attention "things we knew but didn't acknowledge" in order to create a valuable resource for BT people.

Effective client collaboration

Client: eDesign magazine
www.edesignmag.com
Designers: Contempt www.contempt.net

eDesign, which launched in March 2002, is a printed publication and companion Web site covering interactive design and commerce that spans print and the Web. It is published by RC Publications.

eDesign aims to be an information source for new media designers and designers interested in the Web which "will guide, teach, and most importantly be the voice of the community". Founding editor-in-chief Katherine E Nelson wanted eDesign "to allow users to comment on Web culture and industry-sensitive issues or find basic information". Sung Chang, Co-Founder and Creative Director at Contempt, the design company that developed the Web site, adds that eDesign "wanted a resource that really reflects designers' experiences: how can I become like that if I am a student, or how can I be like that person?". He references the online publications K10K and Designers Toolbox, and refers to eDesign as "a *Wired* for designers".

The business goals of eDesign Online are focused on promoting subscriptions and boosting newsstand sales; driving traffic to the Designers Bookstore; and promoting revenue through branded third-party partnerships.

The conception of the print and online offerings were that they would be complementary. Nelson describes a magazine "with windows into other information, including the Web". A story in the magazine may prompt a discussion on the Web site, which, along with other reader feedback and commentary may be showcased in the magazine. The design brief includes the goal that for readers who pick up the magazine and go to the Web site there should not be a disconnect. It also asked for a design that would support content that was fresh, timely and interactive, and that was modular and simple, with a tight structure. In addition it outlined some technology needs, including the requirement of finding a company to host the publication Web site.

eDesign considered the priority of scenarios of use for the site to be subscribing to the magazine; providing information about interactive design as well as a guidance on problem solving; connecting designers with other designers; and providing pointers to other information sources about interactive design.

Audiences were broken down into Web designers, who use the Web as their main source for information, and who are comfortable with reading on screen and using chat rooms; graphic, print and interior designers, who know the Web medium well, but use the Internet mainly for information, research and email communication; and business and other people interested in the Web (those "who hire and fire designers, and who need to know about what design can do for them," according to Nelson), and those who are less likely to have a high-speed connection, and more likely to be looking for company and job listings.

From the brief, which included an initial site map created by the eDesign team, Sung developed the information architecture leading to a more extensive site map (see pages 68–69) which used an axonometric view to help present the depth of each section of the site.

In the process of appointing a design consultancy eDesign approached a number of companies including some larger agencies, giving them the design brief and asking them to develop proposals, including schedules and cost estimates. Commenting on Contempt's pitch, eDesign art director Anke Stohlmann notes that "Sung was good at responding to us," contrasting it to "big companies where you are put in a line". Nelson adds that "the publisher was concerned that budgets weren't exceeded", and the project was deliberately phased to address this. "We didn't get a sense from the other firms we went to that there was a limit to the commitment or budget," she adds.

The Contempt team included HTML and DHTML programmer Eric Jimenez, co-founder Alex Outman as technical consultant, a database and back-end programmer, and Ninja von Oertzen as primary designer. (Contempt also has an India office that does back-end programming though it wasn't involved in the eDesign project.)

Along with their design consultancy Contempt conducted a technical assessment of eDesign's setup and developed some initial strategy recommendations. They also conducted some competitor analysis, looking at sites that serviced similar needs for designers including the American Institute of Graphic Arts and K10K Web sites. One of the challenges they identified was that of creating a design that was easy for a small editorial team to maintain

Direction presentations

Contempt presented a click-through selection of designs for a number of sample pages, including pages from within the site, to show how the design system worked with icons and navigation. In response to the requirement in the brief that there be an obvious connection in look and feel to the magazine, which had already been designed by the time the Web project began, Stohlman extended the magazine's icon system including rollover states, for Concept to build into the navigation.

Right: The first design approach. The second approach (below left and below right) was favoured by the client.

Below left: Von Oertzen notes that it is hard to imagine the site with live adverts. eDesign felt that banner ads down the side of the page were too difficult to distinguish from editorial content. In response, Sung suggested having a separate frame along the bottom only. The bevelled effect around the editorial and advertising makes it 'pop out'.

Below right: Von Oertzen also notes that while it is fairly easy to control the position of graphics, page elements and font sizes the design needed to compensate for slight differences in browsers and platforms. "If you can only come up with a design that can't tolerate running one line extra then it is probably not worth doing," she says.

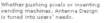

edesign

THE MAGAZINE OF INTERACTIVE DESIGN AND COMMERCE   No.1   Oct 15, 2001

> NEWS
> eFEATURES
> COMMUNITY
> MAGAZINE
> SHOP
> SUBSCRIBE

FEATURES

THIS MONTH IN eDESIGN:

+ ebay under construction
+ The Urban Market: Creating Community Identity
+ e-Business Innovation: IBM Does Design
+ Tuned in to Antenna Design
+ The Urge to Converge: All-in-One Gadgets

PLUS: Personalization, The XML Factor, Hot Product Showcase, Flash Videos, and More

Flash Sites

Lorem ipsum dolor sit amet, consectetuer adipiscing elit, sed diam nonummy nibh euismod tincidunt ut laoreet dolore magna aliquam erat volutpat. /more

Antenna Design

Whether pushing pixels or inventing vending machines, Antenna Design is tuned into users' needs.

Diam nonummy nibh euismod tincidunt ut laoreet dolore magna aliquam erat volutpat. /more

SPOTLIGHTS

Advice
+ Search for Advice
+ View Issues
+ Register to Contribute

Lorem ipsum dolor sit amet adipiscing elit diam euismod tincidunt ut laoreet dolore magna aliquam erat lorem ipsum dolor amet adipiscing elit diam euismod

Careers
+ Search for Jobs
+ View a Job Profile
+ View Education Programs

Lorem ipsum dolor sit amet adipiscing elit diam euismod tincidunt ut laoreet dolore magna aliquam erat lorem ipsum dolor amet adipiscing elit diam euismod

NEWS HEADLINES
+ Lorem ipsum dolor sit amet
+ Adipiscing elit diam
+ Euismod tincidunt
+ Ut laoreet dolore
+ Magna aliquam erat

ADVICE BOARDS
+ Lorem ipsum dolor sit amet
+ Adipiscing elit diam
+ Euismod tincidunt
+ Ut laoreet dolore
+ Magna aliquam erat

REVIEWS
+ Lorem ipsum dolor sit amet
+ Adipiscing elit diam
+ Euismod tincidunt
+ Ut laoreet dolore
+ Magna aliquam erat

EVENTS
+ Lorem ipsum dolor sit amet
+ Adipiscing elit diam
+ Euismod tincidunt
+ Ut laoreet dolore
+ Magna aliquam erat

IdN FRESHCONFERENCE FRI:28.09.01/SAT:29.09.01 SYD CONVENTION CENTRE

syd

Partners :: Contact :: Privacy Policy :: Terms & Conditions :: © 2001 eDesign Magazine

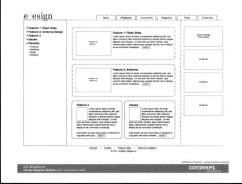

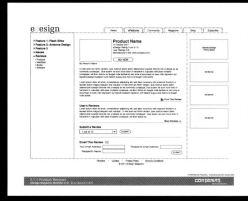

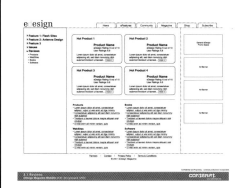

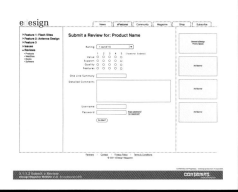

Storyboards (also referred to as wireframes) were developed for each section of the site. As the design matures they provide a reference point that helps ensure it is still on track. The information architecture documentation is useful not just for the designer but for copywriting, sourcing imagery, and collecting project assets.
Top: Storyboards for the features overview screen and a feature page.
Above and right: Storyboards for the reviews overview, a review and the review submission form.

Evaluating design solutions
This was fairly informal, as there was no budget to employ a market research team. Instead the editorial team put itself in the position of its audience, thinking about what they would like to read about, and figuring out the ways it would be most convenient to experience them. "We were our own focus group," says Nelson. The team also made use of industry luminaries who passed through the office to glean expert feedback.

Subscribe

6.0 Subscriber/Account Info

Element Name	Element Type	Navigation	Notes
Register	HTML, with button	6.1	Information on why benefits of registering
Subscribe	HTML, with button	6.2	Information on the benefits of Subscribing
Gift Subscription	HTML, with button	6.3	Information on the benefits of gifting a subscription as a gift
Address Change	HTML, with button	6.4	Information asking users if they want to change their address
Promo	HTML, with image		A promotional space highlighting benefits of the site and subscription

6.1 Register (Subscribe)

Element Name	Element Type	Navigation	Notes
Subscription	Radio button		Asks to see if they are ready to subscribe. If so, only the areas will appear
Email Address	Form Field		Javascript to verify that email address is in the name@address.com format
Username	Form Field	6.2.3.1 already taken after submitting	Enter Username. If a username is already taken then use will be asked to come up with a new one
Password	Form Field		Enter Password
Email Alert	Radio Button		Yes or No to receive email alerts
Submit Button	Button or Image	6.2.7 / 6.2.3	Submit all information

6.3 Register (Gift Subscription)

Element Name	Element Type	Navigation	Notes
Subscriber	Radio Button		Asks to see if they are ready to subscribe. If so, only the areas will appear
Email Address	Form Field		Javascript to verify that email address is in the name@address.com format
Username	Form Field	6.2.3.0 already taken after submitting	Enter Username
Password	Form Field		Enter Password
Notes	2 separate note fields for First Name and Last		This is part of the billing address subscription form
City	Form Field		
State	Pull Down Menu		A pull down menu with all States and Canadian Provinces. Default menu will state 'Select State/Province'
Email Alert	Radio Button		Yes or No to receive email alerts
Subscription	Radio button	6.2 Differ to submitting	Information is confirming. Gives user a brief benefits of a complete or gift subscription
Submit Button	Button or Image	6.1 / 6.2.2 / 6.2.4	Submit all information

Subscribe

6.2 Subscriber/Billing

Element Name	Element Type	Navigation	Notes
Name	2 separate Form Fields for First Name and Last		This is part of the billing address subscription form.
Email Address	Form Field		Javascript to verify that email address is in the name@address.com format.
Address	2 Line Form Field		First line is for Street, PO Box, Route, etc. Second line is for Apt., Suite, Unit, etc.
City	Form Field		
State	Pull Down Menu		A pull down menu with all States and Canadian Provinces. Default menu will state 'Select State/Province'.
Zip Code	Form Field		Zip/Postal Code
Country	Pull Down Menu		Pull Down menu of countries subscribership is expected. Default will be United States.
Different Shipping Address	Radio Button	After submitting, if this is checked it will proceed to 6.2.1	If a user wants a separate shipping address compared to their billing address, they will check this button. Ship your subscription to a Different Location? (U.S. and Canada Only). This is not for Gift Subscriptions.
Credit Card Information	Radio Button / Form Field / Pull Down Menu		Radio Buttons to select the type of credit card: American Express, MasterCard, Visa. Form Field for the Card Number. And a pull down menu for the expiration date (2 number month/4 number year)
Bill Me Later	Radio Button		Button to select whether or not the user would like to be invoiced later through a mailing rather than entering all the info on the site. (U.S. and Canada only)
Gift Subscription?	Radio Button	If users selects either 2 or 3 then will proceed to 6.3 after submitting	Three choices for gift subscription: 1. No 2. Yes, and I'm Subscribing 3. Yes, but I'm not Subscribing
Pricing	Radio Button		The pricing shall be separated for 1 or 2 year subscriptions, U.S. and Canada, and U.S. Maryland residents.
Email Alert	Radio Button		Yes or No to receive email alerts
Register for Site	Radio Button	If yes, then proceed to 6.1 after submitting	Yes or No to register for this site. Advantages to partake in message boards
Submit Button	Button or Image	6.1 / 6.2 / 6.2.1 / 6.2.2 / 6.2.3 / 6.3	Submit all information. If a user selected all possible radio buttons, then the order would be 6.2.1 -> 6.3 -> 6.1 -> 6.2.2

6.2.1 Shipping Address

Element Name	Element Type	Navigation	Notes
Name	2 separate Form Fields for First Name and Last		To see if the name field has changed from billing to shipping
Address	2 Line Form Field		First line is for Street, PO Box, Route, etc. Second line is for Apt., Suite, Unit, etc.
City	Form Field		
State	Pull Down Menu		A pull down menu with all States and Canadian Provinces. Default menu will state 'Select State/Province'
Zip Code	Form Field		Zip/Postal Code
Country	Pull Down Menu		Pull Down menu of countries subscribership is expected. Default will be the United States.
All information from screens 6.1, 6.2, 6.2.1, 6.3. 3.1.2	HTML		An HTML list of all submissions from the user separated by section.
Submit Button	Button or Image	6.1 / 6.2.2 / 6.2.3 / 6.3	Submit all information. If a user selected all possible radio buttons, then the order would be 6.2.1 -> 6.3 -> 6.1 -> 6.2.2

6.2.2 Confirmation Screen

Element Name	Element Type	Navigation	Notes
All information from screens 6.1, 6.2, 6.2.1, 6.3. 3.1.2	HTML		An HTML list of all submissions from the user separated by section.
Change?	Radio Button	6.1, 6.2, 6.2.1, 6.3 (after submitting)	A button after each section asking if the information is correct. If the users selects to change the information, once submit is pressed they will be taken back to that page to change then brought back to this again.
Submit Button	Button or Image	6.1 / 6.2.2 / 6.2.3 / 6.2.4 / 6.3	Submit all information. If a user had selected other settings in 6.2 those pages would be next. If no changes need to be made, users will be taken to 6.2.4

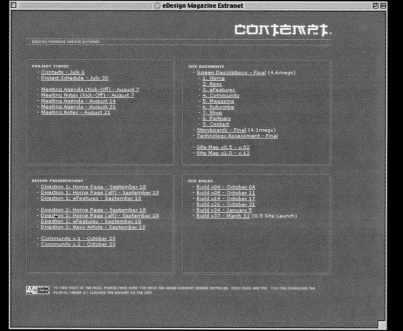

Communication and collaboration

Left: Contempt created an extranet that the eDesign staff could access to find project status, design presentations, related documents and links to the site builds. This created visibility at any time on where the project was and what decisions needed to be made, and ensured that everyone was referring to the same documents. Site builds were reviewed once a week. If an element of the design didn't work well and they had another idea they would ask Contempt to consider it.

Below left: Gantt charts were used for project planning.

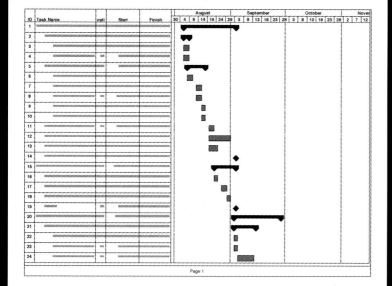

Live design

Although Contempt is keen on creating good documentation, it wasn't felt necessary to create a style guide as, notes Stohlmann, "the site was designed according to a design system established by eDesign".

Conclusion

Stohlmann notes, "we had a vision for the Web site and that helped a lot. We had asked ourselves: who is our audience, what is the site supposed to do for us?" To this Contempt "brought a technical and information architecture knowledge that enabled them to say 'This is how we can make it meaningful to our users'". Additionally "Contempt came up with solutions that were cut out for us, making technology work for the organisation". For instance, eDesign decided that for the first incarnation of the Web site the amount of time saved by implementing a content management system would not justify its expense, which led Contempt to develop the site in a way that made updating manageable for a small team.

The collaboration between Contempt and eDesign worked well. "Sung was extremely organised and meticulous about the organisation, so that everything was agreed on and the structure of the site didn't change once we had started designing," says Nelson. "This helped Contempt come up with the design, as they knew what we wanted." Assistant managing editor and Web editor Ariana Donalds stresses that in such projects it is important to "keep the lines of communication open", adding that "this kind of project is a collaboration between the client and the design firm, so it is important that the client never feels they can't ask questions".

The Contempt team worked well because, according to Outman, "the key people have a good understanding of what the others on the team do and will have to do with your piece of the project". He notes that Von Oertzen has coded HTML, and he has done some design work "so the person doing the information architecture won't create a huge number of pages that need to be designed, and the person doing the design won't create things that are next to impossible to implement".

Mapping design to business value

Client: MONY Independent Network
brokerage.mony.com (not publicly accessible)
Designers: Organic www.organic.com

In 2000, the 158-year-old MONY Life Insurance Company (formerly Mutual of New York) created a new division to begin selling its individual life insurance and annuity products in to independent brokers. Then known as the MONY Independent network (MIN), this division of MONY Life Insurance Co. was charged with addressing the major business objective of migrating delivery of support services for independent agents and broker dealers onto the Internet. MONY's primary objectives were to increase responsiveness and provide better information tools, while decreasing service costs using the Web to enable better customer management.

MONY had hired Chris Owen, a former principal in e-business strategy at IBM, as Vice President of E-business, to lead its Internet group (which included oversight of customer relationship management for MIN). Owen had some familiarity with design, and observes that independent agents wouldn't settle for whatever tool they were given to use. He also recognised that Web design wasn't a core skill at MONY and would need to be hired in.

Owen notes that MONY was also seeking to develop a Web site design solution that better connected the parts of the organisation, working as a window into MONY and increasing the possibilities for product cross-selling among different distribution channels.

He approached a number of companies to pitch for the project. Some he had worked with before and others were known by reputation. All were briefed at the same meeting and asked to prepare a proposal. As part of its presentation and proposal Organic prepared a Flash movie (see page 121) outlining a scenario for a possible 'day in the life of an agent' that showed how far MIN could develop, while recognising that MONY was looking for a more short-term solution.

Although the broader developments weren't part of the pitch Organic also brought up the issue of how the whole branding of MONY would work and how the design of the MIN services would work within that. Owen observes that "one thing that impressed us about Organic was the collaborative approach and personality of the people we met". Organic believes that addressing the wider issues also contributed to winning the pitch.

From this point Organic was careful about planning implementation, narrowing down the scope and complexity of the project to fit within the timeline, and moving elements to the next phase that couldn't realistically be completed. Although they outlined ranges of fees based on project scope and on explicit assumptions lead engineer Godfrey Baker believes that even with good client relations and project administration "success ultimately comes down to massive expectation management". He also observes that "creatives will tend to over-deliver" and the person leading the engagement has to "understand what the client wants and the level of quality they are expecting" and manage delivery accordingly.

Organic's approach to understanding what was needed and developing the product specification was very research-driven, involving the main project stakeholders. Owen also played a key role as an internal salesman. While emphasising that this Web project would be done differently from previous projects at MONY he recognised that stakeholders needed an answer to the question 'What is the benefit to me?'.

Having completed the research phase Organic put together a summary document for the client to reverify the strategy behind the project. Additionally it flagged up three substantial differences, identified from its research, between MONY's plans and the needs and interests of its audiences. Organic also delivered a requirements document within a couple of weeks, along with a document detailing the creative deliverables. This detailed document allows clients to think about cost and helps set expectations. (Typically Organic would first produce a higher level requirements document, with a full requirements document following a couple of months later.)

The collaboration model was kept very fluid, with no gatekeeper, allowing issues to be resolved on the fly. Regular communication meant that there weren't big surprises at the weekly status meetings. According to Baker "the whole process is really about getting people to engage, and think downstream to see where there might be a problem. They might say 'we don't have the data to create that screen', or 'legal may have a problem with that'".

The MONY engineering team tended to see the product as a number of technical systems – a very different view from the users' perspective. Discussing the design solution Baker notes that "we had to sell the IT guys on it", adding that "we also had a strong tool in our hands, which were the interviews with users".

When it came to implementing some of the solutions the team wanted to develop (for instance, showing a policy with the agent's name as well as his number) had to be moved to the next phase as they required integrating data from two systems on the same screen. For similar reasons the design incorporates two search interfaces (see 'Schematics' caption on page 239).

After winning the pitch with the day-in-the-life scenarios (see page 121) and consideration of MONY's overall brand development Organic put together a creative directions presentation for MONY.

Left: Taking the concepts and brand values that MONY indicated they wanted to communicate, Organic brought together a range of brand maps to help narrow down what MONY was saying using pictures.

Informing the client
Presentations included explanations of concepts such as information architecture and its role in online branding.

Setting expectations
Organic also outlined the Web building process to help set client expectations.

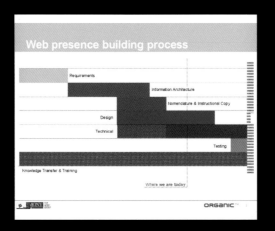

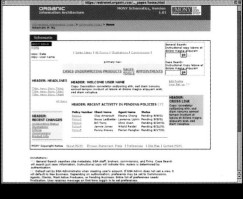

Card sorting
Above left: Exercises were also conducted with insurance agents to help find out what they considered to be the important elements of the site, from which Organic learned that forms needed to be prioritised in a special section of the screen, and that agents wanted a quick link to the commissions area of the site.

Site map
Below: The card sorting exercise informed the creation of the site map and ensured that it was organised according to importance to users rather than to the client.

Schematics
Above: Basic schematics were developed for the main screen types including the home page. The schematics indicate which elements appear on each screen, what the relationship between them is, how they are grouped, what type of content they are and their hierarchy. The schematics don't address layout and 'look and feel' design elements.

Links that would be used infrequently or which agents weren't interested in were placed at the bottom of the screen, as they were used to this format. These schematics were used for testing and agents were happy with the location of the quick-access elements. 'Edit Profile/User Set-up' allows agents to customise the page, for instance setting how many records are displayed after logging in. 'Sales Ideas', 'All Forms', 'Illustrations' and 'Commissions' were the elements the service agents wanted quick access to and they were placed in a special section of the screen. More than one search interface is presented, as contracts are maintained in a separate database from other data.

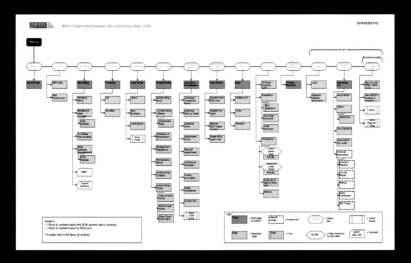

Creative deliverables

Building on the schematics Organic presented four different design directions, reflecting users' desire for functionality over branding and marketing messages. All show policies and status on the first page giving agents an overview as soon as they have logged in.

Right: With this solution it was judged that the sub-navigation didn't work well.

Far right: Icons were introduced with sub-navigation moved to the left, and location indicated using dark blue.

Left: The screen was divided in four areas, with the tabs at the top.

Below: 'Expanding arrows' were added to the navigation and 'quick links' were added to the top.

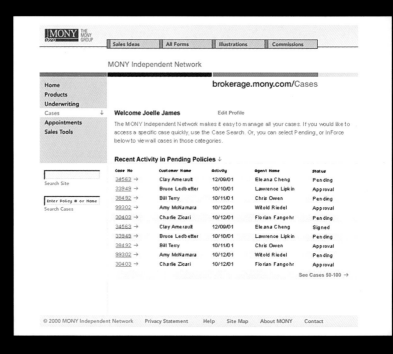

Icons and colour

Right: Icons were developed that related to the tasks the site enabled.

Below: People weren't enthusiastic about MONY's corporate green but everyone likes blue, especially in the financial industry, and it was adopted as the primary colour, with orange for highlights. Varied colour palettes will be used to differentiate other MONY sites.

Contract Status
A BGA and an Agent checking on the progress of a recently submitted application

Sales Tools
An agent searching for sales materials, calling up forms on his screen

Underwriting
An agent offering pen and documents to the viewer/user of the site

Appointments
Two people meeting shaking hands, pretty straight forward

Products
A group of people each holding a document representing a unique MONY product

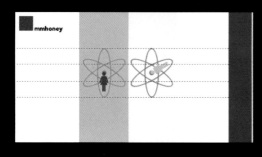

Design revision

Left: MONY asked Organic to develop the first and third directions from the creative deliverables and they incorporated the elements they liked from both.

There was a reluctance to use images on the pages because of the effect on download times, but Organic considered that they added a fun element, and would help agents identify where they were in the site.

It was agreed that imagery should communicate MIN's mission, show diversity, show real and happy people "looking up and directly looking at you", in a warm light, but should "never appear slick or stylised". This imagery would also be used in online marketing and print collateral.

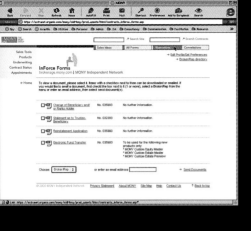

Visual design

The schematics were developed visually and rendered in Photoshop. Typography was addressed and layout developed from the schematics. The colour schemes and icons were incorporated.

Right: The Contracts Inforce Forms, Commissions Results, and Set Preferences screens. Orange is used for the top menu mouseover and, when a section has been selected, to highlight the location of the current screen. The left menu rolls over to white with an arrow pointing to the associated sub-menu. Icons are used in some screens.

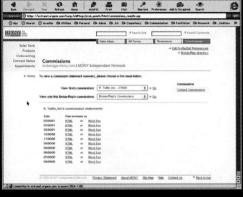

Below: In the Contract Status Overview screen radio buttons are used to sift contracts, and blue highlights the current filter. The navigation now uses an arrow pointing into the page to indicate the current site section, and an arrow pointing out for home.

Conclusion

The independent agents that work with MONY are now able to view all of their contracts and commissions, locate and send forms, determine underwriting requirements and receive sales training via the Web site, while executives receive monthly reports detailing case progression, new users and unique users, downloads and other metrics.

Explicit and implicit metrics by which success has been measured include the number of registered users, reductions in support calls related to technical and policy issues, length of site sessions and number of page views, and the speed with which forms are processed.

Owen feels that for this project success is difficult to measure quantitatively and instead evaluates it based on a mix of subjective and objective measures, one being the response from agents, which he summarises as: "Don't underestimate what you have done; this is a fundamental differentiator in the market."

Beyond its original brief Organic identified a number of enterprise initiatives they believed MONY needed to address, such as the lack of an organisation-wide repository of forms, and the lack of single sign-on access to all client information. Web projects are likely to reveal these kinds of issues as they tend to cut across the organisation. "We are much more prone to put a box around a problem, naming and shaping it, writing up what that thing might look like and surfacing it to the right person," observes Baker. This proactive approach may lead to more projects for Organic, and to projects that can be even more effective for clients.

Further reading

As we have established, design for the Web draws from many different disciplines and relevant books are similarly disparate. As the discipline is also developing we have also listed publications and Web sites which will help keep you up to date with current developments.

All books listed can be found at Amazon by adding the ISBN to the URL: www.amazon.com/exec/obidos/ISBN=
Substitute amazon.com with amazon.co.uk, amazon.fr, amazon.co.jp, or amazon.ca depending on which service, if any, you use. These books and a wider selection are also listed at www.whatiswebdesign.com with additional notes, links to reviews, and links to the book's Web site where appropriate.

Section 1: Issues

A short history of the Internet and digital computing
Where Wizards Stay Up Late, Katie Hafner, Matthew Lyon, Touchstone, 1998, 684832674. One of the definitive accounts of the history of the Internet. The authors interviewed many of the key players, presenting the events factually and dramatically. They are keen to debunk the myth that the creation of the Internet was driven by the desire to create a defensible network.

The Internet Society's 'A Brief History of the Internet' provides a good factual background: www.isoc.org/internet/history/brief.shtml

Background of Web design
Graphic Design: A Concise History, Richard Hollis, Thames and Hudson, 1994, 500202702. Hollis's excellent history of graphic design, organised chronologically and by theme.

See also 'The Best Books' section of *What is Graphic Design?* (page 250).

Technical platforms
For up-to-date information read online and print periodicals:

New Architect (was Web Techniques): www.newarchitectmag.com
ZDNet, Anchordesk: www.zdnet.com/anchordesk
Wired News: www.wired.com/news
Communications of the ACM: www.acm.org/cacm
Technology Research News: www.trnmag.com

Principles of design
Paul Rand: A Designer's Art, Paul Rand, Yale University Press, 1985, 300082827. One of the giants of post-war design, Rand describes and illustrates his approach to design, and discusses his relationship to his clients, his audience and his art. A revision of his classic essay 'Thoughts on Design' is featured.

Screen: Essays on Graphic Design, New Media, and Visual Culture, Jessica Helfand, Winterhouse Editions, 2001, 156898310. US-based designer Helfand's essays "decode the technologies, themes, and visual phenomena that frame contemporary design theory and practice". Helfand is an erudite design writer and her themes offer a welcome counterpoint to so much blinkered writing about design in digital media, though sometimes her ideas seem to be obscure for their own sake.

Bringing Design to Software, Terry Winograd (Ed), Addison Wesley, 1996, 201854910. A wide-ranging and profound collection of essays focused on software design but considering the wider context of design in the organisation and in society. Winograd directs the teaching programs in Human-Computer Interaction at Stanford University, and has been a formative influence in the field of interaction design. Contributors include Gillian Crampton Smith,

David Kelley, Donald Schön, Michael Schrage, Donald Norman, John Rheinfrank and Shelley Evenson.

Elements
Digital, interactive and network art
Maeda@Media, John Maeda, Thames and Hudson, 2000, 500282358. Maeda's investigations into the relationship between computing, programming and graphics have created new aesthetic languages that are integral to the medium.

Forecasting and design trends
There are no substantial books on how to approach forecasting and design trends. For social trends see Viewpoint (www.view-publications.com) and for technology and business trends see Wired (www.wired.com/wired). Social data is published by government agencies such as the Office for National Statistics in the UK (www.statistics.gov.uk) and the Economics and Statistics Administration in the US (www.esa.doc.gov). A private organisation, the Pew Research Center, runs the Internet & American Life Project (www.pewinternet.org).

Designing processes not things
This is still a new area of design and no books currently address it, though *The Secret Life of Information* flags up many of the issues. It is most thoroughly addressed in management consultancy publications such as the *Harvard Business Review* (www.hbr.org), *The McKinsey Quarterly* (www.mckinseyquarterly.com), and *strategy+business* (www.strategy-business.com).

People
Things That Make Us Smart: Defending Human Attributes in the Age of the Machine, Donald A Norman, Perseus Publishing, 1994, 201626950. Norman addresses what differentiates human and machine attributes, and what each is good at, thus investigating the nature of human cognition.

The Society of Mind, Marvin Minsky, Touchstone Books, 1998, 434467588. In a very accessible fashion Minsky's classic develops a theory explaining how humans learn to think, which he applies to understanding cognition and artificial intelligence.

The Design of Everyday Things, Donald A Norman, The MIT Press, 1998, 262640376. This is a sophisticated introduction to human cognition in relation to the design of products and environments. His example of the way door design communicates use (flat panel for pushing, fixed handle for pulling) sticks in the mind of every reader. The book also outlines a useful model for understanding interfaces (see page 80).

The Secret Life of Information, John Seely Brown and Paul Duguid, HBS Press, 2000, 875847625. The authors tackle the conundrum that few of the predictions about technology transforming 'almost everything' have come to pass. The unanticipated factor they find is skeptical users who are exasperated by computer systems and find it hard to get a fix on the true potential of the computer revolution. They argue that "a viable system must embrace not just the technological system, but the social system". This book makes salutary reading for anyone who has been naive enough to see information technology as simple to design and implement, and an end in itself.

Scenarios and personas
Making Use: Scenario-Based Design of Human-Computer Interactions, John M Carroll, The MIT Press, 2000, 262032791. Carroll presents scenario-based design as an alternative to the complexity that results from abstract design approaches. He argues that designers should focus first on the activities that need to be supported and drive development from descriptions built around them.

User research

See the quantitative data sources mentioned in Forecasting and design trends. See also The Design of Sites and Designing from Both Sides of the Screen.

Corporate identity and branding

There are no books which address this area of Web design well, though there are many classic books on corporate identity and many more recent books that pore over every aspect of branding.

Brandchannel (www.brandchannel.com), produced by Interbrand, features book reviews, case studies and white papers, as well as a reasonable discussion debate forum.

Metaphors

Metaphors is a theme addressed in most traditional HCI books. See titles in Interaction design and Interface design.

Information architecture

Mapping Websites: Digital Media Design, Paul Kahn and Krzysztof Lenk, RotoVision, 2001, 288046464. Kahn and Lenk bring academic and teaching experience to this book, along with knowledge and examples gleaned from their years as principals of Dynamic Diagrams, the company they founded. The authors begin by examining maps in general, then move on to look at mapping hypertext, and Web site planning diagrams and maps.

Information Architecture for the World Wide Web, Louis Rosenfeld, Peter Morville, O'Reilly, 2002, 1565922824. In their expanded second edition of their celebrated book Morville and Rosenfeld examine information architecture as an established practice in organisations. They elaborate basic principles around anatomy, organisation, labelling, navigation and search systems, thesauri, controlled vocabularies and metadata. Addressing process and methodology, they outline an approach to a project and look at how information architecture can be most effective within organisations. The book concludes with two case studies. See additional comments on page 66.

See also the American Society for Information Science special interest group on information architecture discussion list mail.asis.org/mailman/listinfo/sigia-l

See the Boxes and Arrows (www.boxesandarrows.com) which publishes regular articles on information architecture and related themes.

Navigation

See *Information Architecture for the World Wide Web*, *Digital Information Graphics*, *Designing Large-Scale Web Sites*, *Designing Web Usability* and *Don't Make Me Think*.

Information design and visualisation

Digital Information Graphics, Matt Woolman, Thames and Hudson, 2002, 500510946. This book starts from the premise that with the volume of information to which we now have access "designers are beginning to realize that what really matters is not just how good the homepage looks, but how quickly and easily information can be displayed, accessed and delivered". It uses case studies and examples from information designers to illustrate four areas: mapping, informing, interacting and exploring.

Interaction design

In the areas of interaction design and interface design Web design can draw from decades of research and learning in HCI, and still has much to assimilate. Much of this knowledge is in the form of peer-reviewed conference papers and articles in journals.

Interaction Design: Beyond Human-Computer Interaction, Jenny Preece, Yvonne Rogers, Helen Sharp, John Wiley & Sons, 2001, 471402494. Written by three senior academics this book is aimed at undergraduate and masters students studying HCI, interaction design or Web design, and at practitioners. It seeks to go beyond the traditional issues, topics and paradigms that frame HCI to address the next generation of interactive technologies, including mobile and wearable devices. It addresses interaction design theory, practice, and evaluation, and its structure is well-considered, including extensive suggestions for further reading, and a student assignment at the end of each chapter. It is supported by a thoughtful Web site (www.id-book.com).

The Art of Human Computer Interface Design, Brenda Laurel and Addison Wesley (Eds), 1990, 201517973. Conceived before the Web by British-born Silicon Valley veteran S Joy Mountford and edited by Brenda Laurel (both then at Apple Computer) many contributions to this book are still relevant, not least for the grander perspective they give on design before the graphical browser. The book is divided into five sections: Creativity and Design; Users and Contexts; Sermons; Technique and Technology; and New Directions. Many contributors are even better known today, and include Bruce Tognazzini, Jonathan Grudin, Alan Kay, Jean Louis Gassée, Gitta Salomon and Howard Rheingold.

HCI Bibliography (www.hcibib.org) is a very extensive resource for information on books and other HCI-related writing and material.

For a two-way discussion CHI-WEB (sigchi.org/listserv/#lists) is a thoughtful mailing list focused on detailed aspects of HCI.

Two valuable periodicals in this area are the ACM SIGCHI magazine *Interactions* (www.acm.org/interactions) and the British HCI Group quarterly *Interfaces* (www.bcs-hci.org.uk/publications.html).

A few of the key journals in this area include *International Journal of Human-Computer Studies* (Academic Press www.academicpress.com/ijhcs), *Interacting with Computers* (Elsevier www.elsevier.nl/locate/intcom), *Human-Computer Interaction* (hci-journal.com) and *ACM Transactions on Computer-Human Interaction* (www.acm.org/pubs/contents/journals/tochi).

Interface design

Designing the User Interface: Strategies for Effective Human-Computer Interaction, Ben Shneiderman, Addison Wesley, 1998, 201694972. Founding director of the University of Maryland's Human-Computer Interaction Lab, Shneiderman's classic textbook offers practical techniques and guidelines for interface design backed up with discussion of the underlying issues and with empirical results. The author also addresses interaction styles such as direct manipulation for graphical user interfaces (see page 76), and extensive discussion of information visualisation. While this book addresses interface design broadly material focused on the Web was introduced in the third edition.

About Face 2.0, Alan Cooper, Robert M Reimann, John Wiley & Sons, 2003, 764526413. Cooper begain life as a software engineer and was best known as the 'father' of the Visual Basic programming environment. Outraged by the "inferior and unusable products that are constantly forced upon long-suffering software users" he became interested in humanising technology and customer-centred design. This book, written with the passion of someone who has been on the inside of the software industry, considers how to fashion intuitive and effective user interfaces for software and the Web.

Making the Web Work: Designing Effective Web Applications, Bob Baxley, New Riders, 2002, 735711968. This book develops a consistent approach to the design of Web applications, and to their

Further reading

implementation, with a view to creating successful products which have clearly presented functionality. It describes how to create a product vision and prioritise design decisions accordingly, discusses how to work through design problems and trade-offs, and presents some best-practice solutions to common design problems. It concludes with case study designs for Amazon.com and Ofoto.

As an example of thorough and well-considered interface guidelines in action see Apple Computer's Macintosh Human Interface Guidelines (developer.apple.com/techpubs/mac/HIGuidelines/ HIGuidelines-2.html or developer.apple.com/techpubs/mac/pdf/ HIGuidelines.pdf).

See former Apple interface guru Bruce Tognazzini's opinionated Ask Tog (www.asktog.com) Web site for insights on interface issues.

For discussion see CHIPlace (www.CHIPlace.org), an informal offspring from the annual ACM SIGCHI conference.

Graphic design and aesthetics
Designing Web Graphics 4, Lynda Weiman, New Riders, 2003, 735710791. Weiman is one of the most prolific writers on the practical aspects of design for the Web. This book considers Web aesthetics and addresses the whole gamut of technical issues that need to be understood to be able to implement design solutions effectively.

Color For Websites, Molly E. Holzschlag, RotoVision, 2001, 288046542. Holzschlag addresses the broad use of colour in design for the Web, also considering 'color psychology' and related cultural understandings of colour. This book also considers the technical issue of using colour across multiple platforms and browsers, working with Web file formats and associated software.

For more general graphic design titles see 'The Best Books' section of *What is Graphic Design?* (page 250).

Typography
Web typography is covered by most general titles on Web design implementation.

Stop Stealing Sheep: & find out how type works, Erik Spiekermann, E M Ginger, Adobe Press, 1993, 672485435. This book presents a rye and engaging introduction to anyone interested in typography. Written in the early 1990s when digital production had made typography but not typographic skills more available, Spiekermann calls for a considered approach to type. Although it pre-dates the graphical Web this book is a useful typographic primer and a reminder of what should be typographically possible with screen-based media.

Text and writing
Content Critical: Gaining Competitive Advantage through High-Quality Web Content, Gerry McGovern, Rob Norton, Financial Times Prentice Hall, 2001, 027365604X. Best known for his opinionated 'New Thinking' newsletter, Norton addresses writing for the Web in a polemical fashion. In particular the authors address information architecture and metadata, search behaviour, navigation issues, the design of email publications and organising a publishing team.

Evaluation
Covered by books under Usability and usability testing.

Usability and usability testing
Designing Web Usability: The Practice of Simplicity, Jakob Nielsen, New Riders, 2000, 156205810. Nielsen can take substantial credit for the successful promotion of usability in the area of Web design, and this book eloquently restates his well-rehearsed arguments. It is

most interesting for the subtle insights the author brings to his subject from his technical knowledge of computing and the Web, and the historical context with which 20 years in the industry privileges him. The book's approach is overly rule-driven and doesn't situate its insights in a real design process. Reservations aside, the author has had a significant, and almost wholly positive, impact on the development of design for the Internet which this book captures well.

Don't Make Me Think, Steve Krug, New Riders, 2000, 789723107. Krug could be considered as a Jakob Nielsen with humility, and his self-deprecating style has considerable appeal. This book is quite accessible, quite short but still packed with valuable insights and tips. It is also engagingly illustrated. The author has considerable experience in the design industry and is more attuned to design and process issues than Nielsen.

Usability for the Web: Designing Web Sites that Work, Tom Brinck, Darren Gergle and Scott D Wood, Morgan Kaufmann, 2001, 1558606580. The authors are principals of Diamond Bullet Design, a company closely associated with usability. The book presents a systematic process for incorporating usability into the solution of almost any business need, with practical advice on project management. The authors are keen to see usability realised in practice, and like Krug have the experience to back up their recommendations.

Usability: The Site Speaks for Itself, Kelly Braun, Max Gadney, Matt Haughey, Adrian Roselli, Don Synstelien, Tom Walter, David Wertheimer, Glasshaus, 2002, 1904151035. This book is built around extensive and thorough case studies of six Web projects, including BBC News Online, Economist.com and eBay.com, and includes an introduction by Molly E. Holzschlag. The style of the book is rather informal which makes it feel less than serious, but this is made up for by the valuable stories "from the code face".

Building Accessible Websites, Joe Clark, New Riders, 2001, 73571150X. The author begins with 'The access manifesto' and the book has a preachy feel, though it is also grounded in real-world examples. It also considers successful accessibility initiatives taken by Web developers, with examples of "before and after" design presented on an accompanying CD-ROM. The design and typography of the book are unusually elegant for a title in this area.

See the online publication *Usability News* (www.usabilitynews.com) published by the British HCI Group, which offers news, paper calls, jobs and original writing on and beyond usability.

Jakob Nielsen's *Alertbox* (www.asktog.com) is the best known online newsletter about Web design and usability. The email alerts are pithy and the articles well reasoned.

User Interface Engineering's *UIEtips* (www.uie.com), edited by Jared Spool, presents usability and interface insights backed up by UIE's research, and often presents surprising conclusions.

Technical testing
Covered by most general titles on Web design implementation.

Creativity, innovation and the big idea
Much innovation related to Web design can be seen in product design, where companies are prepared to invest substantially in research, development and design.

Smart Design, Clive Grinyer, RotoVision, 2001, 2880465249. This book tells the stories of 50 inspirational product design projects, from British Airways' Club Class seat to Apple's iBook, from conception to execution, including the thoughts of the designers.

Future possibilities and challenges

Information Appliances and Beyond, Eric Bergman (Ed), Morgan Kaufmann, 2000, 1558606009. This book is a collection of essays edited by Eric Bergman, a senior interaction designer at Sun Microsystems, looking at the interaction design issues posed by non-PC digital appliances, from hand-held devices and mobile phones to networked automobiles and interactive toys. Introducing the book, Donald Norman notes that designers need to "break away from the tried-and-true methods of the computer and face up to design under new constraints, different environments and restricted technology". Contributors include Michael F Mohageg and Annette Wagner on design considerations for information appliances, Rob Haitani on designing the PalmPilot, Aaron Marcus on user interface design for a vehicle navigation system, and B J Fogg on 'persuasive technologies' and the related ethical issues for designers.

Human-Computer Interaction in the New Millennium, J Carroll (Ed), Addison Wesley, 2002, 201704471. This collection of essays, edited by John Carroll, director of the Center For Human-Computer Interaction at the Virginia Polytechnic Institute, investigates the critical technical challenges and opportunities that will define HCI work in the future. The essays are grouped into seven sections: Models, Theories and Frameworks; Usability Engineering Methods and Concepts; User Interface Software and Tools; Groupware and Cooperative Activity; Media and Information; Integrating Computation and Real Environments; and HCI and Society. Contributions, many of which were peer-reviewed, come from some of the leading researchers and thinkers in the HCI world. This book addresses new and substantial problems which will be commonplace for most designers in their future careers.

The Humane Interface: New Directions for Designing Interactive Systems, Jef Raskin, ACM Press/Addison Wesley, 2000, 201379376. Best known as the creator of the Macintosh project at Apple, Raskin has spent many years arguing why we need to supersede the interface conventions he helped to establish. He believes that people are tired of digital technologies for their own sake and makes a humanist case for more appropriate and hassle-free information technology products. "An interface is humane if it is responsive to human needs and considerate of human frailties," he contends. The author argues that design ideas need to be built on a scientific basis and grounded in cognitive psychology. He proposes a number of innovative and specific interface ideas, and many have subsequently been implemented in exemplary software he has developed.

The Invisible Computer: Why Good Products Can Fail, the Personal Computer Is So Complex, and Information Appliances Are the Solution, Donald Norman, The MIT Press, 1998, 026214065. The subtitle of this book makes for a short synopsis. Norman asks how IT companies can become consumer products companies; how they can reorganise to promote human-centred design; what user experience is and how it can be incorporated into the design process; and why information appliances provide the route to happier customers. He defines information appliances, a term he credits to Jef Raskin, as devices specialising in information, designed to perform a specific activity and able to share information among themselves. He excoriates IT companies for their narrow, technology-driven focus, and argues that they will have to move to being consumer-driven if they are to survive, drawing on the work of Clayton Christensen and others to demonstrate how disruptive innovation can easily unseat apparently dominant companies. As well as looking to the future the author has practical recommendations for the present. From his years in industry, at Apple and then Hewlett-Packard, he has a clear understanding of the relationship of technology, marketing and user experience, which he envisions as the three legs of the product 'stool'. He presents a valuable model for team-based and iterative product development, one element being to write the manual before designing the product, and is quick to point out that designers will need a better understanding of the other elements of business if they are to be effective.

See the MIT periodical *Technology Review* (www.technologyreview.com) for serious reporting on new technology by insightful columnists.

See the ACM online publication *Ubiquity* (www.acm.org/ubiquity) which features articles on the future of IT, innovation and economics, knowledge management and the future of the enterprise, and new challenges for human factors and interaction design.

General

The Design of Sites: Principles, Processes and Patterns for Crafting a Customer-centered Web Experience, Douglas K van Duyne, Dr. James A Landay, Jason I Hong, Addison Wesley, 2001, 020172149X. The authors attempt to bring a balanced approach to Web design, avoiding absolute rules and focusing on patterns to provide a language for building Web sites. These patterns, derived from Christopher Alexander's work, are applied to all areas of Web site design and are complemented by principles and processes that provide instruction on their use. The first section of the book makes the case for customer-centred design and outlines many customer research techniques. Co-author Landay works in the Group for User Interface Research at UC Berkeley in California, which has developed many interesting user interface design tools.

Taking Your Talent to the Web: A Guide for the Transitioning Designer, Jeffrey Zeldman, New Riders, 2001, 735710732. Zeldman is a larger-than-life character in the Web design world. He is responsible for the *A List Apart* online magazine "for people who make websites", and is co-founder of the Web Standards Project, an obsession taken to its apogee at Zeldman.com. This book is aimed at print designers moving to Web design, as well as professionals seeking to learn more. It is divided into three sections: Why: Understand the Web; Who: People, Parts, and Processes; and How: Talent Applied. The author is very focused on coding and technology, but is also philosophical, able to put the Web in a historical context and concrete enough to ask "What is a Web Designer, Anyway?" The most valuable material is in the third section where he focuses on Tools and Techniques for applying design concepts.

The Art and Science of Web Design, Jeff Veen, New Riders, 2000, 0789723700. Veen is an industry veteran who came to prominence at Wired Digital, and is now a partner at Adaptive Path. He presents this book as "the readers' mentor": answering their many questions, teaching them the rules, and showing how they can be broken. The book is organised by: Foundations; Interface Consistency; Structure; Behaviour (on Web technologies); Browsers (on history and characteristics); Speed (on download optimisation); Advertising; and Object-Oriented Publishing. This book will date more quickly than many but is still very relevant. It is well presented and the author's intimate knowledge of good Web design practice along with his technical insights add considerable value.

The Elements of User Experience, Jesse James Garrett, New Riders, 2002, 735712026. Garrett, a veteran information architect and user experience designer, is a partner of Veen at Adaptive Path. Of this

Further reading

slim and thoughtful volume he writes "this is not a book about technology... [or] of answers. Instead, this book is about asking the right questions". The volume is anchored around his now famous diagram of the same name, which he seeks to elaborate on in the text. He begins by asking what user experience is and why it matters. The rest of the book is organised around the diagram's planes: Strategy; Scope; Structure; Skeleton and Surface; concluding with a discussion and examples of their application.

Experience Design, Nathan Shedroff, New Riders, 2001, 0735710783. Shedroff is one of the savviest people in the world of design, and had considerable experience with pre-Web interface design before he co-founded Vivid Studios, one of the most prolific interactive media companies (subsequently acquired by Modem Media). This book is a thinkpiece investigating the nature of experience, and draws on broad and personal examples. The author believes that "the elements that contribute to superior experiences are knowable and reproducible, which make them designable". He presents real-world and online examples of experiences, to facilitate learning how to create more successful experiences in new media.

Designing Business: Multiple Media, Multiple Disciplines, Clement Mok, Hayden Books, 1996, 156830282. Mok is a veteran of the digital design industry, having worked at Apple Computer as creative director before founding Studio Archetype (subsequently acquired by Sapient) and Web software company NetObjects. At the time of publication this was a very far-sighted book, in which the author sought to enlist designerly approaches to text, diagrams and graphics and apply them to digital and networked media. The book begins by examining design in business and the implications of multiple media for the discipline of design. It continues through Identity Design, Information Design and Interactivity Design, concluding with a number of case studies. It is wonderfully illustrated with thoughtful and elegant information diagrams, illustrations, and examples that we should not forget from the history of design.

A number of titles present lessons about Web design by critiquing existing Web sites. The value of their criticism of specific design is limited, as the reviewers rarely know the design brief or the project background. However, the general observations and comments on design heuristics can be valuable e.g. *Homepage Usability*, Jakob Nielsen, Marie Tahir, New Riders, 2001, 073571102X.

See also design company 37signals' 'Design Not Found' Web design critiques (www.37signals.com/dnf)

Many of the general themes of *What is Web Design?* are addressed on the UK Design Council's design resource 'The Brain' (www.designknowledge.net)

For discussion and a place to find and offer answers to questions see the Webdesign-L mailing list for designers and developers (www.webdesign-l.com)

See *A List Apart* (www.alistapart.com) for high-calibre information on Web design and implementation, edited by Jeffrey Zeldman.

Tomalak's *Realm* (www.tomalak.org) provides well-written synopses of news stories related to Web design and technology, as well as broader issues around business, society and technology.

Section 2: Anatomy

Invention by Design: How Engineers Get from Thought to Thing, Henry Petroski, Harvard University Press, 1998, 0674463684. An engaging book that, by telling the stories of a number of engineering triumphs, elucidates what it means to be an engineer, and demonstrates that the boundary between engineering and design is

very porous. Demonstrating his instinct for intriguing stories of human ingenuity the author also wrote *Pencil: A History*.

Web Redesign Workflow That Works, Kelly Goto, Emily Cotler, New Riders, 2001, 735710627. This is probably the most comprehensive book on Web design workflow. It presents a core workflow which aims to be universally applicable, with supporting checklists, worksheets and forms. It also considers the move at the end of the process from site development to maintenance, and presents case studies illustrating the lessons of the book. The book also includes contributions from a number of industry experts, including one entitled 'Knowing your client before you code'.

Designing from Both Sides of the Screen: How Designers and Engineers Can Collaborate to Build Cooperative Technology, Ellen Isaacs, Alan Walendowski, New Riders, 2001, 672321513. This book considers how designers and engineers can collaborate to build cooperative technology. As well as its insights in this area it is valuable for its take on human-centred design, and its recommendations on project development, from understanding users' needs through structuring the user interface to iterative development. It also has an excellent appendix of guidelines covering user needs, requirements gathering, user interface design, project management and development, designer-engineer collaboration and usage studies.

See also the AIGA's 'Standards of Professional Practice' (www.aiga.org/content.cfm?CategoryID=111) which also includes a sample contract (most applicable for the US).

See the AIGA 'A Client's Guide to Design' for a view from the client's perspective (www.aiga.org/content.cfm?CategoryID=313)

Section 3: Practice

Adobe Master Class: Website Redesigns, Darcy Dinucci, Adobe Press, 2001, 201758644. The coverline for this book is 'makeovers from nine top design teams', and it focuses on user-centred approaches to Web site redesigns. Case studies include Method Design's work on TRIP.com, Small Pond Studio's SchwabLearning.org redesign, and in-house design revisions at Epinions.com and IBM.com. The book is well illustrated, showing photographs taken from research, sketches, analytical diagrams and many artifacts from the design development.

See also the AIGA 'Experience Design Case Study Archive' (www.aiga.org/content.cfm?Alias=casestudies), featuring peer-reviewed case studies, many written for conference presentations.

Glossary

If you cannot find a term you are looking for in the text, a more extensive glossary is presented at www.whatiswebdesign.com

Accessibility Also referred to as 'universal usability'. The degree to which a product is usable by people with disabilities or physical impairments. For Web sites aimed at broad audiences and with particular functions accessibility standards are increasingly mandated by laws such as the Americans with the Disabilities Act and the UK Disability Discrimination Act.

Acrobat See PDF

Alt tags Text that describes an image used in a Web page (including images used for navigation) to assist understanding the nature of the image. Alt tags are parsed by the screen readers used by people with sight impairment. Most browsers also display the alt text for an image before it loads, helping users decide whether to move on or back. They are also used by search engines to categorise pages and images. Alt tags typically take the form `<img src="image file name" alt="Image description">`.

ASCII The American Standard Code for Information Interchange, referred to generically as 'plain text', was developed by the American National Standards Institute. It can represent 128 characters, hence characters such as £ are excluded. HTML is encoded in ASCII but as it needs to represent many characters beyond the 128 ASCII characters, 'escape sequences' are used where characters enclosed in an ampersand and a semi-colon indicate to the Web browser a non-ASCII character. The escape sequence for £ is &pound

Bitmap Bitmap (pixel) graphics describe images as a matrix of pixels, each having a size, colour and tone. Photographic (continuous tone) images are best stored as bitmaps. They are typically produced by applications such as Photoshop and saved in formats such as GIF, JPEG and PNG. See also Vector.

Cascading Style Sheets See CSS

Clickstream analysis See Web server logs

Client-side Operations that take place on a user's computer rather than on the server. Such operations include an HTML Web page rendering, a Java applet executing, DHTML code modifying a Web page, or Javascript being used for calculations or form validation.

CSS (Cascading Style Sheets) Cascading style sheets allow multiple-style characteristics (font, size, colour, position, line spacing) to be applied to units of text, in a similar fashion to styles in word processors and page make-up applications. This speeds text formatting and allows this formatting to be changed globally by simply altering a style sheet. Style sheets can be embedded in an HTML page, or referenced externally. By abstracting presentation from content, style sheets also have the potential to allow users to view pages using their preferred style sheet, or appropriate style sheets to be used when a page is viewed on another platform such as a PDA. CSS files have the suffix css. See the diagram How the Web works (page 33).

Discussion list See Mailing list

DHTML See Dynamic HTML

Dynamic HTML (DHTML) An enhancement to HTML that allows Web pages to change dynamically with user interaction and over time. These changes happen without the page needing to be refreshed, allowing for a more satisfying user experience. This is effected by embedding the code for the other elements of the page and their behaviour in the original page. Dynamic user interfaces can be effected with Javascript (to an extent), Java applets, and most commonly with Flash. DHTML is the easiest to author, and is supported by most mature Web editing tools, though as it is implemented by many vendors there are inevitable problems in creating cross-browser compatibility. See examples: Public Lettering Web site (page 82) and BBC Food Web site (page 83). See the diagram How the Web works (page 33).

Escape sequence See ASCII

Ethnography A research practice derived from anthropology. See Section 1: User research (page 80).

Extensible Markup Language (XML) Allows data to be stored in ways that enable it to be flexibly combined and recombined, searched, sorted and exchanged. In XML data is marked up with semantic tags that indicate, in human readable form, the nature and measure of that information; for instance, that it is a last name or a price in a specific currency. XML documents are presented by parsing with Extensible Style Language (XSL). One output might be XML-compliant HTML, referred to as XHTML, for display in a Web browser. XML documents can be altered and restructured using XSLT (XSL Transformations) which allow for considerable flexibility. XML represents a return to the roots of HTML in the structure of markup languages developed for computer-processing of data. The separation of data and meaning mirrors the separation of data and presentation represented by Cascading Style Sheets (CSS). In future the majority of data-driven products are likely to be based, or interchangeable with, XML data. XML files have the suffix xml.

Extranet An intranet accessible from outside an organisation's internal network. Any Web site which displays information directly taken from an organisation's internal network is technically an extranet. See MONY Independent Network case study (page 236).

Flash Flash is a file format that allows presentation of vector-based animation, along with time-based media, via Web browsers that have the appropriate plug-in. We have noted elsewhere that the client-server model of the Web is unsuited to dynamic interfaces, and with the wide distribution of Flash-compatible plug-ins and their inclusion with many default browser installs Flash has almost become a standard form of Web content. Flash (originally known as FutureSplash) was purchased by software developers Macromedia and many of its authoring and server tools have been adapted to support it.

Glossary

Flash supports presentation of high-quality, anti-aliased type (as fonts are vector-based) but this type is more difficult to edit or generate dynamically than HTML text, and is also impossible for screen-readers to parse, though Macromedia is addressing both issues. Flash can be a very powerful tool when used appropriately.

Fonts See Typefaces

Form A form on the Web is very like a printed form, requiring users to give certain responses and constraining the form of those responses. Web forms typically contain fixed character fields and scrolling free-text entry fields, check boxes and radio buttons, single and multiple selection menus, and buttons for initiating data submission and clearing.

Frames Frames were introduced with Netscape's Navigator 2.0 browser in 1995 and allowed multiple, independently updating Web pages to be presented in a browser window within a 'frameset'. As users navigate there tends to be at least one frame which doesn't need to refresh, making the experience less jarring. Frames also allowed for easier site maintenance as the same frame could be used in multiple screens. Web site maintenance has since been facilitated by other methods, such as the use of server-side includes, and limits of frames have been extensively investigated. Frames are most useful for Web applications that don't use the page metaphor, such as banking, or to solve certain performance issues. See Bolt.com case study (page 211).

GIF (Graphics Interchange Format) A format for storing bitmap graphics, primarily for display via a Web browser, and the first image format supported by Web browsers. It can represent colours up to 8-bit (256 colours) and is best used for flat graphical images rather than continuous tone images. GIF also supports animation (a feature often deployed gratuitously) and interlacing, whereby an image loads progressively, helping the user to identify it before it has completely rendered. GIF is a proprietary format and, although free to use, vendors of software that can create GIF files have to pay a licence fee to Unisys. GIF files have the suffix gif. See also JPEG and PNG.

GUI Stands for Graphical User Interface, and typically refers to WIMP interfaces that employ Windows, Icons, Menus and a Pointing device. GUIs were pioneered at Xerox PARC and commercialised by Apple Computer with the Macintosh. Prior to GUIs most user interfaces used a 'command line'. See Section 1: A short history of the Internet and digital computing (page 14).

HTML Hypertext Markup Language describes the codes for formatting documents to be displayed by a Web browser, and the structure documents need to follow. HTML is concerned with presentation, not programming. HTML documents consist of 'head' and 'body', the former containing non-display elements such as meta tags as well as the page title, and the latter containing display elements. Markup includes structural elements such as headings indicated with the tags (or elements) <h1>, <h2> etc, and lists, as well as display elements such as bold and italic <b>, <i>, and formatting of choice of font and colour. A key aspect of HTML is the markup of hypertext links, and HTML documents can also pull in external elements, which are typically graphics but could be movies or Java applets. Although HTML standards are controlled by the Worldwide Web Consortium it is not always implemented consistently across browsers, though inconsistency is tending to decrease. HTML is based on ASCII, using escape sequences for non-ASCII characters, and can be authored in any text editor. Many applications allow HTML documents to be authored more easily using visual interfaces though from an engineering perspective the code produced may need work to optimise. HTML documents can include JavaScript. Dynamic HTML is an enhancement to HTML and XHTML is a HTML re-expressed as an application of XML, which allows authors to add new elements and extend it.

Hypertext Markup Language (see HTML)

Image map A graphic which has been coded to work as navigation, allowing clicks on different parts of the image to map to separate locations (URLs). Early image maps were server-side, making them clumsy to use, but modern browsers allow image maps to be implemented on the client-side.

Intranet An internal collaboration system built using Web technologies, primarily a Web server but also including shared documents, task and contact management and calendaring. See also Extranet. See BT Group HR case study (page 220).

iTV (interactive television) Services delivered via a television set connected to a 'set-top (intelligent) box', itself connected to a network by a combination of phone line, cable, ADSL and satellite links. See 'New devices' in Section 1: Future possibilities and challenges (page 55). Interactive television platforms have tended to use proprietary technologies and only present services which have explicitly signed up to the platform (a model known as the 'walled garden'). As a result they have been complex to develop for, though some are moving to open standards. With iTV interface conventions tend to be tightly controlled by the platform provider.

Java A programming language created by Sun Microsystems that, like C++, can be used to create applications. Traditional applications are 'compiled' to work on a specific platform and chip, such as Windows on a specific Intel architecture chip. Java 'applets' can 'execute' on any combination for which a Java Virtual Machine has been written, which extends to some PDAs and mobile phones, though performance will always be slower as the code has to be interpreted by the virtual machine. Java applets are also designed to be delivered over a network such as the Internet. Sun has developed graphical user interface elements guidelines for Java applets developers, and like

DHTML, Java interfaces are dynamic. See 'Computers and operating systems' in Section 1: Technical platforms (page 14). See Section 1: Future possibilities and challenges (page 107). See also JavaScript.

JavaScript An interpretive scripting language used to implement client-side 'intelligence' such as form validation. It was originally developed by Netscape and has no relationship to Java. Like DHTML it is implemented by many vendors and there are inevitable problems in creating cross-browser compatibility.

JPEG JPEG refers to a number of compression algorithms developed by the Joint Photographic Experts Group, some of which allow compression without any apparent loss in image quality. It is best suited to representing continuous tone or photographic images as it isn't restricted to the colour gamut of GIF and its compression algorithms work well with these kinds of images. JPEG also supports progressing rendering, akin to interlacing in GIF images. Most image-editing applications support saving as JPEG and many allow the user to determine the level of compression, in a trade-off between file size and image quality. JPEG files have the suffix jpg. See GIF and PNG.

Listserver See Mailing list

MacOS See Operating system

Mailing list A tool that allows an email to be efficiently distributed to multiple recipients. They are created by listservers which typically allow users to add or remove themselves to or from the list, and set the listserver to send each individual posting or all the postings over a given period. The lists are a popular way of conducting two-way discussions, or publishing a newsletter to multiple readers.

Modem A device that sends data over an analogue connection between a computer and a remote network using a standard telephone line. (Modem, derived from modulate/demodulate, describes the process of turning digital data into 'sounds' that can be carried along a telephone line.) Fast modems are often referred to as a '56k'.

Mouseover Refers to any change in a Web page that is prompted by the user's cursor moving over a page element. Mouseovers are most typically used in navigation where a navigation element may highlight to indicate it is active and would be selected if the user were to 'mousedown' (click). Today the 'mouse' implied in 'mouseover' is often not a mouse and might be a trackpad, the user's finger (with a touchscreen) or a games controller.

Operating system (OS) Operating systems are discussed in 'Computers and operating systems' in Section 1: Technical platforms (page 26). Common personal computer operating systems include: Microsoft's Windows, by far the most popular on the client-side; Unix, which has many versions including

GNU/Linux and is used mainly on high-end workstations and servers; and Apple Computer's MacOS, which in its MacOS X version is based on one version of Unix.

PDF (Portable Document Format) A format, also known as Acrobat, created by the Adobe software company for exchanging digital documents as 'facsimiles'. Many documents accessible over the Web are in this format. Acrobat files have the suffix pdf. Free Acrobat Reader software is found at www.adobe.com/products/acrobat

Plug-in See 'Browsers and plug-ins' in Section 1: Technical platforms (page 30).

PNG (Portable Network Graphics) A non-proprietary format for storing both bitmap and vector graphics. Unlike JPEG it is not 'lossy', and the original image is presented when it is rendered by a browser. PNG supports transparency and, unlike GIF, multiple degrees of transparency (opacity). It also supports interlacing and gamma correction. Despite its advantages PNG has been slow to be adopted, though software packages that save GIF and JPEG images will typically save PNG files, and the format is supported by most modern browsers. PNG files have the suffix png.

PSD A file created by and stored in Adobe Photoshop's native format. As Photoshop is commonly used to visualise the graphic, aesthetic and typographic aspects of a design, PSDs are commonly exchanged, as in "Have a look at the PSD of that page". PSD files have the suffix psd.

Refresh (browser) A refresh refers to a Web page reloading as the result of a client-side action that requires the server to update the current page. Browsers also cache pages locally and this can result in users receiving out-of-date material, which can be fixed by forcing the browser to refresh the page. (See pages 32, 72 and 82.)

Rollover See Mouseover

Router The devices that direct data traffic around the Internet to ensure that it arrives at its intended destination in tact and as quickly as possible.

Server-side See Client-side

Server-side includes (SSI) A server-side include is a bit of data that is added to a (static) HTML file just as it is requested by a browser. It could be a piece of data as basic as the current date or as complex as an element of the page such as the navigation, which makes the site easier to update. One type of include could be the information about the client browser and version, passed over from the Web server, which could for instance be inserted in a technical feedback form, informing the recipient of a possible browser incompatibility. The concept of 'including' data in a page as it is requested is key to most complex Web products.

Staging server A server used for previewing a Web site before it goes live. The server mirrors the specification of the live server, using the same applications configured in the same way, and the same data (including pages and graphics). A staging server allows aspects of site performance to be tested and the site content to be proofed. See Section 2: Testing (page 158).

SVG SVG stands for Scalable Vector Graphic and is a graphic format that supports vector-based images and is thus scalable, thus able to be presented at an appropriate size on different size displays, and possibly allowing users to zoom in on the graphic. SVG is an application of the Extensible Markup Language. It is not as widely supported as other graphic formats (GIF, JPEG, PNG) and authoring tools for SVG are also much less common.

Typefaces Historically a font was one instance of a typeface, such as roman, italic or bold, though they usually weren't created as part of a typeface family. Today, as a result of the nomenclature used in electronic publishing applications, font tends to be used to mean typeface. See 'Typography' in Section 1: Elements (page 92).

Unix Unix is an operating system, like Windows or MacOS, created at Bell Labs in the early 1970s. It has been extensively developed upon elsewhere as with Sun Microsystem's Solaris, Apple's MacOS X, and the 'open source' Linux (properly known as GNU/Linux) that has been adopted by IBM among others. Unix has traditionally been used on workstations and servers, and much of the early development of Internet protocols and applications was done on Unix platforms, including the first Web server and browser. Some knowledge of Unix can be very useful for designers, particularly if running their own Web server.

URI (Uniform Resource Identifier) See URL

URL URL stands for Uniform Resource Locator, a syntax for pointing to any resource on the Internet and specifying the protocol by which it should be accessed. A URL is one kind of Uniform Resource Identifier (URI). The RFC document which describes URIs has a URL of the form:

`http://www.ietf.org/rfc/rfc2396.txt`

Where http indicates the hypertext transfer protocol should be used, www.ieft.org is the host name of the server on which the resource resides, and `/rfc/rfc2396.txt` is the path to the resource, in this case a text file, though most commonly for a Web server it would be an HTML file. URLs are valuable, as they can point users unambiguously to a resource, and in this respect they are also valuable for teams collaborating on a Web development project, or for a design team sharing references to interesting resources.

Use case Use cases are related to scenarios and originated in software engineering. They are often used in conjunction with the Uniform Modelling Language (UML). See 'Scenarios and personas' in Section 1: Elements (page 58). See Shared Healthcare Systems case study (page 194).

Validation The process by which data submitted by a user (most commonly via a form) is checked to see that all the required fields have been completed and that the data submitted is of the appropriate form. Required fields are typically flagged up, and supporting copy may explain what the appropriate form of data for that field might be, e.g. a login may allow a minimum and maximum number of characters, allowing letters and numbers but no special characters. Validation may be used anywhere from a basic one-field search to verification of payment information, and can take place on the server- or client-side. Client-side validation is usually quicker and provides a better user experience, though server-side validation is often needed for reasons related to security or engineering. Designing unambiguous forms is a major challenge.

Vector Vector-based graphics can be described most efficiently in terms of straight lines and curves, colour, tone and gradation. See also bitmap and SVG.

Web server A computer permanently connected to the Internet that runs Web server software to allow Web pages that you place on it to be accessible on the Web. See 'Web servers and caching' in Section 1: Technical platforms (page 30). See the diagram How the Web works (page 33).

Web server logs Server logs are the files in which activity of server applications is recorded. The log generated by Web server software shows every 'hit' on a site, that is every request made by a Web browser for a file on the server, including graphics, CSS files, server-side includes, and files explicitly intended to be downloaded (perhaps PDFs). The log also records time of access, client IP address, the client browser, version and client platform (Windows, MacOS, Linux, etc) and version, the URL from which the user was referred (if any), and files not found. This log can be processed into a readable report showing the number of page views (a more useful metric than hits), and number of user sessions, pages viewed, and session length, as well as profiling the make-up of browsers and platforms, which is useful for optimising site performance and reporting broken links within the site. This log examination is sometimes referred to as 'clickstream analysis'. See the diagram How the Web works (page 33).

Windows See Operating system

Picture credits

All Web site designs are credits of the Web site owners or designers. All uncredited information diagrams credit of Jack Schulze (www.jackschulze.co.uk).

003: NCSA/UIUC, image by Donna Cox and Robert Patterson, courtesy of the National Center for Supercomputing Applications (NCSA) and the Board of Trustees of the University of Illinois; 008: John Maeda; 012: 'Human-size computing': Lucent Technologies, Inc./Bell Labs; 013: 'Pioneering user interfaces', Photo courtesy of Palo Alto Research Center (PARC); 013: 'PC gets corporate', IBM PC Jr image copyright IBM Corporation; 013: 'PC gets corporate', Bill Gates image copyright Anthony P. Bolante/CHI; 013: 'Operating systems for all', Steve Wozniak image copyright Alan Luckow; 017: 'Inventing the Internet', JCR Licklider image courtesy of the MIT Museum; 017: 'Inventing the Internet', Bob Taylor image courtesy of Bob Taylor; 017: 'Soviet first', image courtesy of Jeff Miller; 017: 'The first router', image courtesy of Frank Heart; 019: 'From the Internet to the Web', Vinton Cerf image courtesy of Vinton Cerf; 019: 'From the Internet to the Web', image courtesy of Robert E. Kahn; 019: 'From the Internet to the Web', image of Tim Berners-Lee copyright Fabian Bachrach; 019: 'From textual to graphical', MSN interface design credits: Agency: Clement Mok designs. Creative Director: Clement Mok. Photography: CMCD. Information Designer: Lillian Svec. Interface Design: Clement Mok; 019: 'From textual to graphical', Amazon.com image copyright Amazon.com Inc.; 022: 'Product design', Palm V image courtesy of Palm Inc.; 022: 'Product design', Sony Airboard courtesy of Sony Corporation; 022: 'Physical ergonomics', all images courtesy of Matt Marsh; 022: 'Architecture', image courtesy of Foster and Partners; 023: 'Games design', images courtesy of Capcom; 023: 'Information design', HMSO; 028: ' 'Classic' computing', The Image Bank; 037: Copyright © 2002 Eames Office (www.eamesoffice.com); 040: The Coca-Cola Company; 041: The Coca-Cola Company; 041: 'Designing forward', eDesign; 042: 'The customer experience from beginning to end', Amazon.com Inc; 046: image courtesy of the Royal College of Art; 047: John Maeda; 049: 'Playing in the kitchen', Philips Design; 049: 'Phones as jewellery', Nokia Corporation; 049: 'The writing is on the wall for paper', E Ink Corporation; 051: Clement Mok; 053: The Image Bank; 057: 'Pogo', Pogo Mobile Solutions; 059: Copyright © 2002 Cooper; 061: 'Innovation beyond research', Sony Walkman, courtesy of the Sony Corporation; 061: Bolt Inc.; 061: 'Users as designers', Fitch: Worldwide; 065: 'Metaphorical books', Voyager/Educorp; 065: 'The literal desktop metaphor', General Magic Inc.; 065: 'The home as interface', Microsoft Corporation; 065: 'Real Things', IBM Corporation; 067: 'Schematics', Dimension Data; 067: 'Wireframes', Contempt Productions; 067: 'Sketching', Dimension Data; 068: Contempt Productions; 078: Copyright © David Small, 1999; 081: 'Enhancing the physical with the digital', Durrell Bishop, photograph courtesy of Bridget Bishop; 081: 'The Design of Everyday Things', portrait courtesy of Donald A Norman; 082: 'Origins of an concept', Photograph courtesy of Bill Moggridge; 082: 'Origins of a concept', Sketch copyright Bill Verplank; 083: 'Integrating hard and soft interaction', Handspring Inc.; 085: ' 'Lean back' GUIs', TiVo Inc.; 084: 'GUI essentials' and 'GUI essentials revisited', Apple Computer Inc.; 086: 'Interface updates', Images copyright © Ebay Inc. All rights reserved; 090: Olivetti SpA; 091: Low bandwidth graphics, Niclas Sellebråten; 091: 'Space and movement', Quantum Business Media; 093: Microsoft Corporation; 094: Matthew Carter image courtesy of Matthew Carter; 098: Organic Inc; 101: 'Testing times', Courtesy of Matt Marsh; 101: Bottom, image courtesy of Flow Interactive; 103: 'Performing for your users', Niclas Sellebråten; 103: Left, Bolt Inc.; 105: 'Xerox Star', Copyright Palo Alto Research Center (PARC); 105: 'Apple iBook and iPod', Apple Computer Inc.; 111: 'Interactive commercial spaces', IDEO; 111: 'Counteractive', MIT Media Lab; 113: British Broadcasting Corporation;113: 'New devices', Ambient Devices; 113: 'New devices', 3Com Corporation; 113: 'Portable and locational' Palm Inc. All rights reserved; 115: Copyright © 2002 Chris Pacione. All rights reserved. With acknowledgement to Barry Boehm, PhD; 117: 2001 © Dubberly Design Office; 121: Organic Inc; 125: Images courtesy of Bolt Inc.; 127: 'Changing order', 2001 © Dubberly Design Office; 131: 'Shared workspace', Image courtesy of BodyMedia Inc; 131: 'Shared virtual workspace', Copyright © 2000–2003 Groove Networks; 127: 'Visualising timelines', Contempt Productions; 135: 2002 © Dubberly Design Office; 141: Trilogy; 142: Trilogy; 145: Chris Edwards; 147: Cooper; 149: Spy; 153: 'Exploring possibilities', MetaDesign; 155: 'Engineering communication', MetaDesign; 157: 'Design for the back room', Guardian Newspapers Limited; 163: Top, Organic Inc; 163: Bottom, Images courtesy of MetaDesign; 168–177: FordDirect and Trilogy; 178–185: Manchester United plc and Dimension Data; 186–193: The Ocean Conservancy and MetaDesign; 194–199: Shared Healthcare Systems and Cooper; 200–205: Visual I|O; 206–213: Bolt Inc; 214–219: BodyMedia Inc; 220–227: BT Group and Xymbio; 228–235: eDesign and Contempt Productions; 236–241: MONY and Organic Inc.

Index

Acknowledgements

For advice on all aspects of the book: Andrew Zolli, Ann Light, Gill Wildman, Ian Worley, Jack Schulze, Martyn Perks, Michael Andrews, Nick Loat, Peninah Goldman and Rachel Abrams.

For providing technical reviews: Heath Kane, Lou Rosenfeld and Margaret McCormack.

For assistance with case studies: FordDirect: Jared Rowe and Tim Pulliam at FordDirect and Drew Mille, John Morkes and Jay Kamm at Trilogy; ManUtd.com: Bill Galloway and Antony Webster at Dimension Data, Matt Aubrey-Batchelor and Nicky Smyth at TWI Interactive, and Ben Hatton at Manchester United plc; The Ocean Conservancy: Mary Tesluk and Rick Lowe at MetaDesign, North America, and David Peters formerly at MetaDesign, North America, Steve Knox at IS², Stephanie Drea at The Ocean Conservancy. Shared Healthcare Systems: Robert Reimann at Cooper, David West at Shared Healthcare Systems; Compass: Angela Shen-Hsieh, Mark Schindler and Scott Listfield at Visual I|O, and Christine Vander Vorst at SPS Infoquest; Bolt.com: Hafeez Raji, Thalia Kamarga, Tom Plunkett and Jane Mount at Bolt Inc.; BodyMedia: Chris Pacione, Chris Kasabach and Eric Hsuing at BodyMedia Inc.; BT Group Human Resources: Nick Loat, Kath Stynes, Ruth Miller and Karen Mahony for Xymbio, and Phil Edwards at BT Group; eDesign magazine: Sung Chang, Ninja von Oertzen and Alex Outman at Contempt Productions, Katherine Nelson, Ariana Donalds and Anke Stohlmann at eDesign; MONY Independent Network: Fanny Krivoy, Godfrey Baker and Liza Koreer at Organic and Chris Owen at MONY.

And for help sourcing case studies: Lesley Allan, Max Gadney, Nathan Shedroff, Simon Darling, and Terry Irwin. For assistance with research Colin Searls, Debra Zuckerman, Eric Kindel, Gerry Leonidas, Lydia Thornley, Marc Millon, Rakhi Rajani, Romaine Delaney, Simon Esterson and Steven Hoskins.

For assistance sourcing visual material: Bill Moggridge, Bill Verplank, Clement Mok, Colin Burns, David Peters, David Rose, David Small, Durrell Bishop, Fiona Raby, Hafeez Raji, Hugh Dubberly, John Maeda, Laura Borns, Lauralee Alben, Liz Sanders, Martin Dodge, Matt Marsh, Michel Beaudouin-Lafon, Nick Loat and Niclas Sellebråten. And Amanda Bown at RotoVision and Jack Schulze for overall assistance.

For general assistance: Jennifer Carlson, Gong Szeto, Miranda Filbee and Paul Kahn. Thank you to all the organisations who invited me to report on or present at design events, from which I have drawn extensively.

To people who have kindly given their time to interviews for my writing. And to the editors I have worked with who have helped focus my thinking and writing, including Rick Poynor, Max Bruinsma, Janet Abrams, John Walters, Steven Heller, David Brown, Antonia Ward, Steve Hoskins and Roy McKelvey.

Thanks also to everyone who has presented at conferences and events I have programmed, including the continuing AIGA Experience Design London series (and to Ewa Spohn, Gill Wildman and Ellie Runcie at the UK Design Council for their support of the series).

And finally thanks for inspiration to Gilbert Cockton and the British HCI Group committee, Clement Mok and Terry Swack of AIGA Experience Design, Ric Grefé of AIGA, and my colleagues Lauralee Alben, Shelley Evenson, Ken Garland, Kevin McCullagh, Bill Verplank and James Woudhuysen.

For design: David Hawkins at Untitled Studio for book design, Luke Herriott at RotoVision for design consultancy and Jack Schulze for information diagram concept and design.

At RotoVision: Aidan Walker, Chris Foges, Jeremy Hammond and Laura Owen.

And thank you to Zara Emerson, my stalwart editor.

Finally thank you to Juliet Tizzard for her generous assistance and unwavering support, and to Gabe, who never knew what was going on.

Nico Macdonald

Nico Macdonald has been writing about design for the Web since 1995, for renowned design publications including *Eye*, *Blueprint*, and *AIGA Gain*. His consultancy, Spy, focuses on design strategy and management for the Web. For a decade from the mid-1980s he focused on print and editorial design, advising leading designers and publishers on IT strategy. He was involved with Web design from its inception, and from his consulting work is familiar with many of the key tools used in Web development. In the mid-1990s he co-programmed the first significant European conference on Web design, and at the end of the decade pioneered understanding of usability and user experience with the 'Design for Usability' conference, co-programmed with Jakob Nielsen. He is on the steering committee of AIGA Experience Design, and programmes its London events, which constitute the most significant design series in the UK in the last decade.